Happy Birthday
Mabel
Jan. 9, 1999

Thought you would
enjoy Norman's devotions
each day—

Love,
John & Sarah

FOLLOW *the* LEADER

A DAILY SPIRITUAL JOURNEY

NORMAN G. WILSON

TABLE OF CONTENTS

TABLE OF CONTENTS

TABLE OF CONTENTS

TABLE OF CONTENTS

TABLE OF CONTENTS

TABLE OF CONTENTS

PREFACE

J esus was the Master Storyteller. In each of the lessons He taught, he seemed to reach out to everyday life experiences and turn them into word pictures of eternal truth. A farmer sowing seed, a rebellious son running away from home, a poor widow searching for a lost coin, a rich man building bigger barns — in these stories we see ourselves (or more likely, someone we know).

While still in my teens, I preached my first sermon. Over the years, these messages have been received with a variety of responses — from enthusiastic affirmation to . . . well, let's just say to something far less than that. However, without question, the most encouraging comment I ever received after one of my sermons was to hear two young boys tell their parents, "He's a good storyteller." Preaching never comes closer to its original purpose than when the story is told, and told with such simplicity, that even a child can understand it.

This book is a collection of some of the stories I've told over the course of forty years. My purpose in telling them as I preached was to open the windows of understanding and let the light of truth shine through. If you will follow the suggested Bible reading for each day, you will have read the entire Bible by the end of the year. I would be satisfied if this book accomplishes nothing more than that. However, if the daily vignette helps to shed some light from God's Word on the path you are called to follow, that will be a double reward. Your personal "Life Response" may differ from what is suggested, but I do hope that after each day's reading, you will at least take a moment to reflect prayerfully on what you have read. You may find a ray of "Sonlight" to illuminate your path.

Norman G. Wilson

ACKNOWLEDGMENTS

As a universal truth, Sir Walter Scott is right. We cannot exist without mutual help. As a specific example, I know that this book could not exist without it. Therefore, it is with deep gratitude that I acknowledge all of those who contributed to the success of this project.

First of all, all glory, praise and honor to our Lord and Savior Jesus Christ, whose love, mercy and grace are what this book is about.

Many thanks to all of the personnel of the Department of Communications, but especially to the two who worked specifically on this book. To Jerry Brecheisen, whose encouragement and prodding kept the book on the front burner, and whose hours of editing, formatting and contributions to the LIFE RESPONSES were invaluable. To Alberta Metz, who combed through years of messages to dig out the illustrations and stories that make up the core of many of the daily devotional thoughts.

The race of mankind would perish did they cease to aid each other. We cannot exist without mutual help."

Sir Walter Scott

I am also grateful to the thousands of individuals whose life experiences have contributed such richness to my own.

And finally, thanks to my wife Nancy, who has been my partner and helpmeet through forty years of ministry.

GIVE ME TOMORROW

One New Year's Eve in the 1950s, a newspaper correspondent with the troops in Korea noticed a big Marine standing near a tank. His uniform was frozen stiff, his beard encrusted with mud and he and his buddies were eating cold beans out of cans. They were on the front lines and the situation was precarious. The newspaper man said to the Marine, "If I were God and could give you the one thing you would rather have over anything else in the world, what would you ask for?" The Marine was silent, thinking of his many possible wishes. Then slowly he replied, "I would ask you to give me tomorrow."

Why, you do not even know what will happen tomorrow.

James 4:14 (NIV)

Give me tomorrow! When you think about it, that's what most men want. When faced with the brevity of life — whether on the battlefield or at home — most of us are anxious about tomorrow.

There is a time to live and a time to die, the writer of Ecclesiastes reminds us. Too many people do not use their time to live as a preparation for their time to die. Actually, dying is a part of living — the necessary transition from physical life to eternal life. Are you ready for your tomorrow?

LIFE RESPONSE:

What do I need to do *today* to prepare for my *tomorrow*?

THROUGH THE BIBLE

Genesis 1-3

TAKE OUT THE TRASH

On a bitterly cold night my wife and I were on vacation in Rome. We were warned not to go out that evening as midnight approached. It wasn't safe, we were told, because of a strange Roman custom. Every New Year's Eve at midnight, Romans throw something old out of the window into the street below. If you were out walking, you could be hit on the head. We stayed in our hotel and, just as we had been warned, at midnight we heard the noise of things being thrown out.

Get rid of all bitterness, rage and anger, brawling and slander . . .

Ephesians 4:31 (NIV)

The next morning we went out to see all kinds of things littering the streets — old furniture, shoes, just about everything imaginable.

The symbolism of the custom has some merit. The beginning of a new year is a good time to throw out old habits, prejudices, hatreds, failures and sins. We need to get rid of excess baggage that has accumulated, hindering us on our Christian walk. A house cleaning is in order periodically, to rid ourselves of "spiritual trash."

Replace these sinful, negative things with forgiveness, compassion, love and thanksgiving.

You've heard it said that today is the first day of the rest of your life. What better time to take out the trash?

LIFE RESPONSE:

I will determine to get rid of attitudes, affections, or associations that will hinder my walk with the Lord.

THROUGH THE BIBLE

Genesis 4-7

MAKE TODAY COUNT

In a book on time management, I read a suggestion that we could make better use of our time if we kept track of how we spent it. I began to take a notebook with me everywhere. Every fifteen minutes throughout the day I would jot down what I did during that segment of my life.

When I saw the record of my time in black and white, I was amazed at how much of it was wasted — time spent doing nothing, or at least nothing of eternal significance.

I decided that life is too short to waste. It is too short for me to remember insults and carry grudges. Too short to allow the sins and blunders of the past to put a cloud over today's usefulness. Too short to miss the joy of family and friends while I'm busy pursuing a career. Too short to give the devil part of today while I reserve only a portion of tomorrow for God.

We could do more with our lives if we only recognized how brief they are. Evangeline Booth of the Salvation Army said, "It is not how many years we live, but what we do with them that counts." How swiftly time passes! What we are going to do, we had better be doing. Don't put off until tomorrow what you should be doing today.

> *The path of the righteous is like the first gleam of dawn, shining ever brighter till the full light of day.*
>
> *Proverbs 4:18 (NIV)*

LIFE RESPONSE:

I will set spiritual, social, and financial priorities in keeping with the principles of God's Word.

THROUGH THE BIBLE

Genesis 8-11

No Christianity Without Christ

O n a visit to Israel I had a guide who had been born in Jericho and raised in that part of the world. Quoting freely from both the Old and New Testaments, his knowledge of biblical facts was amazing. He spoke with respect and reverence about Jesus. But He was not a Christian. He was a Muslim.

I questioned him regarding his opinion of Jesus Christ. He said Jesus was a great prophet sent from God, but the guide would go no further.

Thou art the Christ, the Son of the living God.

Matthew 16:16 (KJV)

A great man. A prophet. He came from God. Those are true statements, great truths, but they are not enough.

Who was Jesus? Whose Son is He? The carpenter's son? Joseph's son? Mary's son?

Many in the Bible confessed Christ as the Son of God. At His baptism, God himself said Jesus was His beloved Son (Matt. 3:17). The disciples watched Him still the storm and said, "Of a truth, thou art the Son of God" (Matt. 14:33). The centurion at the cross exclaimed, "Truly this was the Son of God" (Matt. 27:54b). Even the unclean spirits cried out, "What have I to do with thee, Jesus, thou Son of the most high God?" (Mark 5:7).

There is no Christianity without Christ. If the doctrine of the deity of Christ is lost, Christianity no longer exists. Who is Jesus to you?

LIFE RESPONSE:

I will discover for myself, the Christ of the Scriptures. I will not only learn about His words, I will discover His ways — and walk in them.

THROUGH THE BIBLE

Genesis 12–16

THE QUICK FIX

People these days are looking for the quick fix. We want easy answers and we want them now. Television has taught us to expect fast results. On TV, life is divided into neat thirty-minute intervals. Mysteries are solved, broken hearts mended, diseases cured, crises averted — all within a thirty-minute time slot.

Commercials are even more miraculous. Asthma sufferers find relief, headaches are cured, overweight people become slim, and the ugly become beautiful — all within a thirty-second time slot. No problems in your life are too big for the thirty-second commercial!

As a result, we grow impatient with the real world. Extra pounds don't melt away overnight, headaches persist, and miracle products don't do what they promise. In the real world, bodies grow sick, cars break down, investments go sour, houses need repairs, young people die.

When he heard that Lazarus was sick, he stayed where he was two more days.

John 11:6 (NIV)

When Lazarus died, some commented that surely Jesus who opened blind eyes could have kept this man from dying. Instead, Jesus stayed where He was two more days.

It is hard for modern people to understand that God transcends the time and space of our world. His purposes may take longer, but we can count on it that He is at work!

LIFE RESPONSE:
Where do I see Christ at work in my life right now?

BE CONTENT IN ALL CIRCUMSTANCES

Just after I received my pilot's license, I took one of my nephews for his first plane ride. I was amused as I watched him out of the corner of my eye. While we climbed higher, he was doing his best to mentally keep contact with the ground. After reaching our desired altitude and flying for several minutes, I pushed the nose of the plane forward and dropped down several feet. My nephew looked as though he could keep himself up in the air by the sheer force of his will.

Finally I said, "Son, if you would just relax and go where the plane goes, you'll enjoy the ride much more."

Often people struggle to keep life on an even keel. But life isn't like that. It has its ups and they are great. But life also has its downs, and sometimes they come swiftly and abruptly.

Paul says we need to learn contentment in all circumstances. The poor need to have simple trust, believing God will take care of them. The rich must understand that all they have belongs to God and they are simply stewards who must give an account.

> *I know what it is to be in need, and I know what it is to have plenty. I have learned the secret of being content in any and every situation . . .*
>
> Philippians 4:12 (NIV)

LIFE RESPONSE:

In what area of my life am I discontent? What can I do to "learn to be content" in that area?

THROUGH THE BIBLE

Genesis 20-23

HAPPINESS: KNOWING YOUR GOAL

A little boy saw a beautiful butterfly in his backyard and decided he wanted to have it. Leaving all his toys, he began chasing the butterfly, sure he would be happy if he owned such a lovely thing. With a mighty effort, he lunged for the butterfly and grasped it in his hand. But when he opened his little fist, the brightly colored creature he had been chasing was crushed and broken.

Life is like that for many people who strive to attain happiness. They think more money, a bigger house, a new job, or perhaps a new marriage partner will bring them happiness. But when they get what they thought they wanted, they are as miserable as before.

It is reported that Sigmund Freud said, "The chief duty of a human being is to endure life." But Jesus offered more than endurance, He promised happiness. He said those who are poor in spirit are happy. They are happy because they know where they are going — for theirs is the kingdom of heaven.

Happy . . . are the poor in spirit . . . for theirs is the kingdom of heaven.

Matthew 5:3 (ANT)

Recognizing one's own spiritual poverty is the beginning of the solution to unhappiness. Happiness comes from knowing you are right with God and that you are going to heaven. Happiness is not the goal of life but the by-product.

LIFE RESPONSE:

I will determine to make my relationship with God — and not material things — my source of happiness.

THROUGH THE BIBLE

Genesis 24-25

GOD IS IN CONTROL

I once had the experience of flying in a private plane that was on automatic pilot. Sitting next to the pilot, I watched the yoke move almost mysteriously, turning the plane. It might have looked to the casual observer as if the plane was out of control and turning capriciously. The fact is, an outside power was directing us. A radio signal from the airport of our destination was guiding our flight and drawing us closer and closer to itself. We were steadily and confidently being directed toward our goal.

I am the Lord your God, Who teaches you to profit, Who leads you by the way you should go.

Isaiah 48:17 (NKJV)

We are tempted at times to think that our lives and the whole world are out of control, with no direction or destination. But God still sits at the controls. God does everything with a careful plan and a perfect design. The universe itself is remarkable, not only for its immense size but for its perfect orderliness. Nothing is haphazard.

And He has planned carefully for each of us, arranging Christ's sacrifice for our sins, even before the foundation of the world! Doesn't it make sense for us to cooperate with God so His plan works in our lives as He intended?

LIFE RESPONSE:

Is my spiritual life on "automatic pilot" or do I insist on taking control?

THROUGH THE BIBLE

Genesis 26-28

CULTIVATE CHEERFULNESS

A doctor said, "It is chemically and physically impossible to be angry or to get ulcers while you are laughing." Most of us have come to accept a certain level of depression as normal. We talk about blue Mondays, thinking that after an exciting weekend, the routine of beginning another work week is a signal for our emotions to drop and our spirits to lag.

Although discouragement plagues most of us at times, we do not have to give in to it, allowing it to take the delight out of our life or the song out of our heart.

It is our personal responsibility to learn the secret of rejoicing, of maintaining joy even in the midst of distressing situations. David encouraged himself in the Lord. Sometimes we have to do just that.

Sirs, be of good cheer: for I believe God . . .

Acts 27:25 (KJV)

When the Apostle Paul was on his way to Rome the ship was caught in a terrible storm. But Paul stood on the rolling deck and called to the others on the storm-tossed boat, "Be of good cheer." Every time Jesus came to His disciples during distressing circumstances, He spoke the words, "It is I; be of good cheer."

Laughter and cheerfulness make us healthier both physically and spiritually.

LIFE RESPONSE:

With a smile, a word of encouragement, or laughter, I will purposefully bring cheer into someone's life today.

THROUGH THE BIBLE

Genesis 29-30

Shut
The Door!

O ne successful executive maintains a small inner room next to his office. During his busy day, he often slips into this room to seek God's guidance.

Many Christians have such a place. It is called a prayer closet. But shutting the door is not easy. The door of the room may be closed, but distracting thoughts clamor for attention.

> *When you pray, go into your room, and when you have shut your door, pray to your Father . . .*
>
> Matthew 6:6 (NKJV)

I have found something helpful in my own prayer life. When I am plagued with distractions, I use a pad and pencil to jot down things I need to do or remember. Once these things are gotten out of the way I can concentrate on prayer. I have finally shut the door.

Occasionally, God has to use drastic measures to get people quiet long enough to pray. More than one busy person has chafed when laid low by illness or injury. But as a result, they were able to shut the door and pray.

A place of prayer is important. John Wesley's mother, used to sit down and cover her head with her apron in order to be shut in with God. Do whatever you have to do to shut the door and pray.

LIFE RESPONSE:

I will give my time alone with God a prominent place in my daily calendar.

THROUGH THE BIBLE

Genesis 31-33

LIVE IN DAY-TIGHT COMPARTMENTS

A man who had been worrying and fretful was making each day miserable because of his thoughts about yesterday's failures and tomorrow's fears. One day he visited a ship and was taken below deck. There he saw water-tight compartments with steel doors. He was told that if there was trouble in one section of the ship and a leak occurred, the steel doors could be closed and each compartment sealed from the next. The ship could withstand considerable damage in one area and still remain afloat.

The man thought, "I could live a life like that. I could live in day-tight compartments." He decided to close off yesterday and seal off tomorrow, and live today without worry.

This is the way God intends for us to live. Today is a day the Lord has made. Don't be plagued by yesterday's failures and tomorrow's fears. Most of the circumstances which can make today less than a good day are related to some other day!

> *Do not worry about tomorrow . . . Each day has enough trouble of its own.*
> Matthew 6:34 (NIV)

Seal off yesterday and tomorrow and trust God today. Rejoice and be glad in this moment. Make today count. Fill each day with joy, love and service to God.

LIFE RESPONSE:
How can I live this day in faith and not fear?

JESUS:
CHART AND RUDDER

One of man's first successes in flying was by hot air balloon. It has never become a popular means of transportation, however, because it has no rudder, no means of guidance. The least maneuverable of all aircraft, it flies only where the wind may blow it. Although hot air balloonists have accomplished some remarkable feats, they can never be sure where or when they will arrive.

As ye have therefore received Christ Jesus the Lord, so walk ye in him.

Colossians 2:6 (KJV)

In order to achieve success in life, we must have both an external guidance system and some internal method of control. Every man is dependent upon a course, a chart or an indication of the way he should go. And he must have some means by which he can choose the direction of his life in order to follow that course.

According to Paul's words to the Colossians, Jesus is both the chart and the rudder. He is the external guide and is the internal power that enables us to follow His direction. When we start our walk with the Lord, we cannot see the end from the beginning. But we continue our walk the same way we began it — by faith. We do not need to see the end of the road. Our job is to trust and obey. We cannot go astray as long as we stay close to our Guide.

LIFE RESPONSE:
    I will allow Jesus Christ to be my "chart" and "rudder."

THROUGH THE BIBLE
Genesis 37-39

GOD GIVES US JOY

The college I attended employed a handyman who appeared to be very stern and severe. He looked as if he never enjoyed life. Perhaps it was because he lived in a small apartment in the basement of the boys' dorm. Perhaps it was his menial job. But he often reprimanded us when we were laughing and having fun. As a result, of course, he was often the target of practical jokes. Scowling in disgust, he would scold, "Foolishness, foolishness."

His reputation as a sourpuss went back to his youth when he told two of his friends that they would never amount to anything because they were too silly. One of those fun-loving friends became a respected church leader and the other was president of the college where the handyman worked.

I have told you this so . . . that your joy may be complete.

John 15:11 (NIV)

The frowning, serious-minded Pharisees were not happy men. Strictly religious, they were full of prejudice and hatred. Jesus' positive zest for life —mingling in the happiness of people's lives, attending wedding feasts, sharing in people's joy — left the religious leaders shocked and dismayed.

Yes, Jesus was also a Man of sorrows, but He must have smiled, for children were drawn to Him. He gives His joy to us!

LIFE RESPONSE:
How can I bring joy to someone's life today?

THE MEANING OF FORGIVENESS

Several years ago, a man and his wife drove nearly 2000 miles from Michigan to California, to visit a man in prison who had murdered their daughter. The purpose was not revenge, nor was it to see that the killer was suffering as much as he should for his heinous crime. It was rather to tell him of the love of God in Christ Jesus, and to tell him that they forgave him. Calling it a journey of forgiveness, they said they harbored no hatred or revenge.

For if you forgive men their trespasses, your heavenly Father will also forgive you.

Matthew 6:14 (KJV)

The murdered girl's mother told of first hearing the news of their daughter's death. "We suffered the normal human reactions of grief and anguish," she said. "Didn't I have the right to be filled with red-hot hate? But where would that have gotten me? It wouldn't bring my daughter back. We believe God can make good come out of this pain."

This couple said that their greatest joy would be if their daughter's murderer would accept Jesus Christ as his personal Savior. According to the newspaper report, the convicted murderer said, "People like this give a new meaning to the word forgiveness." But it's not a new meaning. It is understanding what true forgiveness is.

The meaning of the word forgiveness is not justice, it is mercy. It is love expressed.

LIFE RESPONSE:
I will not hold someone hostage by my unforgiveness.

THROUGH THE BIBLE
Genesis 43-45

SIN BRINGS DEATH

A barber noticed his customer had a sore on his lip. The customer told him cigarettes had done it, but he was sure it would soon heal.

A month later the man's lip was split and ugly, and the barber expressed concern. "I've switched to a cigarette holder. It will soon heal," the man said.

The barber obtained medical photographs showing what lip cancer looked like. The man admitted that his sore lip looked like the pictures. "But I'm not worried," he said.

On the third month the man did not come in for his regular haircut. When the barber called to inquire about him he was told his customer had died of cancer two days earlier.

Sin is like a cancer. It destroys. Slowly, sometimes without our realizing what is happening, it keeps getting worse and worse until it results in death.

> *The soul who sins is the one who will die.*
>
> *Ezekiel 18:4b (NIV)*

Rationalization is dangerous and foolish when it comes to cancer or to sin. Prevention involves "nipping sin in the bud." The remedy for sin is application of the blood of Jesus. He alone can deal with the sin of the human heart.

LIFE RESPONSE:

What areas of my life need cleansing?

ENVY: THE ROBBER OF HAPPINESS

I saw a cartoon which illustrates four cows grazing in the corners where their separate pastures came together. Each cow was straining to get its head under the barbed wire fence to eat the grass in its neighbor's pasture.

How much we are like that, each envying our neighbor and never realizing that someone else is envying us! Envy robs us of happiness. As long as you look with longing at either the position or the possession of someone else, you will never find satisfaction in your own.

For where you have envy and selfish ambition, there you find disorder and every evil practice.

James 3:16 (NIV)

One man said, "Lots of people know a good thing the minute the other fellow sees it first." You may have seen a child lay down an expensive toy and begin to cry because another child is playing with the box the toy came in.

Martin Luther said, "Too many Christians envy the sinners their pleasure and the saints their joy, because they don't have either one."

A child of God has no reason to envy anyone. If we are in right relationship with our Heavenly Father, He satisfies the longings of our hearts. "The Lord is my shepherd, I shall lack nothing" (Ps. 23:1 NIV).

LIFE RESPONSE:

I will learn to be content with the things God has brought into my life.

INTOXICATED WITH JOY

Several preachers were once invited to a dinner party at which a number of Hollywood personalities were being entertained. Among them were comedians who made their living making others laugh. The preachers also began telling wholesome human interest stories that were very funny. One eighty-year-old preacher was especially entertaining. An actress asked him, "Did you by any chance have anything to drink before you came to this dinner?"

One of the men started to say, "Of course not!" But the older preacher stopped him.

"You're right," he said to the actress. "We are intoxicated with the joy that flows from Almighty God through our Lord Jesus Christ." The actress, with tears in her eyes said, "I'd like to have what you have."

There is something dynamic and irrepressible about the life that is in Christ Jesus. The 120 who came from the Upper Room had tasted the wine of the Spirit, and onlookers thought they were intoxicated.

Some . . . said, They have had too much wine.

Acts 2:13 (NIV)

Are you experiencing the vitality, the joy, the freshness of life in Christ? If your Christian life has become stale, come to Him for renewal and refreshing!

LIFE RESPONSE:
I will be a witness of Christ's joy, as well as His love, to others.

DO WE GET ALONG WITH THE WORLD?

Some years ago, a young man told me he had joined a rock group which performed in taverns and night clubs. His motive was to win those people to Christ. I don't question his motive, but I have serious reservations about his method.

The world is not won by our compromises, but by our contrast. Something is wrong when the church strives to win the approval and affirmation of the community. Jesus told His disciples the world would hate them because it hated Him. I frankly wonder about a church's relationship with Christ if it gets along so well with the world. Where is the hostility that holiness provokes?

> *Do not love the world . . . For everything in the world . . . comes not from the Father . . .*
>
> *1 John 2:15-16 (NIV)*

John said the sinful cravings, the lust of the eyes and the boasting of man is not of God but of the world.

After Uncle Buddy Robinson, the renowned evangelist, visited New York and saw the sights, he said, "Thank you, Lord, for letting me see New York, and thank you that I didn't see anything I want!" Longings for the trinkets and treasures of the world cannot live in the same heart with love for God.

LIFE RESPONSE:
   I will let the beauty of Jesus — not the world — shine through me.

Life's An Adventure

D L. Moody was once describing the leap of faith. "If I stood at the bottom of the stairs in the dark and said to my little girl, 'Jump and Daddy will catch you,' she might say, 'But, Daddy, I'm afraid.' I would assure her, 'It's all right. I'm here and I will catch you.' She would jump, trusting me. Faith is like that. It's a leap into the dark."

Someone commenting on Mr. Moody's statement, took exception to it and said, "Faith is not a leap into the dark, but a leap from the dark into the light." And it is that, but for the one who has not yet made the jump, it looks frightening. It is a risk.

Sometimes the Christian life has been portrayed as flat and unexciting. According to the TV commercials the only life worth living, the life with gusto, is the sinful life. As a result of this misunderstanding, many run away from Christ. In his poem "The Hound of Heaven," Francis Thompson tells of running away from Christ: "For I was sore adread, lest having Him/I should have naught else beside."

I consider everything a loss compared to the surpassing greatness of knowing Christ Jesus my Lord.

Philippians 3:8 (NIV)

Satan lies when he says Jesus takes away everything that makes life worth living. Only Jesus can give abundant life and fill the heart with peace and joy.

Life Response:

Is there anything in my life that means more to me than Christ?

GOD HAS NO GRANDCHILDREN

There is no place in the New Testament that speaks of second-generation Christians, God's grandchildren. One lady boasted that her grandchildren were the sixth generation of the family to be members of their 275-year-old church. Their great-great-grandfather was one of the founders and their father had been on the consistory for forty-six consecutive years.

I hope she knows her grandchildren are not God's. Their long family record of faithfulness to that church is admirable, but does not give those children a favored status with God. Our relationship with God is purely a personal matter.

How great is the love the Father has lavished on us, that we should be called children of God!

1 John 3:1 (NIV)

I have always appreciated the benefits of a Christian home, perhaps not as much when I was younger as I do now. I was taken to church when only a few weeks old. I don't remember anything other than going to Sunday school and church on Sunday. For years, my father was the volunteer church custodian. We were the first family to arrive so he could open the church and the last to leave after he closed up. During that faithful attendance, I learned many things. But one day as a teenage boy, I repented of my sins, received Jesus Christ as my personal Savior and became a child of God.

Becoming a Christian is a personal matter.

LIFE RESPONSE:
When was my SPIRITUAL birthday?

THROUGH THE BIBLE
Matthew 10-12

THE POWER OF THE HOLY SPIRIT

I once saw a picture of a piece of straw that had pierced a solid piece of wood. The straw had been driven by the power of a tornado. I'm told that if all the wind in the world stopped blowing, it would take the force of all the atom bombs and nuclear warheads of all of the countries combined to get it moving again. There is tremendous power in the movement of air currents.

One of the basic needs of mankind is the need for power. We need power to drive machines and we need power to light and heat our homes. We also need another kind of power, the power of authority. Some have the power that comes from position and influence and some have the power that comes from physical strength.

. . . being fervent in the Spirit . . .

Acts 18:25 (KJV)

The Holy Spirit is the power we need in our lives. His power provides the strength, the light, the heat, and the authority and influence every Christian needs.

A man once sent his New Testament to be rebound. The binder could not fit the words *The New Testament* on the spine of the book, so he abbreviated it *TNT*. The Holy Spirit puts TNT into our lives. He gives the power to accomplish what we can never do on our own.

LIFE RESPONSE:
I will live a "Spirit-propelled" life, not a self-propelled life.

THROUGH THE BIBLE
Matthew 13-14

WORKS DON'T SAVE

Yawiya Tukuya was a nineteen-year-old Papua New Guinean trained to be a warrior like his father. When missionaries arrived in his region, he was hired to work at their mission station. Hearing that he needed to be saved, he decided one day to become a Christian. He thought baptism would do it, so he put his head under water in a nearby stream. But nothing changed.

Then he thought if baptism didn't do it, communion would. So he filled a large jug with water and drank it down, refilling and drinking it three or four times. But he wasn't changed.

That night as he lay in his house, God spoke to him and told him that none of the things he had tried could take away his sins. He would need to repent, humble himself and make restitution. Yawiya decided he would put his trust in the Lord. He prayed that God would protect him from the wrath of people he must confess to. And God took care of it.

So many people try doing good works or going through rituals in order to be saved. But only Jesus Christ can make us different!

> *Not by works of righteousness which we have done, but according to his mercy he saved us, by the washing of regeneration, and renewing of the Holy Ghost.*
>
> *Titus 3:5 (KJV)*

LIFE RESPONSE:
Do others see the difference Christ has made in my life?

THROUGH THE BIBLE
Matthew 15-17

OWNER OR HONORED GUEST?

Quite often when I am invited to homes during my travels, people say to me, "We're so happy to have you here with us, and we want you to make yourself right at home." But I know, and they know, they do not mean that I should act in their home just like I would in my own. They don't expect me to go upstairs, or open closet doors, or look in private places. They mean I'm welcome. They want me as their guest, they want me to be comfortable with them, but they don't want me to move in and take over.

Many born-again Christians who have welcomed God through His Holy Spirit into their lives, tell Him to make himself right at home. Then they treat Him only as an honored guest. They keep Him restricted to certain areas of their lives. They want His help and fellowship. They want Him to be comfortable and abide in their hearts, but they don't want Him to take over and control them.

> *Don't you know that you yourselves are God's temple and that God's Spirit lives in you?*
>
> *1 Corinthians 3:16 (NIV)*

To have the fullness of the Holy Spirit means He is not just a guest, He is Lord of all. He becomes the one who holds the key to every door.

LIFE RESPONSE:

Does the Holy Spirit have ownership of my life or is He just an honored guest?

THROUGH THE BIBLE

Matthew 18-20

SACRIFICIAL GIVING

Many people have perverted the truth of this verse and made it a blank check for all of their selfish desires. Empty promises have been made regarding the prosperity of the saints, saying God's blessing is their right.

One of the sad commentaries of this age is the fact that, for the past few years, people have spent ten times more for luxuries and nonessentials than for all charitable and religious purposes combined.

Jesus said, "It is more blessed to give than to receive" (Acts 20:35).

> *Give and it shall be given unto you . . .*
>
> Luke 6:38 (KJV)

In a church I pastored, one lady cleaned other people's houses for a living. She lived very simply in a humble home and walked all over town to do her work. Her clothing was not fashionable or stylish. She had very little of this world's goods. But she seldom missed an opportunity to contribute to the church's offerings. By the end of the year, she had given more money than many of the other members who were quite well-to-do. In God's sight she gave far more because, like the widow in the Bible, she gave out of her need.

I have found over and over again that the real work of building the kingdom of God and meeting the needs of our fellowmen is carried on by those who do not have much. But with a spirit of sacrifice, they share what they have.

LIFE RESPONSE:
I will make it a practice to do more "giving" than "getting."

THROUGH THE BIBLE

Matthew 21-22

GOD OF THE SECOND CHANCE

He is the God of the second chance. He lets us start over.

I read a newspaper account of a young woman caught in a blizzard who was found frozen. Her rescuers couldn't even penetrate her skin with a needle. But to everyone's surprise, she thawed out and lived! A second chance!

A thirty-seven-year-old man was released from prison after spending all his adult life behind bars. Abandoned and neglected as a child, he got into trouble early and at age sixteen, was the youngest person ever sent to Soledad Prison in California. He had never been a free man. But within thirty days of his release, he committed a violent crime and was back in prison. He was given a second chance and threw it away.

> *The pot he was shaping . . . was marred . . . so the potter formed it into another pot . . .*
>
> *Jeremiah 18:4 (NIV)*

Most of us have had many chances. God patiently molds and remolds us, offering us repeated opportunities to choose the right way. We have been risen with Christ so that we can walk with Him in newness of life. Like Lazarus we have died and been buried under a mountain of sin, but by the resurrection power of Christ, we have been given a second chance.

LIFE RESPONSE:
What "second chance" has God given me?

GOD'S BUSINESS

A young boy once asked his father, "Dad, what does God do all day?" How you answer that question will depend on your opinion of God.

Some would answer, "Nothing." It appears to them that God is unemployed. Their opinion of Him is described in an old song, "Like that lazy old sun, he's got nothin' to do but roll around heaven all day." For them God is a far-off mystery or a forgotten nonentity. He may have created the world, but He has left it to drift by itself. If He were involved, they argue, He would be feeding the hungry and relieving suffering, stopping wars and ending violence.

My Father is always at his work to this very day . . .

John 5:17 (NIV)

Yet some would answer the question "What does God do all day?" with "Everything." They give God credit or blame for every detail, from making the sun rise each morning to the flat tire they had on the way to work. I heard a lady in a Sunday school class ask, "What does God have against me? Does He think I'm such a bad person? Why would He cause all seven of my electrical appliances to break?"

God is not in the business of causing flat tires or breaking your appliances, but He is in the business of redeeming (buying back) what was His by right of creation. Every act of God in history has been part of His plan. Are you involved in that plan as a co-laborer with Him?

LIFE RESPONSE:

What is God doing in me right now? What am I doing for God right now?

THROUGH THE BIBLE

Matthew 25-26

SAVED BY SINCERITY?

I read of a young lady in New York who had opened a bottle of pain remedy medicine. She may have had a simple headache. She sincerely believed that one or two of the capsules would relieve the pressure and alleviate the pain. She obviously had no way of knowing that someone had tampered with that particular bottle of medicine and that what she was taking was, in fact, cyanide poison. Her sincerity didn't save her. The end of that way was death.

I'm sure you've heard it said many times that it doesn't really matter what you believe as long as you're sincere. Many people, even in the church, are trusting in sincerity to save them. They may hold tenaciously to their convictions, but the tragedy is, although sincere, they are wrong. Their faith is not founded in God. They have been deceived.

> *There is a way that seems right to a man, but in the end it leads to death.*
>
> *Proverbs 14:12 (NIV)*

Paul wrote to the Thessalonians that when the Antichrist came, the power of Satan would be displayed in counterfeit miracles and all sorts of deception. "They perish because they refused to love the truth and so be saved" (2 Thess. 2:10 NIV). It is not true that there are many ways to be saved. We are not all going to the same place by different paths.

The way to be saved is to sincerely believe the truth as it is in Christ Jesus.

LIFE RESPONSE:
I will preach and practice the gospel of "one way."

THROUGH THE BIBLE

Matthew 27-28

THE GIFT OF LAUGHTER

Among the sermons I have preached is one on laughter. One winter I had occasion to "take a dose of my own medicine."

My wife and I were privileged to spend a weekend in Florida, at exactly the same time Indiana was experiencing record-breaking cold. My son called on Sunday to inform me our water pipes had frozen and a pipe had burst. When we arrived home on Monday night, with frigid temperatures and blowing snow, we had car trouble. My son used our snow-blower the next day to help a neighbor and broke part of the steering mechanism. That same day, we received word that a supplier could not fill an order we desperately needed in the office.

> *A merry heart maketh a cheerful countenance: but by sorrow of the heart the spirit is broken.*
>
> Proverbs 15:13 (KJV)

When all of these mishaps piled on top of each other, I began to feel a little put upon and, I must admit, a little irritable. I said to my family, "I need to listen to my own sermon and laugh." You know, listening to that tape helped. It didn't fix the pipe, or the car, or the snow-blower, or fill our order, but it did change my disposition. None of our problems seem quite so grave if we can laugh.

We need to learn that a smile, a pleasant word, a happy thought, a cheerful countenance, will not only brighten *our* day — it may lift a neighbor's heavy load as well. Sunshine in our souls should lighten our countenances!

LIFE RESPONSE:

I will determine to face my circumstances with contagious cheer instead of resentment.

THROUGH THE BIBLE

Exodus 1-4

IS STATIC KEEPING YOU FROM HEARING?

In Jesus' parable of the sower, He spoke of those who let cares of this world drown out the message of the Word. Their anxiety divides their minds.

One day I was listening to a Christian radio station in my car. The announcer was talking about the local tornado warning system. But something was wrong; another broadcast was coming in over the satellite feed and going directly on the air. I could hear both broadcasts, but it was extremely difficult to concentrate on either one. I missed much of the important warning about tornadoes because my attention was diverted by the other voice.

Many voices call to us today — materialism, secularism, humanism. Prosperity and pleasure call loudly to so many. Where we once spent most of our time and energy barely eking out an existence, now our work week has been shortened and our leisure time lengthened.

. . . the man who hears the word, but the worries of this life and the deceitfulness of wealth choke it, making it unfruitful.

Matthew 13:22 (NIV)

The Apostle Paul said there are so many kinds of voices in the world (1 Cor. 14:10 KJV) it can be confusing trying to sort through them all. We must be sure we are listening to the voice of truth.

LIFE RESPONSE:

I will not let the "static" of the world keep me from hearing God's message.

THROUGH THE BIBLE

Exodus 5-7

GOOD SOIL

I n Dr. Billy Graham's book, *Facing Death and the Life Hereafter*, he writes of the 1978 arrest of Velma Barfield for the murder of four people, including her mother and her fiance. A victim of both incest as a child and the abuse of prescription drugs as an adult, she admitted her guilt, was taken to prison and confined alone to a cell.

One night the guard tuned his radio to a gospel station. Velma heard the words of an evangelist and allowed Jesus Christ into her life. She had been in church and had heard the gospel, but this was the first time she understood that Jesus had died for her.

The one who received the seed that fell on good soil is the man who hears the word and understands it.

Matthew 13:23 (NIV)

Velma's conversion was genuine. For six years on death row she ministered to many of her cell-mates. She wrote to Mrs. Billy Graham and a friendship developed between them. Mrs. Graham wrote to Velma, "God has turned your cell on death row into a most unusual pulpit. . . . As long as God has a ministry for you here, He will keep you here."

Velma was the first woman in twenty-two years to be executed in the United States. But she was a living example of the good soil in Jesus' parable. She brought forth fruit a hundredfold.

LIFE RESPONSE:

I will not just read my Bible, but read to understand it and apply it to my life.

THROUGH THE BIBLE

Exodus 8-10

ARE YOU DEFEATED BY SELFISHNESS?

When Socrates chose young men to be his students, he had them look into a clear pool of water and tell him what they saw. If they saw the beautiful fish swimming in the pool they were chosen as students. If they saw only their own image reflected in the surface of the water, they were not chosen, for they were in love with themselves.

William Gladstone said, "Selfishness is the great curse of the human race." Too much concern about self stifles fruitfulness and frustrates ambitions. It is when we get beyond ourselves and live for others that true greatness can be achieved.

"For whosoever will save his life shall lose it: and whosoever will lose his life for my sake shall find it" (Matt. 16:25 KJV). Some people sit around in selfish isolation, crying about the emptiness and meaninglessness of their existence. Life is not a fragile gift that must be pampered to be preserved. It is a strong, powerful tool that must be exercised to find its total usefulness. If we lose our lives for Jesus' sake, we will find life comes flooding back in abundance. No one is truly alive until he is part of something bigger than himself.

> *We were therefore buried with him through baptism into death . . .*
>
> Romans 6:4 (NIV)

LIFE RESPONSE:
Whose reflection is more important in my life, Christ's or my own?

CHOOSE YOUR MASTER

Most of us like to believe that we are our own masters. Ever since the Emancipation Proclamation ended the practice of slavery in America, we have prided ourselves on being a free and independent people. We love to sing about ours being "the land of the free and the home of the brave." But we are all under authority.

It is never a question as to whether or not you will serve some master; the only question is which master will you serve? Edward Howe said, "We are not free; it was not intended we should be. A book of rules is placed in our cradle, and we never get rid of it until we reach our graves."

Choose for yourselves this day whom you will serve.

Joshua 24:15 (NIV)

Many people say they want to be in control of their own lives. They do not want to answer to anyone. "I don't want to serve any god at all," they say. But that option is simply not open to any of us. Everyone chooses to be a slave of Jesus Christ or of Satan. We must choose our master.

Some choose alcohol or drugs or sex or pleasure as their "recreation," not realizing that they are actually choosing their master.

What master have you chosen?

LIFE RESPONSE:

I will not be a slave to anything or anyone other than Jesus Christ.

THROUGH THE BIBLE

Exodus 14-16

A CONTRADICTION?

A young skeptic walked in a garden with an old preacher. The young man didn't understand how such an intelligent person could be a Christian.

"How can you believe the Bible, with all of its contradictions?"

"I'm not aware of any contradictions."

"Doesn't the Bible say that God is love and then say that He is a consuming fire?" asked the young man. "How can God be love and a consuming fire at the same time?"

In the garden path lay a flower that someone had broken off. All around were beautiful flowers still growing. "Didn't all this color come from the sun?" asked the preacher. "Yet this flower here on the path is withering and dying. What made it dry out?"

"The sun, I suppose."

"Yes," said the old preacher, "the same sun nourishes and destroys. The only difference is the relationship of the flower to its source of life."

God is love.

1 John 4:16 (NIV)

God is a consuming fire.

Hebrews 12:29 (KJV)

As long as we are properly related to our source of life, God's presence is a comfort and strength. But the same God will surely slay the wicked. God is love and God is justice, and they are both compatible with His perfect nature.

LIFE RESPONSE:

Does the light of God's presence make me blossom in love or wither in fear?

A PERSONAL RELATIONSHIP

A lady in Africa was ill. A member of her family brought her a tape recorder with a tape of "The Wesleyan Hour." She didn't want to listen, but since she was confined to her bed, she was a captive audience. Later, she wrote a letter telling what happened. She said that she had been a church member for years and had been faithful to the services and ordinances of her church. But as the message of the gospel was presented from the tape recording, God began to speak to her heart. She wrote, "I found tears flowing down my cheeks, and as you prayed, I prayed."

Does God give you his Spirit and work miracles among you because you observe the law, or because you believe what you heard?

Galatians 3:5 (NIV)

For the first time in her life she discovered what a personal relationship with God is. Worship for her had been forms and ceremonies. Now it is a dynamic experience as she is able to worship God in Spirit.

In the Old Testament many of the people worshiped God in fear. God was sealed off behind a thick veil separating the Holy of Holies from the rest of the sanctuary.

Now we can come boldly to the throne of grace.

LIFE RESPONSE:

Am I taking advantage of the opportunities of my personal relationship with God by spending time with Him in prayer and the reading of His Word?

THROUGH THE BIBLE

Exodus 21-23

CHOOSE FOR ETERNITY

I t is an indication of maturity to be able to accept responsibility for our own choices. Too many people blame someone or something else for their wrong choices. If I hadn't been born into this family, or if I were a different race, or if we weren't so poor, if I had a better education, or lived in a nicer neighborhood, or if society hadn't put so much pressure on me . . . and on and on.

Viktor Frankl, in his book *Man's Search for Meaning*, describes the reactions of two brothers with the same heredity and environment, who were in the same concentration camp under the Nazis. One became a saint and the other a swine. Frankl tells us the reason why. "Each man has within him the power to choose how he will react to any given situation."

Each of us is going to give an account to God for what we have done. No one else can answer for us. It would seem that it is much better to face the responsibility for our decisions and our actions now than to wait and face them before the judgment seat of Christ.

Do not envy a violent man or choose any of his ways.

Proverbs 3:31 (NIV)

You have a choice. You are not like a puppet on a string, forced by fate or circumstances or heredity or any other external factors. Assess the alternatives and choose wisely. Your eternal destiny is at stake.

LIFE RESPONSE:
I will make my earthly choices with eternity in mind.

THROUGH THE BIBLE
Exodus 24-27

We Need Guidance

This morning, perhaps millions of Americans received some kind of prompting, leading or intuition that affected their decisions. Many would say that leading came from the stars. Perhaps you have consulted your horoscope in the newspaper this morning. Most newspapers carry such columns daily. With more than ten million Americans steeped in astrology and another forty million dabbling in it from time to time, it has taken on the proportions of a major religion.

I will instruct you and teach you in the way you should go.

Psalms 32:8 (NIV)

Generations have looked to the stars, to prophets, fortune tellers, palm-readers, tea leaves and tarot cards for information regarding the future. While many play a dangerous game with Ouija boards, it is really a serious and dangerous practice.

Every day we make dozens of decisions, many of them without a second thought. Yet some seemingly insignificant decisions turn out to be of major importance. It is not surprising that people look for outside help.

Following the right guide is crucial, and God has promised guidance for His children through His Word, through the Holy Spirit and through prayer.

LIFE RESPONSE:

I will seek God's guidance first in making my life decisions.

THROUGH THE BIBLE

Exodus 28-30

UNLIMITED POWER?

A farmer was watching his fourteen-year-old boy drive the pickup truck around the farm. Rounding a curve in the lane too fast, the boy lost control and flipped the truck into a ditch containing about two feet of water. The father came running and found the unconscious boy pinned under the truck with his head half submerged.

Although the man was only five feet seven inches tall and weighed about 155 pounds, without a moment's hesitation he jumped into the ditch and lifted the truck off his boy. A farm hand ran up and pulled the boy out. Later the man could not budge the truck. The doctor explained that under crisis, a man's physical system can send an enormous discharge of adrenaline through his body, bringing forth superhuman strength.

Man is capable of accomplishment beyond his imagination. It is my opinion — and that of others as well — that man has never seen the limits of the human spirit.

Add to this unexplored potential the power of the Spirit of God dwelling within,

I am crucified with Christ: nevertheless I live; yet not I, but Christ liveth in me . . . I do not frustrate the grace of God . . .

Galatians 2:20-21 (KJV)

and the limits are pushed much farther. According to Paul's words to the Galatians, only uncrucified self can limit what man, plus God, can do.

LIFE RESPONSE:

I will let Christ's supernatural power work in me and through me.

THROUGH THE BIBLE

Exodus 31-34

SEEKING FOR FULFILLMENT

I often hear people say, "I don't feel fulfilled. I feel there is something lacking in my life. I haven't reached my full potential as a person."

The problem is that the world suggests fulfillment in the wrong way. It tells us we'll find fulfillment in a career, or in marriage, or in friendship, fame or fortune. But as someone has put it, there is a God-shaped vacuum inside each of us, and we can never know fulfillment until He dwells within.

You have been given fullness in Christ.

Colossians 2:10 (NIV)

Too many people feel empty, cold or dead when they are not high on drugs or drunk on alcohol. They cannot bear for the party to end. They don't want to go home to their lonely apartments.

You may know someone like this, or maybe have experienced it yourself. Sometimes, such a person is sure that fulfillment is just around the corner. If they can just find the right formula, meet the right person, or make the right deal, they will be on top. Happiness will be theirs.

God created us and He can recreate us in His image, no matter how marred and scarred we may be. Martin Luther said, "God created the world out of nothing, and as long as you are yet nothing, He can make something out of you."

LIFE RESPONSE:

I will seek "fulfillment" in Christ alone.

REBELLION OR RECONCILIATION?

Sin alienates us from God. It results in a broken relationship, a sense of being lost. Sin destroyed the beauty of God's perfect creation, His masterpiece — man. What was rightfully God's was usurped and stolen away.

After giving a series of radio talks on marriage and divorce, I received a letter from a very troubled listener. This lady had been a Christian but had fallen away. Her backsliding had resulted in a great deal of heartache, some of which she recounted in the letter. "I lost my children, I lost my husband, I lost my home, I lost my testimony, I lost my credit, I lost my health and I have almost lost my mind."

Then she said, "How sorry I am today. May God have mercy on me. How does a backslider return home? Do you honestly believe that God will take me back? Is there hope for someone like me with the Lord?"

Once you were alienated from God . . . But now he has reconciled you . . .
Colossians 1:21-22 (NIV)

What an illustration she is of the alienation that follows rebellion against God. Christ has become the visible evidence of God's willingness to be reconciled with us.

Is there hope for her? Yes! Just as there is hope for you. You can be reconciled to God through Jesus Christ.

LIFE RESPONSE:
I will take definite steps today to keep from "sliding back" in my faith.

BE NOT AFRAID

I remember that as a small boy during World War II, we experienced air raid drills and blackouts. My father was an air raid warden. When the sirens began blowing, Dad would leave the house and go through the neighborhood to see that all lights were out.

We sat in the darkness, listening to the sad wail of the siren. I didn't understand why the lights had to be out. Sitting there with Dad outside and the siren moaning, I was afraid.

Then in a matter of minutes, my father would come back into the house, the all clear whistle would blow, the lights would be turned on, and our spirits would brighten. It didn't seem nearly as frightening because Dad was close by.

Take courage! It is I. Don't be afraid.

Mark 6:50 (NIV)

Fear can have devastating physical effects, even causing actual illnesses. Far more serious, however, are the spiritual conditions caused by fear: double-mindedness, instability, inconsistency, unhappiness, lack of contentment, and backsliding. Fear is the enemy of faith and the great disrupter of the spiritual life which is lived by faith.

Fear dissipates in the presence of Christ. As long as the Apostle Peter kept looking at Christ, he was able to walk on the water. By keeping our eyes on Jesus, we will be more aware of His love and care than of the storms around us.

LIFE RESPONSE:
I will consciously surrender my fears to the Lord Jesus Christ.

THROUGH THE BIBLE
Mark 1-3

JESUS HELPS US CARRY OUR LOAD

W e visited a lumber camp museum in northern Michigan. The old bunk house, store, dining hall and workshop were all there. Displayed inside the workshop were some of the yokes used on the oxen that pulled logs. They were great carved pieces of wood with sticks that fastened the yoke around the neck of the animals.

The yokes looked heavy, cumbersome, almost unbearable. What were those yokes for? Were they designed to weigh the beast down and torture it? The very opposite is true. The yoke is made to make the burden lighter. In fact, attached by any other means, the load would be unbearable. Pulled by the yoke, the heavy burden is made light.

A yoke makes hard work light. It relieves pain instead of causing it. Jesus offers His children a way of making the suffering and pain of life more bearable. He spent His early years in the carpenter shop and knew well the importance of a well-fitted yoke.

Take my yoke upon you, and learn of me . . .

Matthew 11:29 (KJV)

Jesus invites us to share the yoke with Him. He helps us bear life's burden of trouble and pain. We who are weary can take His yoke and find rest. His yoke is easy and His burden is light.

LIFE RESPONSE:

I will put on the "yoke" of faith and let Christ share my burdens.

FAMILY PRIORITIES

When Jesus visited the home of Martha, Mary and Lazarus at Bethany, He got right into the middle of a family quarrel. Mary sat at Jesus' feet to hear His words, but Martha was concerned about keeping house. She may have been fixing a meal for their guest, or taking care of household routines. Those things are necessary.

Martha may have had a legitimate complaint about Mary's failure to help carry her share of the load. But Martha allowed the chores of the house to destroy the cheerfulness of the home. She allowed herself to be weighed down with work while Jesus was giving the Word of God.

Martha, Martha, . . . you are worried and upset about many things, but only one thing is needed.

Luke 10:41-42 (NIV)

When she came to Jesus to complain, He helped her establish proper priorities. Some things are more important than a neat, clean house. Loving family relationships and time spent with one another far outweigh the shine on the floor or the arrangement of the knickknacks. When the children have grown and gone, it is not the spotlessness of your kitchen that will make them long to come home. It is the spot you gave them in your heart.

LIFE RESPONSE:

As much as it depends on me, I will straighten the family priorities in my home.

NEVER ALONE

Late one night, I was driving home from a preaching assignment while a storm was blanketing Indiana with ice and snow. Several large trucks had slid off the highway and my route home was blocked. The road was getting more treacherous by the minute. The words of the Apostle Paul came to my mind and I said, "Lord, like the Apostle Paul, I am in danger on the highway, in danger in the storm, and like the apostle, I need your sustaining presence." I can tell you, I was no longer alone in the car that night.

So many people feel alone. I have visited the elderly who often live out their last years in heart-breaking isolation. I remember one lady who boasted of her son, telling of his successes and how busy he was. But behind her boasting, I could hear the cry of her lonely heart. She really wanted her son to visit, to call, to show some attention. Her talk of his busyness was her way of covering up her disappointment.

My Presence will go with you, and I will give you rest.
Exodus 33:14 (NIV)

But no one needs to feel alone. Children or parents may neglect you. Your companion may be gone. Neighbors may not drop in to visit — but you are not alone.

Best of all, we know we won't have to cross the Jordan alone!

LIFE RESPONSE:
I will reflect on the presence of Christ in my life today.

THE COMFORTER IS HERE

A familiar comic strip character carries with him his faithful and familiar blanket. For him, happiness is a warm blanket. Adults, as well as children, often need a security blanket. We mourn and need to be comforted.

Look at what has become the most recognized symbol of Christianity throughout the world — the cross, an emblem of suffering and shame. All of the tragedy, pain, anguish, injustice, suffering and sorrow of human existence are wrapped up in that old rugged cross. By taking that cross, Jesus Christ brought us the greatest source of happiness available to the human heart. Even in your time of mourning you can be happy, Jesus says, because you will be comforted.

. . . walking in the fear of the Lord, and in the comfort of the Holy Ghost.

Acts 9:31 (KJV)

The Apostle Paul, in the midst of great suffering — beatings, stonings, shipwreck, imprisonment, hunger, thirst and danger — knew he was not abandoned by God (2 Cor. 4:8-9).

Before Jesus left this earth, He promised He would not leave His children as orphans. He would give them a Comforter who would stay with them at all times. We have the confidence that we do not face life and death alone. We have the Comforter.

LIFE RESPONSE:
I will concentrate on the Comforter and not the crisis.

THROUGH THE BIBLE
Mark 10-11

ARE YOU A PRACTICAL ATHEIST?

Some time ago, because of an error by the bank, I overdrew my checking account. I received a notice from the bank that I did not have funds sufficient to cover the checks I had written. It was an embarrassing situation which had to be rectified immediately — especially since one of the checks was written to the IRS to pay my income tax. Because of my previous record the bank had paid the check but, even though it was their error, they expected me to correct the situation immediately.

Sometimes we draw upon our resources, only to discover to our dismay that they are insufficient. We lack the strength, the talent, the wisdom, or the ability to accomplish what we attempt. Our spirit of independence must give way to dependence, and our self-sufficiency must become a spirit of trust. It may hurt our pride. It may be embarrassing, even humiliating, but when we reach the end of ourselves and put our trust in God, we can experience our best accomplishments.

Without me ye can do nothing.

John 15:5 (KJV)

A few people may be *avowed* atheists, but many more are *practical* atheists. Regardless of what they claim to believe about the existence of God, they live their lives as though there is no God. The truly wise person knows how dependent he really is upon God.

LIFE RESPONSE:
How can I depend more on God in my daily life?

CAST YOUR CARE UPON THE LORD!

Some years ago, a terrible flood hit the area of Stroudsburg, Pennsylvania. On my way to college, I drove through the beautiful Pocono Mountains and viewed the flood-stricken valley. Homes had been ripped from their foundations. Cars had been carried for miles and left on the river bank, or against trees. Buildings had been smashed to piles of sticks.

It didn't make any difference whether the homes belonged to the rich or the poor. Mansions were destroyed, as were humble cottages. The river did not pick and choose. Everything in its path was flooded.

> *Casting all your care upon him; for he careth for you.*
>
> *1 Peter 5:7 (KJV)*

Some people are almost paranoid when trouble comes into their lives. "Why me?" they cry. But trouble is universal to the human family. Only the foolish man is unprepared for the floods and storms of life.

A Christian man from India wrote and asked me how he could better witness to his non-Christian friends and neighbors. He wanted to convince them that God is love, even when the same troubles come to Christians as well as to non-Christians. An effective witness is when Christians have the right attitude toward their troubles. Non-Christians often turn to drink, drugs, bitterness or suicide. Christians can cast their care upon the Lord.

LIFE RESPONSE:

Am I carrying my concerns or casting them on the Lord?

THROUGH THE BIBLE

Mark 14-16

THE WOUNDED HEALER

Before going to the pulpit for his first Sunday, the new pastor of a large church visited one of the elders. "If you could say one thing to me before I enter the pulpit of this great church on Sunday morning, what would it be?" The elder thought for a moment and then replied, "Just remember this: Each person that you look out upon as you are speaking, is sitting beside his or her own pool of tears."

Each of us sits by our own pool of tears. In his book *The Wounded Healer*, Henri Nouwen writes to those who would minister to the hurting. "His service will not be perceived as authentic unless it comes from a heart wounded by the suffering about which he speaks."

I visited a friend in the hospital. A fine surgeon and a Christian gentleman, he has performed surgery on members of our family as he has on thousands of others. We have always found him to be a considerate, caring doctor. But this time he was the one forced to lie in bed, to be cared for by others, to heed the advice of his doctors. He said it gave him a different perspective on hospital care. He was now the wounded healer.

Jesus, our suffering Savior, is our Wounded Healer. He was tempted as we are tempted, He hurt as we are hurt.

He was wounded for our transgressions . . . and with his stripes we are healed.

Isaiah 53:5 (KJV)

LIFE RESPONSE:
I will bring my wounds to the Wounded Healer.

THROUGH THE BIBLE
Leviticus 1–4

BAD THINGS . . . GOOD PEOPLE

In recent years, we have seen many powerful demonstrations of nature's force and fury. A hurricane levels much of the lower peninsula of Florida. A flood in the Midwest destroys crops, homes, businesses and whole towns. An earthquake makes a shambles of buildings, bridges and freeways in the West. Blizzards wreak havoc and take lives.

At times, it seems that nature is bent on wiping humanity from the face of the earth. Why must calamity strike even the best of people? If God is just, why doesn't tragedy come to bad people, not good people?

The Lord gave and the Lord has taken away; may the name of the Lord be praised.

Job 1:21b (NIV)

Is it true, as some preachers say, that if you serve God you will prosper? Can it be that if bad things happen it is because our faith is weak or we are disobedient?

The book of Job puts a different perspective on such theories. Here was a man who was wealthy, had a wonderful family, and served God so well that God pointed it out to Satan. When Job lost everything, he did not understand — but he still trusted the Lord.

In a fallen world, bad things happen to good people. But for a redeemed person, even bad things can work for good (Rom. 8:28). We can praise God even when we suffer loss and heartache.

LIFE RESPONSE:

I will learn to trust and praise God, even when bad things happen.

THROUGH THE BIBLE

Leviticus 5-7

God's Word — A Treasure

When the famous John Wanamaker was eleven years old, he bought a Bible. Years later he said, "I have, of course, made large purchases of property in my time, involving millions of dollars, but it was as a boy in the country, at the age of eleven that I made my greatest purchase. In the little mission Sunday school I bought a small, red leather Bible for $2.75 which I paid for in small installments. Looking back over my life, I see that the little red book was the foundation on which my life has been built, and the thing which has made possible all that counted in my life."

I have treasured the words of his mouth more than my daily bread.

Job 23:12b (NIV)

The holy books of other religions begin with flashes of light and have smatterings of truth, but they all end in utter darkness and leave us in despair. The Bible, in spite of the onslaughts of its enemies through the centuries, has withstood every attack and has been more widely distributed than any other volume. Why?

God's Word offers hope, salvation, the way to God and to heaven. It is the only safe and complete guide for faith and practice. God's Word has transformed the lives of unnumbered multitudes.

How important is the Bible in your life? Do you treasure it more than necessary food?

LIFE RESPONSE:

I will treasure the nourishment of God's Word even more than the nourishment of daily bread.

THROUGH THE BIBLE

Leviticus 8-11

IT IS FAITH
THAT SAVES

S halom aleichem," the letter began. I immediately suspected it was from a converted Jew. I was right. The writer continued, "I am Jewish . . . now of course a Messianic Jew, a born-again Jew. Nine months ago I heard a radio speaker discuss how Jesus is the Messiah. Of course, my Jewish mind said, No! This is nonsense. Jesus has nothing to do with us Jews. The week which followed I could not sleep at night. I finally wrote for some literature and read what was sent. I realized everything I read was true. I prayed to the God of our fathers and asked forgiveness, and asked Christ Jesus into my heart to become my only Savior and Lord. It was like a veil was lifted from my eyes. I could see how He, the crucified One, is the one for whom we have waited so long. The most wonderful moment of my life was when I knew in my heart of hearts my sins were forgiven."

> *Believe on the Lord Jesus Christ and thou shalt be saved . . .*
>
> *Acts 16:31 (KJV)*

No matter how religious this person may have been before this, he had not found peace with God or assurance of eternal life. Why? Because the Spirit does not come through our efforts and works but through faith in the work of Christ on the cross.

LIFE RESPONSE:

I will depend on the Lord Jesus Christ — not the church — for my salvation.

THE DARK TIMES

In *The Hiding Place*, Corrie ten Boom tells how her family sacrificed themselves in order to hide Jewish neighbors during the Nazi occupation of Holland in World War II. After being a prisoner in Ravensbruck, the infamous women's concentration camp, Corrie traveled worldwide telling her story. For thirty-three years she had no permanent home. When she was eighty-five, some of her supporters provided her a lovely house in California. It was a luxury she never dreamed she would have.

One day as her friend, the late movie director Jimmy Collier, was leaving her home, he stopped at the door and turned around. "Corrie, hasn't God been good to give you this beautiful home?"

His wife said to him, 'Are you still holding on to your integrity? Curse God and die!'

Job 2:9 (NIV)

She replied firmly, "Jimmy, God was good when I was in Ravensbruck, too."

There is a mistaken notion prevalent in church circles today that only health, wealth, prosperity, ease and comfort reflect God's goodness. What is implied is that God cannot be seen in the darkness.

Job's wife made the same mistake. In his trouble and torment, she urged Job to curse God and die. Never forget, God is good in the dark times, too!

LIFE RESPONSE:

I will look for God's goodness in the shadows as well as in the sunshine.

DO YOU BOSS YOUR BODY?

They called him Lucky Lindy, but he was proof of the old adage, "The harder I work, the luckier I get." Charles Lindbergh's nonstop flight across the Atlantic in May 1927, was not the careless fling of a daredevil. It was the culmination of long months of planning and preparation.

A man shared a hotel room with Lindbergh while he was in San Diego waiting for his plane, "The Spirit of St. Louis," to be prepared. Sometime after midnight, the man woke up and realized Lindbergh was not in his bed. "What are you doing?" the man asked.

"Practicing," Lindbergh replied.

"What in the world are you practicing in the middle of the night?"

I beat my body and make it my slave . . .
1 Corinthians 9:27 (NIV)

"I'm practicing staying awake all night." He had worked out a flight plan which would take him 3,600 miles and would last for over thirty-three hours. He wanted to be prepared in every way possible.

If a man disciplines himself to accomplish such a task (which brings only earthly rewards and recognition), how much more should we as Christians discipline ourselves to accomplish the task given to us by God (which promises rewards in heaven)?

Isn't "lazy Christian" a contradiction in terms?

LIFE RESPONSE:

Are my words and actions "out of control" or under God's control?

LIVING FOR SELF OR FOR OTHERS?

Is it true that all men are created equal? Or is the Declaration of Independence wrong? Obviously, there are many inequalities.

I once shook hands with a man who was called the strongest man in the world, a former weight-lifting champion. When we shook hands, I couldn't close my hand around his hand at all. For some time, he held the record for lifting the greatest bulk weight — 6,270 pounds! In terms of strength, he probably had no equal in the world.

Inequalities in wealth are also very obvious, as are inequalities in intellect and health. The only way we are at all equal is that we are all human beings, with (at least theoretically) equal rights, responsibilities and the obligation to live in concert with our fellowmen.

Human beings do not come off an assembly line. Each is as unique as our fingerprints. We have individual strengths and individual weaknesses, and we have a responsibility to use our strengths, abilities and talents to offset the weaknesses of others.

For none of us lives to himself alone . . .

Romans 14:7 (NIV)

"We then that are strong," Paul said, "ought to bear the infirmities of the weak" (Rom. 15:1 KJV).

LIFE RESPONSE:
I will make it my goal to live for others and not for self.

Time To Come Home

A pastor received a phone call from a friend who said, "You have to help me. I'm in hell." The pastor invited him to his office so they could talk.

When the man came in, he repeated his statement, "You must help me. I'm in hell."

"What do you mean?" the pastor asked.

"I mean I'm in torment. I'm miserable." He then told a tale of the most wicked kind of life. He was weighed down with guilt. Finally he said to the pastor, "Do you remember when we were young they used to preach that you could repent of your sins and be forgiven?"

. . . his father saw him and was filled with compassion for him; he ran to his son, threw his arms around him and kissed him.

Luke 15:20 (NIV)

The pastor said, "Yes, and some of us still preach it. You need to get on your knees and quit running away from God." The man fell to his knees and began the road back to God. He found the Father waiting with open arms. He left the office saying, "I haven't been this happy in years."

A person may have everything that it is possible to attain in this world, but he can never be happy dragging around a load of sin and guilt. It's time to come home!

LIFE RESPONSE:

Am I carrying any guilt that needs to be "carried" to the Father for His forgiveness?

THROUGH THE BIBLE

Leviticus 24-25

HEAVEN WITHOUT HELL?

During the nineteenth century William Booth, founder of The Salvation Army, concerned himself not only with the spiritual needs of people, but with their total well-being. The social and physical problems faced in the slums of London had to be addressed. Yet Booth said before he died, "I am of the opinion that the chief danger which confronts the coming century will be religion without the Holy Spirit, Christianity without Christ, forgiveness without repentance, salvation without regeneration, politics without God and heaven without hell."

You need someone to teach you the elementary truths of God's word all over again.

Hebrews 5:12 (NIV)

Someone recently asked students at Harvard about their views on God, the afterlife and Jesus. One said, "I would conceive of what you call heaven but I have no concept of hell. I can't picture God being all-punishing." And another, "I don't believe in hell. I believe more in degrees of heaven." Here are some of the brightest young people of our day saying what Booth predicted would come to pass.

When Christianity loses those ingredients which make it distinct, it sinks to the level of just another religion, one among too many religions of mankind.

LIFE RESPONSE:

I will learn the great truths of God's Word so that I will be able to defend them before others.

ACCEPT THE CHALLENGE OF JESUS

A director of a camp whose purpose is to lead young hoodlums to Christ says, "Being a Christian is the toughest thing in the world. What is tougher than loving your enemies?"

One of the boys who later developed into a rugged disciple said, "In this outfit we are all brothers and we're all men. It was too tough for me at first, but then I heard that through Christ all things are possible. I say a man is not a man, not a full man, until he gets to know Jesus Christ."

The Christian life is rough and that is what makes it challenging. When you pick up the cross to follow Jesus, you have accepted the greatest challenge you will ever face, and only those who can take it will stand.

> *If anyone desires to come after Me, let him deny himself, and take up his cross, and follow Me.*
>
> *Matthew 16:24 (NKJV)*

A trained horse is far more valuable than a wild one. Every athlete knows if he is to be at his best, he must accept the discipline of training. The player who cuts corners with the training rules and doesn't want to bother with practice, will never make it.

Discipline in the Christian sense is not meant to break you, but to make you. The uncontrolled energy of our lives will destroy us, but God can channel it into productivity.

LIFE RESPONSE:

In what areas of my life do I need to strengthen my discipline?

THROUGH THE BIBLE

Luke 1

YOU CAN CLAP AND CHEER

Handicapped from birth, Little Jamie was in first grade. He and his classmates were organizing a play for their parents and Jamie was hoping to get a leading part. Day after day he talked to his mother about their plans and how much he wanted a part in the play.

An excited Jamie eagerly went to school on the day of the tryouts. But all day long his mother worried. She intuitively knew he would not be selected because of his handicap. When it was time to pick Jamie up after school she went anxiously to meet him. The boy she had worried about came running and laughing. "Mom, guess what!" he exclaimed. "The teacher says I've been specially chosen to clap and to cheer."

Encouragement is one of the most necessary ingredients of life. Letting people know what you appreciate about them may help them realize the love of God more fully. Last year more than one million teenagers ran away from home, many of them yearning to be appreciated.

Let us encourage one another.
Hebrews 10:25 (NIV)

There are many things to clap and cheer about. When you are not center stage, be sure to encourage those who are. When someone else is down, be the one to encourage and uplift.

LIFE RESPONSE:
Who needs me to "clap and cheer?"

GUARD
YOUR MIND

O liver Wendell Holmes once said, "The human mind is like a checking account. As long as you keep putting money in the bank, a checkbook is like a book of magic. But stop making those deposits and the magic evaporates with a rude statement from the bank — no funds."

Thou wilt keep him in perfect peace, whose mind is stayed on thee: because he trusteth in thee.

Isaiah 26:3 (KJV)

If you keep putting into your mind those things that are pure, honest and of good report, you will have a reservoir from which to draw power, strength and peace. But if you put into your mind things that are evil and sinful, you have nothing from which to draw. Peace of mind is for those whose minds are stayed on God.

In order to have peace of mind, you must learn the secret of disciplining your mind. Bring your thoughts into captivity. Fill your mind with good things. Meditate on the Lord and His goodness. Reject worry and fear, and rejoice in the salvation God provides. Learn to be grateful — cultivate the habit of thanksgiving, the attitude of gratitude. Guard your mind.

LIFE RESPONSE:
What can I do to protect my mind from evil?

SUFFERING BRINGS UNDERSTANDING

Queen Victoria, a story goes, learned that the wife of a common laborer had unexpectedly lost her baby. Having experienced deep sorrow herself, the Queen called on the bereaved woman and stayed with her for some time. After she left, the neighbors gathered around, curious to know what she had said.

"The Queen said nothing," the grieving mother told them. "She simply put her hands on mine, and we silently wept together."

A few years ago, I was preaching at a camp meeting in the east when my wife and I received word that our five-month-old granddaughter had died. Many of our friends came to us and expressed their sympathy, and we appreciated all of them. But, visiting the camp that same weekend was a young couple who had lost their daughter just a short time earlier. We sensed that they understood our pain perhaps better than most others. They had been there.

When you endure suffering, keep in mind that you will be able to help others realize the comfort of Christ better as the result of your pain. Jesus Himself identifies with our pain because He, too, suffered.

> *. . . the God of all comfort; Who comforteth us in all our tribulation, that we may be able to comfort them which are in any trouble.*
>
> *2 Corinthians 1:3-4 (KJV)*

LIFE RESPONSE:
Who needs the comfort of Christ through me?

GOD NEVER FORGETS

A woman in Chicago was arrested for child neglect. Intending to fly to Puerto Rico for a vacation, she had taken her three-year-old son with her to O'Hare International Airport. The mother mistakenly believed the child could fly free by riding on her lap. When she attempted to check in for the flight she made two discoveries: first, that she would have to purchase a ticket for the boy and second, that she did not have enough money to pay for it. Her solution was to simply leave her child at the snack bar in the airport and go on the vacation by herself. When the plane landed in Florida, the woman was taken into custody and sent back to Chicago to face charges.

Can a woman forget her nursing child? . . . Surely they may forget. Yet I will not forget you.

Isaiah 49:15 (NKJV)

The prophet Isaiah asked, "Can a woman forget her nursing child? And not have compassion on the son to whom she has given birth?" It seems inconceivable. Maternal instinct is normally the deepest and strongest bond known to the human family. A woman who has gone through birth pangs to bring a child into this world may be expected to suffer any hardship or danger to insure that child's health and welfare. And yet the Lord says, "Surely they may forget, Yet I will not forget you."

Although mother's love has been known to fail, God promised He will never forget.

LIFE RESPONSE:

I will praise God for His constant love and care for me.

Grow Up!

Following the funeral of one of the older members of my congregation, I asked the question one Sunday, "Who will take the place of these who have been pillars of the church? We have leaned on them, looked to them for counsel, felt secure in their care. Now these older saints are dropping out of the ranks. Who will step into the gap? We must be maturing in the grace of God so we can become the means of support to others."

One young lady responded to my challenge. She said, "As one who has been raised and nurtured in the church, I recognize my responsibility of taking up the torch." That young lady eventually went to the mission field.

In all things grow up into him who is the Head, that is, Christ.

Ephesians 4:15 (NIV)

It is possible to become a Christian and then fail to grow to maturity in the faith. Christian maturity means stability and steadfastness, not being tossed about by winds of doctrine. Maturity means service, not being waited on. Mature Christians help support others, edifying the body by their words and actions.

Don't let your spiritual life suffer from arrested development. Put away childish things and mature into a productive saint in the kingdom of God.

LIFE RESPONSE:

By God's grace, I will "grow up" and not "slow up" in my faith.

A RIGHT TO BE SELFISH?

The philosophy of the world is, "Do your own thing, please yourself." Plenty of people encourage us in such selfish motivation. The business world bombards us with advertisements promoting the principles of personal pleasure and instant gratification: "You deserve a break today." "Have it your way." "Sure it costs more, but you're worth it."

We are living in a generation that is impatient with restraint of any kind. Young people, as well as many older ones, know little of delayed gratification. Although "I want it, and I want it now," is the driving force of too many people, self-centeredness is the basic cause of much of life's distress.

I'll say to myself . . . Take life easy.

Luke 12:19 (NIV)

Jesus underscored the fact that His followers were to live lives that flow outward rather than inward. He offered the rich young man a way to have eternal life. But the young man "went away sorrowful" (Matt. 19:22 KJV), unwilling to take an unselfish course.

The foolish farmer was a success in worldly terms. In Luke's account of the parable, the farmer used personal pronouns at least eleven times in those few sentences. His life was wrapped up in himself. God said he was a fool.

Where is your focus?

LIFE RESPONSE:

Am I trying too hard to take care of "number one"?

THROUGH THE BIBLE

Luke 10-11

GOD ON OUR TERMS?

I lived in a community some years ago in which a wealthy man built his own church. He hired a preacher to come every Sunday to his estate and conduct services in this private little church. That way, he could have it entirely on his own terms.

Many folks are like that. They want religion to some degree. They want the church and the preacher in their community to do their job. In their own way, they want God. But that is the problem. They want God on their own terms.

That was the tragic mistake made by Saul, the first king of Israel. From the humble, God-fearing man who hid when the people wanted to crown him king, Saul became a self-reliant, self-centered leader who presumptuously assumed the place of the priest in offering sacrifices to God. As a result, Saul also became a casualty in the battle between self and God.

You acted foolishly . . . You have not kept the command the Lord your God gave you.

1 Samuel 13:13 (NIV)

The prophet Samuel told Saul that God was more interested in obedience than He was in sacrifice. Religious observances and ceremonies are not pleasing to God unless they are accompanied by obedience in heart and life. If we think differently, we are only rationalizing.

LIFE RESPONSE:

I will determine to seek God on His terms.

❈

BRAIN TRANSPLANT?

Modern medicine, with its miracles of transplant surgery and genetic engineering, has raised serious questions and interesting speculations. Major organ transplanting is now commonplace. With what appear to be medicine's unlimited capabilities, many fear the possibilities and implications ahead. One such speculation involves brain transplants. What would happen if the brain of one person could be successfully transplanted into the body of another?

God promised through Ezekiel that He would take the old heart of His rebellious people — the heart of stone — and put in a new heart of flesh (Ezek. 11:19).

Paul urged the Romans to be transformed by the renewing of their mind (Rom. 12:2). But he tells the Philippians, to have the mind of Christ. Obviously, God's Word speaks of the spiritual heart and mind, not the physical counterparts.

Let this mind be in you, which was also in Christ Jesus.

Philippians 2:5 (KJV)

Having the mind of Christ will make us new people. Think of the attitude change! A new attitude of selflessness, of laying aside our rights; a new attitude of service, taking the very nature of a servant; and a new attitude of submission, obedient even to death.

Oh, to be like Thee, blessed Redeemer!

LIFE RESPONSE:

I am determined to think Christlike thoughts, say Christlike words, and do Christlike deeds.

THROUGH THE BIBLE
Luke 14-16

MIDDLE AGE

That is the story of life. When Konrad Adenauer was chancellor of West Germany, he was chafing under the inconvenience of an illness. "I'm not a magician," his doctor said. "I can't make you young again."

"I'm not asking to become young again," the chancellor responded. "All I want is to go on getting older."

But many young people today are pessimistic about growing older. Part of that may be due to the threat of nuclear holocaust. Part may be the growing incidence of suicide, or deaths from alcohol, drugs and AIDS. But in spite of many fears, even these pessimistic young people will, for the most part, move on to adulthood and middle age. Since the average life expectancy in America is about seventy years, "middle age" is around thirty-five.

Middle age can be a dramatic and traumatic time for many people. It may be a time of success for some, and disillusionment for others. Jesus told of a rich man who had "arrived." He had the wealth to make plans for a comfortable future filled with ease and plenty. Yet he had reached middle age without making any plans for the world beyond. He thought that for himself, life was really beginning at forty! Jesus said this man was a fool because he had not planned ahead for his immortal soul.

I was young and now I am old.

Psalms 37:25 (NIV)

LIFE RESPONSE:

Have I planned for eternity as much as I have planned for this life?

WISE CHOICES

A farmer hired a man to dig postholes. The fellow finished the job in no time. The next day he told the man to clear stumps. That, too, was done in record time. The third day, the farmer decided to reward such hard work by giving the man an easy job — sorting out bad potatoes. After about three hours the man quit. "The job was easy enough," he said, "but the decisions got me down."

Every one of us is faced with making decisions every day. We recognize some of these decisions, even as we make them, as being important. We make other, less significant decisions, however, almost without a second thought. But all of these decisions, whether we realize it or not, work together to determine our destiny.

By faith Moses . . . chose to be mistreated along with the people of God.

Hebrews 11:24-25 (NIV)

William Jennings Bryan said, "Destiny is not a matter of chance, it is a matter of choice. It is not a thing to be waited for, it is a thing to be achieved."

In order to make an intelligent decision, we must assess the alternatives. Moses chose to suffer affliction rather than to enjoy pleasures. That doesn't sound very wise, does it? But Moses wasn't making a decision for this life only. He had his eternal destiny in mind.

LIFE RESPONSE:

What are the eternal consequences of the choices I am making right now?

READ AND HEED!

S ome years ago, *Reader's Digest* ran an advertisement captioned, "Send me a man who reads." The advertiser believed that a man who reads will be more intelligent, more informed and of greater value than the man who does not read.

We are rapidly becoming a people who do not read. Many students in our high schools and even our colleges are functionally illiterate.

It has been said, "The pen is mightier than the sword." But it appears the pen is losing some of its potency. What is written can have an impact only if it is read.

To date, the Bible is the best-selling book of all time. Millions of copies are printed every year. Yet a great number of people in our country admit that — even though they own a copy — they never read the Bible. Somehow, they think the message of God's Word is not relevant to their lives and problems.

God's Word is displayed prominently in many homes and is dusted every week. Yet the message remains untapped. It is merely a status symbol or a "good luck charm" for the home.

Give attendance to reading.
1 Timothy 4:13 (KJV)

The Word of God is powerful, but we cannot experience that power unless we read it, meditate on it, heed it, and hide it in our hearts.

LIFE RESPONSE:
Am I plugged in to the power source of God's Word?

DON'T PROCRASTINATE

While driving down a street in our city one day, I saw a long line of people. For a moment I wondered what had brought so many people to the same place. Then I saw that the line began at the License Branch and I remembered it was the last day to renew automobile licenses for another year. All these people, who had known for a year the expiration date of their license plates, had waited until the last minute to purchase new ones.

Be ye also ready.
Matthew 24:44 (KJV)

It seems to be human nature to procrastinate and then scramble at the last minute. Jesus knows human nature. The Bible says He doesn't need anyone to tell Him about man because He knows what is in man. He knows that if He told us the day and the hour that He was coming, we would attempt to be ready just for that hour.

The uncertainty of the future, of death, of Jesus' second coming, should motivate us to prepare and stay prepared every day — even every hour. He said His coming would happen very quickly, like lightning flashing across the sky (Matt. 24:27). Two shall be sleeping in a bed; one will be taken and the other left (Luke 17:34). The one who is prepared will meet the Lord in the air while the one who is unprepared will be left behind.

LIFE RESPONSE:

I will not put off the most important things. I will prepare to meet the Lord today!

THROUGH THE BIBLE
Luke 23-24

STAND UP FOR YOUR RIGHTS?

Stand up for your rights!" is shouted by every conceivable minority and interest group today. People promoting their rights (the new heroes of modern society), parade up and down the streets of America. The unalienable rights to life, liberty and the pursuit of happiness affirmed by our nation's founding fathers have grown and multiplied. Liberty has become license. The pursuit of happiness has degenerated into the pursuit of pleasure, while the right to life is denied to millions at both ends of the age scale.

Jesus did not consider His own rights something to be clung to. He never said, "I have my rights." A man of sorrows and acquainted with grief, He was denied the right to pursue happiness. Falsely accused, arrested and given a mock trial, he was denied the right to liberty. Never resisting His enemies, He was denied His right to life.

Your attitude should be the same as that of Christ Jesus . . . he humbled himself.

Philippians 2:5, 8 (NIV)

His spirit was one of total selflessness. This attitude of servanthood is the same attitude His followers should have. Jesus demonstrated this at the Last Supper when He washed His disciples' feet.

LIFE RESPONSE:

I will not be so busy demanding my rights that I fail to be a servant of the Lord Jesus Christ.

Playing Second Fiddle

A ndrew is almost always referred to as Simon Peter's brother. Constantly living in the shadow of his better known brother, we could say he played "second string."

Generally, we have little regard for "second string." I once saw an illustration of that as I watched a football game on TV. A young quarterback was running the team with great success, while the crowd cheered him on. On the sidelines stood the man who had previously been the first-string quarterback. Known by everyone, he had won many honors and was a superstar.

. . . Andrew, Simon Peter's brother . . . first findeth his own brother Simon . . . And he brought him to Jesus.
John 1:41-42 (KJV)

But age had begun to catch up with him. Too many hard tackles by gigantic linemen had resulted in injuries. He lost his starting job to the rising new star. There he stood, looking rather dejected, watching someone else get the applause.

Unlike the aging football star, Andrew never looked dejected, never resented his brother's position as leader of the apostles. He seemed to understand that it's the second stringers that help make the first stringers what they are. Not everyone can be quarterback and not everyone can play first violin! Andrew may have been "second string," but he was always introducing people to Jesus, including his own brother.

Can you play second fiddle effectively?

LIFE RESPONSE:

If I am called upon to play "second string," I will do it with grace and effectiveness.

THROUGH THE BIBLE

Numbers 3-4

DEDICATED DEPENDABILITY

Dependability is a rather quiet inner quality, not immediately obvious. It doesn't make much noise or attract much attention. It doesn't show on your face. You cannot wear a uniform that says, "I'm dependable." It sometimes takes years for anyone to notice. It means doing what is asked of you, whether anyone sees you or not. It means staying with your task when everyone else is off following the excitement of the day. It sometimes means being ignored, left out, even forgotten.

On a special feast day with an important visiting prophet, David the shepherd boy was away from it all, out in the pasture with the sheep. But dependability was one of the qualities God saw in him that was overlooked by his father.

A missionary was sent to a difficult and unresponsive field. For years he worked, prayed and preached, with negligible results. When a visitor to his field asked how many converts he had, he was told a very small number. "Why do you stay here?" the visitor asked. The missionary replied, "Because this is where God sent me. He wants me to stay."

That's dedication. That's dependability.

> *There is still the youngest, Jesse answered, but he is tending the sheep.*
>
> *1 Samuel 16:11b (NIV)*

LIFE RESPONSE:

By God's grace, I will make dedicated dependability one of my character qualities.

BEARING FRUIT

Have you ever thought about the difference one piece of fruit can make? One piece of fruit has within it the potential of producing an entire orchard. One piece of fruit has the seed power to feed millions. One piece of fruit is part of a chain of production and reproduction that can continue for centuries.

As someone has said, "Any fool can count the seeds in an apple, but only God can count the apples in a seed." What a difference one piece of fruit can make in God's scheme of things! And that is why your life can, and should, make such a difference. Jesus chose you to bring forth fruit that will remain.

I chose you and appointed you that you should go and bear fruit, and that your fruit should remain . . .

John 15:16 (NKJV)

Jesus was often criticized and ridiculed. But He simply kept on producing the fruit of righteousness in the lives of others, and that fruit has continued the reproductive process down through the centuries. Today, you and I can share in the same abundance of life He had.

We choose the kind of fruit we bear by choosing the kind of tree we will be. A good tree bears good fruit and a corrupt tree bears corrupt fruit. If Jesus is the Vine and we are the branches, it is obvious what kind of fruit we will bear, isn't it?

LIFE RESPONSE:

I will be the kind of "tree" that bears good "fruit."

CAREFUL LIVING

O ne of the problems most of us face is "busyness." We look longingly at the simpler, quieter days of our forefathers when the pace of life was seemingly slower and the strain less intense. We get flustered and pressured because most of us have not learned how to say a constructive "No."

Self-discipline is both negative and positive. Every day we should say a definite "No" to some activity, some personal desire, something that will not noticeably improve our lives. And we should say a definite "Yes" to some discipline which will add to our stature.

A thirty-five-year-old man told a psychologist that he wished he had gone to college. The psychologist suggested that he go now. The man said it would take ten years to get through college, going nights while he worked at a job. He said, "I'll be forty-five before I finish." The psychologist asked him how old he would in ten years if he didn't go to college.

Be very careful, then, how you live . . . making the most of every opportunity.

Ephesians 5:15-16 (NIV)

Establish what is most important in your life and discipline yourself to accomplish it. Careful living — with an eye to priorities — uses self-discipline to improve the quality of life.

LIFE RESPONSE:

I will treat every moment as a gift from God.

CHOOSE LIFE!

D r. J. C. McPheeters, former president of Asbury Seminary, Wilmore, Kentucky, was struck with tuberculosis while in his twenties. Although the prognosis was death, God saw fit to heal him. As a result of that illness, Dr. McPheeters began a program of regular and rigorous exercise, which he maintained for many years. He celebrated his 90th birthday by going water-skiing. He was truly a remarkable man who lived a productive and exemplary Christian life. At the age of 94 he suffered a stroke and died six months later.

I have set before you life and death . . . therefore choose life.

Deuteronomy 30:19 (KJV)

We can certainly prolong our physical lives by careful diet and exercise. Life is set before us, and we can choose to make the most of it. But the years inevitably take their toll. When the time comes to leave this world, it then becomes clear that another choice is even more important than the one that has to do with physical life.

God offers us the choice of spiritual life or death. That decision is, by far, the most crucial one we will ever make. It determines our eternal destiny. Every day, we make choices that impact that ultimate destination.

LIFE RESPONSE:
By my daily decisions, am I choosing life or death?

THE WISDOM OF A DAY OF REST

I have a friend who taps maple trees on his farm each spring to make maple syrup. He once told me that he does not gather the sap or boil it on Sunday. "I work all week," he said, "and I need that day of rest."

His neighbor argued that it was necessary to gather the sap during the relatively short period of time that it runs. So he worked seven days, not attending church for several Sundays because the boiling shed was in operation. His family worked with him to bottle the syrup.

But the man who rested on Sunday discovered he had better results and produced more syrup in six days than his neighbor did in seven.

Remember the sabbath day . . .
Exodus 20:8 (NKJV)

Whether you fight deadlines, travel widely, struggle with youngsters in a classroom — however you earn your living — you still need to rest one day in seven. The pace of modern man demands more than ever before, a Sabbath — a day of rest and restoration.

God planned this day for our benefit, then honors those who keep His day holy! Worship in God's house revives and renews our spirits. People would have fewer ulcers, less high blood pressure and heart disease, and would live longer if they heeded God's wise plan for a day of rest that honors Him.

LIFE RESPONSE:
Do I faithfully observe a day of rest?

KNOWING CHRIST PERSONALLY

What is your opinion? Who is this Jesus? One of my seminary professors wrote a little booklet titled "Liar, Lunatic, or Lord of All." Was He a liar? Were His claims of divinity, of oneness with God, carefully calculated falsehoods?

Was He a lunatic, an egomaniac? Did delusions of grandeur plague Him? He believed himself to be a god. The statements He made would be madness if they were not true.

The only other option is, He is the Lord of all. He said, "All authority in heaven and on earth has been given to me." (Matt. 28:18 NIV). The resurrection of Jesus Christ from the grave is the most remarkable event in history, because when He came forth from the grave, He had the keys of death and hell.

I want to know Christ . . .

Philippians 3:10 (NIV)

How would you answer the question, "Who is this Jesus?" Is He the living Savior? More importantly, is He *your* personal Savior? It is possible to believe the truths told about Jesus and yet not yield your own heart and life to His claims.

What a tragedy, to know about Him and yet not know Him personally!

LIFE RESPONSE:
I will do everything I can to enhance my relationship with Christ.

LET JESUS LIGHT YOUR WAY!

When a city has a high crime area, the installation of better lighting curtails criminal activity.

At my last pastorate, there was a problem with nighttime break-ins at our church. Someone was able to break through a basement window, enter the church, and search for valuables.

After trying and failing to stop these break-ins, we finally installed lights at each corner of the building. These lights automatically turned on at dusk and switched off at dawn. When lit, the entire area around the building was as bright as noonday. Immediately the burglaries stopped.

Light has come into the world, but men loved darkness instead of light because their deeds were evil.

John 3:19 (NIV)

All kinds of fears hide in the dark. I remember as a child looking at the pattern in my bedroom wallpaper and imagining all kinds of creatures and monsters. When the lights were turned out, some of those imagined creatures would seemingly come out to haunt me. By daylight, they had once again faded into the wallpaper.

Jesus is the Light and when He is present, sin ceases. He drives the darkness out of people's hearts and lives. He sheds light on life's pathway so that no one needs to stumble in the dark.

LIFE RESPONSE:

How can I bring the light of Jesus Christ into the lives of others?

THROUGH THE BIBLE

Numbers 21-23

Conquering Our Fears

An older lady was making her way up the stairs of her apartment building when she saw a figure in the shadows of the hallway. At first she began to panic, thinking someone was waiting to attack or rob her. Then, words of a song came to her mind and she began to sing, "When you walk through the storm / hold your head up high . . . / you'll never walk alone." Past the shadowy figure she walked, singing until she was safe in her apartment.

I sought the Lord, and he heard me, and delivered me from all my fears.

Psalm 34:4 (KJV)

The next morning, a note had been slipped under her door. The person hiding in the darkness thanked her for singing. Deeply despondent, he had contemplated taking his own life. But when he heard her singing, "You'll never walk alone," something in him said, "Try again!"

The lady had defeated her fears and more than that, had inspired a defeated soul. Her song reminded him, as it had reminded her, of the nearness of God.

Most of our troubles are magnified by fear. Many people let fear make monsters out of mice and mountains out of mole hills. With God, we can conquer our fears and face our problems.

LIFE RESPONSE:

Rather than being controlled by my fears, I will put them under God's control.

FRIEND OF SINNERS

When Mrs. Catherine Booth (who with her husband, William, founded the Salvation Army) was a young girl, she was running along the road one day with a hoop and a stick. She saw a prisoner being dragged away by the Constable to be locked up in the local jail. A mob followed along, hooting, yelling and threatening the prisoner.

It seemed to Catherine that he looked lonely and helpless, and that there wasn't one friend in the world for that poor culprit. Quickly, Catherine pressed through the crowd. She wanted him to know that there was at least one soul who felt for him. Whether he was guilty or not, he needed a friend, and Catherine wanted to be that friend.

The Son of Man . . . a friend of tax collectors and sinners!

Matthew 11:19 (NIV)

Jesus was accused by the Pharisees of being a friend of publicans and sinners. A stinging accusation, it was and still is true. He is a friend to all, not just to saints who seem to deserve His friendship, but to sinners who have no one else to care. One of our best-loved gospel songs says it well, "What a friend we have in Jesus / All our sins and griefs to bear."

He is a Friend who will always be there for us.

LIFE RESPONSE:

Do I know someone who needs to meet my friend Jesus?

ALL THE MONEY YOU NEED

Have you ever wished you could have all the money you need? Have you ever noticed how quickly a raise in pay is absorbed into a higher standard of living?

One way to have all the money you need is to distinguish between your needs and your wants.

My father was born in a simple log cabin home without electric power, running water or labor-saving devices. Today, my family lives in a totally electric house, filled with appliances and gadgets we think we can't do without. A disruption of power during a thunderstorm is a major event. We light candles and it seems like a nice change. But as time goes on, we realize there is very little we can do in our house without electricity.

My God shall supply all your need.

Philippians 4:19 (KJV)

What were luxuries to a previous generation seem to be absolute essentials now. All the money we need is far less than all the money we want.

We also need to differentiate between treasures and trash — determine what is *real* treasure, what is valuable. Henry David Thoreau said, "Money is not required to buy one necessity of the soul."

Gold can never satisfy, but God supplies all our needs.

LIFE RESPONSE:

I will praise God for supplying everything I *need*.

THROUGH THE BIBLE

Numbers 31–33

THE GOOD SHEPHERD

When my wife and I visited Italy, we toured the ruins of Pompeii one afternoon. We were climbing a tower on the outer wall when we heard a loud commotion. Hurrying to the top of the tower, we looked out over the wall. There we saw the most beautiful illustration of the truth of the Good Shepherd that I have ever seen.

The noise we heard was a large flock of sheep coming in from their pasture. At the head of the long line was the shepherd, carrying a tiny lamb. Kept from their mothers during the day, the baby lambs were now about to be reunited for the night. One of the little ones could not get over a section of fence that had separated them, and the shepherd boosted him over. It was a beautiful and moving sight.

I am the good shepherd: the good shepherd giveth his life for the sheep.

John 10:11 (KJV)

One well-known painting of the Good Shepherd pictures Him walking with a staff in one hand and a little lamb cradled in the other. Another artist portrays the Good Shepherd reaching out to rescue a lost sheep.

Jesus is our Good Shepherd, tenderly demonstrating His love, protection and care. He knows each of us by name and has proved His love by laying down His life for us.

LIFE RESPONSE:

Am I filled with anxiety or am I resting in the care of the Good Shepherd?

THROUGH THE BIBLE

Numbers 34-36

LIFE CAN BE BEAUTIFUL

O ne rainy morning, a man sat down in a hotel dining room next to a preacher and said, "Isn't this a terrific morning?"

"Well, I guess it is," the preacher responded. "It's raining though."

"But just look at those raindrops glistening like diamonds," the man continued brightly. "It's beautiful."

"How did you get to be so enthusiastic?" asked the preacher.

I am the resurrection, and the life: he that believeth in me, though he were dead, yet shall he live.

John 11:25 (KJV)

"Some time ago I was in an accident," the man replied, "and the doctors were not sure they could save my life. It was touch and go for some time, but by the grace of God, I got well. Now, everything is so different for me. It seems like I never really lived before. The world is beautiful. Simple things are so exciting. I feel like I'm really alive now."

What happened to this man? He had come to see the preciousness, the *value* of life. When he almost lost it, he realized that what he wanted most was life. And having that, everything about life became beautiful.

Jesus, the Risen Lord, came to remind us that life is more than just an earthly existence. But He also came to make this earthly existence an experience of abundant life and joy.

LIFE RESPONSE:

I will make every day a "resurrection day" — abundant and joyful.

GRACE, OUR TEACHER

G race is the teacher of a great lesson. The function of grace is to bring salvation. Grace, as you may already know, is the unmerited favor of God. It cannot be bought or earned. It is a demonstration of God's unconditional love to us. Grace teaches us — not out of any obligation on God's part — but because of His love.

I remember my seventh and eighth-grade English teacher, Miss McQuaid. A tough teacher, her lessons were hard and her standards high. She was a strict disciplinarian. Although I did not appreciate her at the time, I now see that she was one of the most outstanding teachers in my educational process. That is because I learned something from her. She did one thing and she did it well. She taught us English grammar. It was her function as a teacher.

The grace of God that bringeth salvation hath appeared to all men. Teaching us . . .

Titus 2:11-12 (KJV)

The grace of God brings salvation. "For by grace you have been saved through faith" (Eph. 2:8 NKJV). Grace teaches us to say "no" to wrong and "yes" to right. It teaches us to live godly lives in this present age. It teaches us to be ready for the glorious appearing of Jesus Christ.

Grace, like any top-notch teacher, makes a tremendous contribution to our lives. We can show our appreciation by listening and putting her lessons into practice.

LIFE RESPONSE:
What are some lessons God is trying to teach me?

THROUGH THE BIBLE
John 4-5

COMFORT OR THE CROSS?

A pastor remarked that less than 100 years ago, members of the church he currently pastored were ridiculed and their pastor hissed at as he walked down the street. The old-time religion sought to be at odds with the world. The world and the church met at right angles and formed a cross. Today we run in parallel courses and have lost the reproach.

Some Christians think they are bearing their cross when they have a headache or some other minor inconvenience. But that is not the cross either Jesus or Paul the apostle refer to. Too many Christians today know little or nothing about the crucified life, the life of self-denial.

> *Jesus Christ laid down his life for us. And we ought to lay down our lives for our brothers.*
>
> *1 John 3:16 (NIV)*

We leave our comfortable homes, ride in our comfortable cars, sit in comfortable churches and hear comforting sermons. One pastor said he was called to comfort the afflicted and to afflict the comfortable. We have eloquence in the pulpit and elegance in the pew. But God still calls for self-denial in the hearts and lives of His people.

The real cross is not a pretty decoration but a rugged place of decision and death — death to sin, to self and to the world.

LIFE RESPONSE:
"Lord, help me to die to sin, self and the world."

JESUS IS PREPARING A PLACE

Several years ago, there was a television special about one of the tragic aftermaths of war — Amerasian children, the offspring of American GIs and Vietnamese women. Deserted by their fathers, unwanted by their mothers, rejected by society, these children were searching for identity and acceptance. A few of them have been found and claimed by their natural fathers. Some have been adopted. But the majority are not accepted in either Asia or America.

Everyone needs love and acceptance. There is no greater acceptance than that found in the Lord. Jesus said He was going to prepare a place for us so we could be with Him where He is.

What is heaven like? The description in the book of Revelation indicates something of its beauty, size and splendor. But the Bible doesn't tell us everything. One reason is that heaven is beyond the limits of human language to describe.

I go to prepare a place for you . . . I will come again, and receive you unto myself . . .

John 14:2b-3 (KJV)

The greatest thing that can be said about heaven, though, is that it is home, and that it is where Jesus is. Are you ready for that heavenly home?

LIFE RESPONSE:
Am I prepared to live in the place Jesus has prepared?

THE FELLOWSHIP OF HIS SUFFERINGS

A young woman doctor with much ability and a brilliant future was working at a leprosarium. One day, the car in which she was riding went down an embankment and turned over. She was severely injured and was never able to walk again.

At first, she thought her medical career was over. But with the help and encouragement of others, she began treating her patients again — even though she was confined to a wheelchair.

. . . the power of his resurrection, and the fellowship of his sufferings . . .

Philippians 3:10 (KJV)

She began to discover that something wonderful was happening. The leprosy patients displayed less of the self-pity, hopelessness and sullenness that had been evident among them before. When they were treated by a doctor who herself had to work from a wheelchair, a doctor who, in some cases, was more disabled than her patients, they had a different outlook and a greater hope. They recognized the fellowship of suffering.

With the right attitude toward our suffering, we can identify with Jesus who suffered on our behalf. We can also be a blessing to others who suffer.

LIFE RESPONSE:
I will look for a "sufferer" to bless today.

DO YOU TRUST HIM COMPLETELY?

Many years ago, my wife and I went to visit my brother and his family. They put us in their guest room, which was furnished with some second-hand furniture. None of us had much by way of possessions in those days.

Sometime near midnight, we were suddenly jarred out of a sound sleep by a loud bang and a quick drop. The slats, which held the springs and mattress of the bed, had fallen out, tumbling us to the floor. I fixed the bed as best I could and then tried to sleep. But I couldn't relax. I didn't trust that bed. I felt at any minute it would fall down again. I was tense all night attempting to hold myself up.

You may have had everything you trusted — everything you thought would hold you through any difficulty — fall out from beneath you. You woke up to the fact that nothing was left as a foundation for life.

Trust in the Lord with all your heart and lean not on your own understanding.

Proverbs 3:5 (NIV)

Every foundation for man's trust has sooner or later failed him, except when he puts his trust in God.

You can put your trust in Him with full assurance and confidence. The psalmist said, "Let all those that put their trust in thee rejoice: let them ever shout for joy, because thou defendest them . . ." (Ps. 5:11 KJV).

LIFE RESPONSE:

"Lord, help me to trust You in the 'tense' areas of my life."

WHAT'S THE GOOD OF SUFFERING?

A church leader visited a leprosarium in India and was amazed to hear the patients' testimony. They thanked God for their disease because it had brought them to the leprosarium where they had heard the gospel and been saved.

Helen Keller said, "I thank God for my handicaps, for through them I found myself, my work and my God."

Before I was afflicted I went astray: but now have I kept thy word.

Psalm 119:67

The psalmist found affliction an experience that turned his life around.

Would Fanny Crosby have given the world so many songs if she had not been blind? Could George Matheson have written "Oh Love That Wilt Not Let Me Go" if he hadn't passed through the trial of heartbreak? Would the "Hallelujah Chorus" have been so magnificent if Handel had written it *before* he suffered paralysis of his right side?

Dr. Edward Judson, son of the missionary statesman, Adoniram Judson, said when speaking at the dedication of Judson Memorial Church in New York City, "Suffering and success go together. If you are succeeding without suffering, it is because others before you have suffered. If you are suffering without succeeding, it is that others after you may succeed."

LIFE RESPONSE:

I will acknowledge that my suffering is part of the process of succeeding.

BELIEVING IS SEEING!

Of all the historic relics kept by the Roman Catholic Church, I suppose none has ever aroused more interest or provoked more controversy than the Shroud of Turin. You may have read about it. The image on the ivory-colored linen cloth appears to be that of a bearded man who has been beaten and wounded. Almost everything about the image on the shroud corresponds in some way to the biblical accounts of the crucifixion of Jesus.

Is this shroud authentic or is it a fraud? Has the actual burial cloth in which Jesus was wrapped been preserved through the centuries? Or has someone cleverly reproduced an image to fit the Bible record? This controversy has been going on for many years, and rather persuasive arguments for both sides have been presented.

Blessed are they that have not seen and yet have believed.

John 20:29 (KJV)

To my mind, the real question is not whether or not the Shroud of Turin is the actual burial cloth of Christ, but: What difference does it make? Would it change anything if it was found to be authentic, or if it is proven false? Would it make any difference in your faith?

I do not need a burial shroud to convince me of the reality of Christ's death or resurrection!

LIFE RESPONSE:

I will believe the fundamental truths of the Bible even though I may not fully understand them.

THROUGH THE BIBLE

John 18-19

ARE YOU CONTENTED?

One man spent much time in art galleries admiring great works of art. One day he was asked how he could get so enthused over things he could not even afford to have. He answered, "I would rather be able to appreciate things I cannot have, than to have things I cannot appreciate."

Someone has said, "You will never enjoy what you get until you learn to appreciate what you have."

Godliness with contentment is great gain.

I Timothy 6:6 (KJV)

What is the secret of contentment? How much could you give up — or have taken from you — and still be contented? Can you give up some of the trinkets, the luxury items, the expensive toys we have come to expect in our affluent society and still live with joy and peace and contentment?

There is a Christian discipline for the ups and downs in life: that in success you are not proud, and in failure you are not defeated. If your contentment depends on your circumstances, on your job, your car, your house, or even your health, then it is not deep enough.

It is only when our sufficiency is in God that we can truly be contented in every situation of our lives.

LIFE RESPONSE:

"Lord, help me to appreciate the 'things' You have already given me."

THROUGH THE BIBLE

John 20-21

Playing A Duet With God?

Paderewski was scheduled to perform in a great American concert hall. In the audience was a mother and her young son. The boy grew weary of waiting for the concert to begin. While his mother talked with friends, and drawn by the shining Steinway grand piano, he slipped out of his seat, walked down the aisle and stepped onto the huge stage.

Unnoticed by the sophisticated crowd, the boy sat on the bench and began to play "Chopsticks." The crowd at first grew quiet and then increasingly irritated. They shouted for the boy to be taken away. They had come to hear Paderewski, not "Chopsticks."

Strengthen the feeble hands . . .
Isaiah 35:3 (NIV)

Backstage, the great master overheard the commotion and looked out onto the stage. Hurriedly, he grabbed his coat and approached the piano. Standing behind the boy, he instructed him to keep playing. Then Paderewski, reaching around the boy on both sides, began to improvise a counter melody. The crowd was awed at what a master pianist could do to turn a child's song into a beautiful accomplishment.

How much like that little boy we are! How feeble our hands and how weak our efforts! But the Master comes and places His strong hands alongside ours, and begins to make something beautiful of our lives, all the while whispering, "Don't quit. Keep on playing!"

LIFE RESPONSE:
I am determined to rely on God's strength in Christian faith and service.

ARE WE MARKED BY THE CROSS?

A s a boy, one of my favorite radio programs was about the Federal Bureau of Investigation. The stories were reported to be taken from actual case histories in the FBI files. To add to the authenticity of the program, descriptions of fugitives were given at the end of each broadcast — descriptions of men and women on the FBI's ten-most-wanted list. Identifying marks were mentioned: scars, birthmarks, physical deformities, or other peculiarities that would make the person stand out.

. . . I bear on my body the marks of Jesus.

Galatians 6:17 (NIV)

We can often identify people by the uniform, badge or insignia they wear. Many Christians wear lapel pins, tie tacks and other things with symbols of the Christian faith. Perhaps the most recognizable symbol of our faith is the cross. We have gilded and adorned it. But in so doing, we may have forgotten that the cross originally was the most cruel means of torture and death.

Because Paul was a follower of Jesus Christ, he suffered for His sake. The stonings, beatings, shipwrecks and imprisonments left him scarred. Yet, Paul gloried in the cross — embraced it, preached about it — for he knew that we rise to walk in newness of life only after we have been crucified with Christ.

LIFE RESPONSE:
Do I wear the cross or am I marked by it?

THROUGH THE BIBLE
Deuteronomy 3-4

Jesus
Is With Us

A man gave a testimony on television of how God had protected him. He and his wife heard a noise in their house at night, and when he went downstairs to investigate, he found a masked burglar. The man began to pray, "The blood of Jesus be upon this house and upon this family." As he prayed, something happened to the burglar. He lost his nerve and left the house, without taking anything and without harming anyone. God was with them in the time of danger.

It is true that Christian people *do* get robbed or injured. But God's promise is that we don't have to face the danger alone. The writer of Hebrews reminds us, "The Lord is my helper; I will not fear. What can man do to me?" (Heb. 13:5-6 NKJV).

He Himself has said, I will never leave you . . .

Hebrews 13:5 (NKJV)

When David Livingstone — bearing in his body the marks of his African struggles — spoke to Glasgow University students, he told them what had supported him through his lonely, difficult years. He had staked everything on Jesus' words, "Lo, I am with you always, even to the end of the age."

That promise is for us today.

LIFE RESPONSE:

"Lord, help me to consciously think of Your presence in my daily activities."

GLORY IN THE CROSS!

Centuries ago off the coast of South China, Portuguese settlers built a massive cathedral on a hill overlooking the harbor of Macao. It seemed indestructible. But the awesome velocity of typhoon winds nearly leveled the entire structure. Only the front wall, topped by a huge bronze cross, was left standing. It seemed to challenge the elements, as if to say, "You may destroy everything else, but you cannot destroy the cross."

God forbid that I should glory, save in the cross of our Lord Jesus Christ . . .

Galatians 6:14 (KJV)

In 1825, Sir John Bowring was caught in a terrible storm in that same harbor and suffered shipwreck. Clinging to a piece of the wreckage, he had no idea where to find land. Then he caught sight of that bronze cross high on the hill. His dramatic rescue prompted Bowring to write a poem. Sometime later someone else put the words to music. For over 170 years, God's people have been singing, "In the cross of Christ I glory / tow'ring o'er the wrecks of time."

It isn't, of course, the blood-soaked wood of the cross that saves us, but the Savior who died there. It's what the cross represents and the covering it provides for our sins.

LIFE RESPONSE:

I will praise the Lord for the cross on which Jesus Christ died for my sins.

CHRIST DIED FOR SINNERS

A large apartment building was burning and people were trapped on the top floor. The firefighters put up ladders and began rescuing some of the tenants. But the longest ladder on their fire truck was several feet short of the top-floor window where people were calling for help.

Suddenly, one of the firefighters went up the ladder, stood on the top rung, and reached to the windowsill above. Then he called the people to climb down over him to the ladder and to safety. He literally became the ladder for them. When everyone was rescued and they helped the heroic firefighter down, his hands and arms were terribly burned. He had sacrificed his hands to fill the gap between those people and safety.

He died for us so that . . . we may live together with Him.

1 Thessalonians 5:9 (NIV)

"Scarcely for a righteous man will one die," Paul says, "yet . . . for a good man, some would even dare to die" (Rom. 5:7 KJV). But God showed His love by sending Christ to die for the ungodly. Not because we deserved it! Not that we have any merit of our own!

Christ became the ladder. His own body bridged the gap between guilty sinners and a holy God.

LIFE RESPONSE:
"Lord, thank You for Your great sacrifice."

THE EYE OF THE STORM

I remember seeing a satellite picture of a hurricane on the evening news. Weather tracking stations use such pictures to determine the intensity of a storm and to chart its course. I was particularly interested in the center of the storm, the eye of the hurricane. At the outer edges of the storm were the strong winds and heavy rains that cause extensive damage.

Yet in the center there was an almost perfect calm. The sky was clear and only a gentle breeze was blowing. Those in the "eye" of the storm may have been unaware of the violence not far away.

> *Fear not . . . When you pass through the waters. I will be with you.*
>
> *Isaiah 43:1b-2a (NIV)*

Sometimes life is like that. The storms rage all around us, but at the center of life there can be an inner peace. Yes, Christians go through storms just like everyone else, but the secret is to find that place of inner peace.

How is that done? By taking time to get quiet each day before God, by listening to what He says to us through His Word and His servants. Learn to wait upon the Lord, to slow down, to get free from the pressures and stress. Cultivate the carefree attitude of children who know their parents are taking care of everything.

Those who wait upon the Lord will renew their strength and live in the eye of the storm!

LIFE RESPONSE:

I will trust the Lord to protect me in the storms of my life.

THROUGH THE BIBLE

Deuteronomy 16-19

JUDGE NOW, JUDGED THEN

I met a family by the name of Smart when I was in South Africa. They had listened to "The Wesleyan Hour" for about a year and a half and had all the printed sermons stapled together. They happened upon the program quite by accident on TransWorld Radio from Swaziland. The husband and wife had experienced a particularly strong conviction while listening.

Before accepting Jesus as Lord and Savior, Mr. Smart went back into the Scriptures. Checking references in five encyclopedias, his conviction remained. His conversion was not an emotional one. He examined the facts, weighed the evidence and reached a verdict. Not everyone's conversion is that calculated, but each of us is called upon to reach a judgment and answer the question Jesus asked, "Who do you say I am?" (Matt. 16:15 NIV).

We shall all stand before the judgment seat of Christ . . .

Romans 14:10 (NKJV)

Is He God incarnate? Is He the Lamb of God slain for the salvation of the world? Is He who He claims to be? Our judgment of Him determines our destiny. And someday, we will no longer be making a judgment on Him. He will be making a judgment on us. When we stand before Him as our Judge, we can be very sure of one thing: His judgment will be righteous, for He will know everything about us. I want to face Him with the confidence born of knowing Him as my Savior. Don't you?

LIFE RESPONSE:

With God's help, I will live so that I will be able to stand before the Lord with confidence.

COMPLETE IN CHRIST

W hen I was a boy, one of our favorite family pastimes was piecing together beautiful jigsaw puzzles. But before we would begin, we would always check to be sure all of the pieces were present. Even a thousand-piece puzzle was counted to be sure it was complete. There were five children in a rather small house. Since everyone would get into the puzzle building, sometimes one or two pieces would get lost. No matter how beautiful the picture, it was always spoiled for me if one piece was missing.

Stand firm in all the will of God . . .
Colossians 4:12 (NIV)

I think God must feel like that when He looks at the human family. Having created man in His own perfect image, He now sees incompleteness.

Thousands of people admit they are unhappy. Economic security, recreation, pleasure, a good community to live in — none of these things has brought the peace and happiness they are looking for. The reason is that man was created in the image of God, and he cannot find complete rest, complete happiness, or complete peace until he finds himself in God.

"Ye are complete in him," Paul says (Col. 2:10 KJV). Only Christ Jesus offers complete forgiveness from sin and complete freedom from its power.

LIFE RESPONSE:
Do I have a feeling of completeness in Christ?

WITH YOUR WHOLE HEART

Many graphic and moving images were broadcast from Desert Storm. Among the most dramatic was the surrender of a group of Iraqi troops. Hands held above their heads, they emerged from their bunkers. As an American soldier motioned them to kneel on the ground, one of the prisoners grabbed his hand and kissed it. Their relief at being captured alive was evident. It was later reported that these troops had been cut off from their companions — communication was nearly nonexistent, their supply lines had been severed, they had been surviving on one meal a day, and they did not want to fight.

War is no place for halfhearted effort. A soldier with no will to fight is bound to lose.

Do you remember Mary Lou Retton, the energetic, vivacious teenager who won a gold medal in the 1984 summer Olympics? Her infectious smile was captured on a cereal box and she was in great demand for appearances on various television programs. What was the secret to her success? Training, of course. But the intangible element not found in training is wholeheartedness. Success as a Christian is no different. "Love the Lord with all of your heart."

> *Amaziah did what was right in the eyes of the Lord, but not wholeheartedly.*
>
> *2 Chronicles 25:2 (NIV)*

LIFE RESPONSE:
Am I wholeheartedly serving the Lord?

THROUGH THE BIBLE

Deuteronomy 28-29

CHOOSE A WORTHY HERO!

W hen I was a boy during World War II, General Douglas MacArthur was the hero of many young boys. We had posters with his picture on the walls of our bedrooms, and we wore broken-down army caps like his.

It is natural to look for someone we can admire and emulate. Every year, a list of the most admired men and women is published. Many of today's heroes come from the world of sports or entertainment.

. . . Christ Jesus: Who, being in very nature God . . . being found in appearance as a man.

Philippians 2:5, 8 (NIV)

Usually our heroes of the past, whether in fact or fiction, have been given godlike characteristics. But the Bible reminds us that Elijah was a man subject to passions like ours. The Bible characters were not supermen, or half-gods. They had physical limitations, shortcomings and infirmities like we do. But they were God's men and women.

In all of history, there has been only one person who combined the attributes of God and the body of man, and that is the God-Man, Christ Jesus. He was God in human flesh, the omnipotent God clothed in infant weakness, the eternal God wrapped in mortal flesh, the omniscient God increasing in wisdom and stature.

He is the only hero worthy of emulation!

LIFE RESPONSE:
What Christlike qualities should I imitate in my daily living?

LIKE A
LITTLE CHILD

As a child, I would say my evening prayers, jump into bed, and drop immediately and blissfully into restful sleep. I didn't listen for leaky water pipes or dripping faucets. I didn't hear malfunctioning appliances or worry about leaking roofs. Whether or not the mortgage payment on the house had been made didn't concern me in the least. I knew that my father took care of all those things.

Jesus said that when we become converted we must be like little children. One childlike trait that each of us must have in order to know the richness and fullness of eternal life is simple trust. As a child trusts his father's love and care, so we must become like little children and trust our Heavenly Father.

Whoever does not receive the kingdom of God as a little child will by no means enter it.

Luke 18:17 (NKJV)

We should begin our day with a recognition of God's presence, trusting to Him the unknown events of the next few hours. We should end the day with thankfulness for His care and commit all worrisome concerns into His hands. Then we can lie down and enjoy a good night's sleep. Our Father is watching over His children.

LIFE RESPONSE:
    I will commit my earthly concerns to my heavenly Father.

CHRISTIANITY ROSE AGAIN!

I n 1948, a Romanian Christian pastor was taken prisoner by the Communists. For sixteen years, he was moved from one camp to another, brutally beaten, drugged and tortured. He underwent brainwashing of the most diabolical kind. After years of imprisonment, he almost reached the breaking point. One day, the prisoners were given postcards to send, inviting their families to visit them. Their hopes rose as they shaved, washed and were given clean shirts. But no one came to visit. He did not know then that the postcards had never been sent.

Mary stood outside the tomb crying.

John 20:11 (NIV)

That night the loudspeakers blared, "Nobody loves you now, nobody loves you now." The next day he was told that plenty of other wives had come to visit. They told him his wife was unfaithful to him. That night the loudspeaker blared, "Christianity is dead, Christianity is dead." He almost believed it. He thought the time of great apostasy had arrived.

Then he remembered Mary Magdalene, who wept and waited at the tomb of Jesus. He decided that if Christianity was dead, "I will weep at its tomb until it arises again, for it surely will."

The words written by that pastor have come true. Christianity has risen again in Romania.

LIFE RESPONSE:
"Lord, help me to concentrate on the hope of the Resurrection."

THROUGH THE BIBLE

Acts 1-3

STRENGTH IN WEAKNESS

I remember a windstorm one spring in Indiana. A few days earlier, my wife and I had transplanted some young pine trees to the front of our yard. I watched them bend and sway in the wind. They were so young and tender. Their trunks were thin and looked so fragile. It appeared as though the strong gusts would tear them from the earth. But when the storm had passed and the wind was calm, those tiny pine trees had bounced back and were standing straight and tall.

Down the street, my neighbor had not fared as well. Lying across his lawn was a giant of a tree which had probably stood forty or fifty feet tall, and was at least four feet around. One strong gust of wind, it seemed, had been too much for that old giant. Then we saw something none of us had been aware of. Within the broken trunk, the center of the great tree was rotten. Its heart was dead. Although it was large and appeared to be strong from the outside, it had been weakened from within and was no longer able to bend in the wind. While little wispy pine trees bent and swayed, the giant tree broke.

When I am weak, then I am strong.

2 Corinthians 12:10b (NIV)

When vital life is at my center, I may appear weak — but I won't break when storms come.

LIFE RESPONSE:

I will actively seek to strengthen my inner self.

A WALKING SERMON

When I was learning to preach, students in homiletics class were required to write different types of sermons on various subjects. I went to the library and researched each subject carefully. Then I wrote out my sermons precisely and with much care. When the course was completed, as I recall, I received an acceptable grade on those sermons.

A few years later when I began pastoring, I tried unsuccessfully to use those sermons in my church. I found that very few of them had much effect on real people who worked and played, who laughed and cried, who lived and died in a very real world. These sermons were all recitations of truth, but they were not related to real life experience. A real sermon is not just an academic discussion or a philosophical dissertation, even though it must deal with truth. A real sermon is the application of eternal truth to real life situations.

> *Who is wise and understanding among you? Let him show it by his good life . . .*
>
> *James 3:13 (NIV)*

The poet Edgar Guest wrote,

"I had rather see a sermon/Than hear one any day /I'd rather one should walk with me/Than merely tell the way."

If that is the case, every Christian can be a walking sermon!

LIFE RESPONSE:
What kind of a "sermon" am I preaching to those around me?

WHERE CAN I FIND HIM?

Where can you find God? Can you find Him while gazing into the starry heavens? In a beautiful cathedral or temple? While listening to an organ play or a choir sing? Yes, He can be found in all these places.

But we need to look for Him right where we are. Like the disciples on the road to Emmaus that first Easter Sunday, we can find Him while taking a walk or sitting at the supper table.

Life has not been the same since that first Easter. When Jesus Christ defeated Satan and sin, death and hell, He brought the reality of God's presence into the everyday routine of human existence. He's walking the road, talking with friends, breaking bread.

. . . the presence of the Lord . . .

Psalm 97:5 (NKJV)

A little motto that used to be quite common says, "Christ is the head of this house, the unseen guest at every meal, the unseen listener to every conversation." Wouldn't your home be a better place if you could recognize the presence of God in the daily bustle of your family life?

Look for Him on the bus or train, on the way to work, in the routine of your day. If you really want to find God, you can, but you must search for Him with your whole heart. Life can never be boring when Jesus is by your side.

LIFE RESPONSE:

I will look for God in the daily routines of my life.

THROUGH THE BIBLE

Acts 9-10

THE RIGHT SIDE OF EASTER

Although Jesus had risen from the dead, the disciples were cowering in fear behind locked doors. They were living on the wrong side of Easter, locked in with their fear and doubt.

Yes, Mary Magdalene had told them she had seen Him. But Mark records in his account that they did not believe her. The reality of the truth had not yet come through to them. They were still thinking about a dead Christ and they were filled with fear.

... the doors where shut where the disciples were assembled for fear of the Jews ...

John 20:19 (KJV)

Our world is no less devastated by fear. It stalks our streets like some animal of prey. Many live in fear behind locked doors. Crime, racial tensions, terrorism and other horrors paralyze people and strip the joy from life.

But that's because they are living on the wrong side of Easter. For into the locked compartments of our isolated lives there should stride the steady, confident steps of the risen Lord with the reassuring words He spoke so often to the disciples, "It is I, be not afraid."

Now that doesn't eliminate the sources of our fear, but it does reveal an answer. Easter means that when men have done their worst, God is still able to outdo them with His best.

LIFE RESPONSE:
"Lord, help me to live on the 'right side of Easter.'"

THE PEACE JESUS GIVES

Some years ago, a machine was invented to promote sleep, relaxation and concentration. Screening out noises and controlling tones from bass to treble, it simulates "white sound." It is capable of filtering out unwanted noises, producing single breaking wave patterns, random surf effects, and rain in either light or gentle downpour. It can even simulate a waterfall.

No doubt such a machine would bring soothing comfort to some people. But no amount of external sound conditioning can bring peace to a troubled heart. Someone who is filled with anxiety, tension, guilt, fear or any of the disturbing emotions that keep us on edge, needs the peace of God that passes all understanding.

When you have peace *with* God, you can have the peace *of* God. Then you can live at peace with your fellow men.

All the peace treaties signed by men, all the weapons bans cannot remove bitterness and hatred from people's hearts. Wars between nations are caused by the same evil attitudes that cause bickering between neighbors and among family members. Only Jesus can give peace.

> *These things I have spoken unto you, that in me ye might have peace.*
>
> *John 16:33 (KJV)*

LIFE RESPONSE:
I will earnestly seek peace with God and my fellow men.

How Strong Is Your Desire?

Jesus uses our strongest cravings — hunger and thirst — to characterize the passion for goodness which is found in the man or woman determined to find God. It is like the person who has gone without food or water for an extended period of time. Sir Ernest Shackleton said that when he and his men faced extreme and continuous hunger on their polar expedition, they found it difficult to think about anything else but food.

Give me this water . . .

John 4:15 (NIV)

Our search for righteousness cannot be an afterthought, a casual inquiry, something done in our spare time, with whatever energies are left after our pursuit of everything else has ended. Our soul's deepest desire must be for God. That is the only way to receive the filling God has to give us.

The psalmist experienced this thirst. "As the deer pants for streams of water, so my soul pants for you, O God. My soul thirsts for God, for the living God" (Ps. 42:1-2 NIV). This is much more than wishing for a cool sip of an iced drink on a summer's day. This is the perspiring laborer gulping water down his parched throat.

LIFE RESPONSE:
How great is my thirst for the "Living Water?"

No "If" About It

Some time ago, a society of atheists in London commissioned two lawyers to prove that the resurrection of Jesus Christ never took place, that it was a hoax or a scheme concocted by His followers. After a period of investigation, the lawyers gave their report, saying, "We have proven to our satisfaction beyond doubt, that Jesus Christ did rise from the dead. Furthermore, we have accepted Him as our personal Lord and Savior and urge you to do likewise."

If Christ did not rise from the dead . . . that is the most important IF in the world. The entire superstructure of Christianity rests upon it. That is why men have tried down through the centuries to discredit the truth about the Resurrection.

Each person must reach the personal decision that was made by the two lawyers who investigated the Resurrection. Either Christ did rise or He didn't. If He did, everything else He claimed can be believed. He is the Son of God and has power over death and hell. We can pin our hope and our eternal souls on His promise of eternal life.

If Christ has not been raised, your faith is futile; you are still in your sins.

1 Corinthians 15:17 (NIV)

"If in this life only we have hope in Christ, we are of all men most miserable" (1 Cor. 15:19 KJV). There is no "if" about it. He did rise from the dead and our hope in Christ makes us joyful!

LIFE RESPONSE:

I will live in the power and joy of Christ's resurrection.

THROUGH THE BIBLE

Acts 20-22

ARE YOU AN HEIR?

I would never have believed that brothers and sisters, aunts, uncles, cousins and other close relatives could be so greedy about getting a share of someone else's wealth. But one day I was called upon to mediate a family quarrel over the distribution of the household possessions — and we hadn't even conducted the funeral service for their departed relative yet!

Some attorneys are using modern technology in the preparation of wills. Along with the legal documents, they record the person reading his own will on a video tape recorder. After the client's death, the lawyer simply plays the tape, and the family members see the reading of the will by the deceased relative

You may never have been the recipient of an inheritance. Don't feel too badly about that. The Apostle Peter assures us that each of us will receive our share of a greater inheritance, one that is "kept in heaven for you."

In his great mercy he has given us new birth . . . into an inheritance . . . kept in heaven for you . . .

1 Peter 1:3-4 (NIV)

But to be an heir, you must be born into the family.

LIFE RESPONSE:

I will be sure of my inheritance because I will know for sure that I have been born again.

DON'T BE A WASTER

Jesus multiplied the loaves and fishes. He could have made more, but He did not want to waste that which they already had. It is not wise or scriptural to waste any of the blessings God has bestowed upon us.

It seems that extravagance, rather than frugality, is a popular lifestyle in our society. But it is amazing what can be accomplished by saving even small amounts. One pastor never made a large salary in all his years of ministry. In fact, he lived on what must be called the poverty level. But he and his wife were frugal, never borrowing money. They educated their children, paid their tithe plus offerings and lived simply, counting their pennies, saving what they could. When it was time to retire, they had over a quarter of a million dollars in savings!

Gather up the fragments that remain, that nothing be lost.

John 6:12 (KJV)

Most people are impressed with extravagance and, as a result, attempt to impress others. Expensive clothes, unnecessary jewelry, big car, mansion — all designed to make the neighbors sit up and take notice. But extravagance leads to waste and waste leads to want. Remember the old adage, "Waste not, want not."

LIFE RESPONSE:
I will use the resources God has given to me wisely.

FORGIVE AND BE FORGIVEN

A Filipino pastor, as a young boy during World War II, saw the enemy wipe out the population of his village. His father was murdered before his eyes. He and his mother miraculously escaped, fleeing to the mountains and hiding until the war ended.

> *. . . I forgave thee all the debt . . . Shouldest not thou also have had compassion on thy fellow servant . . .*
>
> Matthew 18:32-33 (KJV)

An American pastor who had been in the Philippines as a soldier during the war, returned for a visit. He met the Filipino pastor and heard his story — a story of suffering, fear and torment, all caused by the war.

When the visitor was about to leave, he shook the pastor's hand, looked him in the eye, and asked, "With all you endured, can you forgive your enemy, the people who caused you such anguish?"

The Filipino pastor's face beamed. "Oh, yes, I can. That is no problem at all. All I need to do is remember what my Lord has forgiven me, and I can forgive anything that has been done to me."

If God's forgiveness of your sins is directly related to your forgiveness of your fellow men, how forgiven are you? Is any sin worth missing out on God's forgiveness and salvation?

LIFE RESPONSE:

What action by another person needs my immediate forgiveness?

THROUGH THE BIBLE

Joshua 1-4

WORSHIP OR ENTERTAINMENT?

I once heard the director of children's ministries in a large church talk about the children's services that were conducted simultaneously each Sunday morning.

"We want to have worship for all of the children at the level of their understanding," she said, explaining why they have four or five services for different age levels.

That sounded good to me until she made this concluding statement: "We entertain them at each age level so they will be excited about church and want to come back again."

O come, let us worship and bow down: let us kneel before the Lord our maker.

Psalms 95:6 (KJV)

I was immediately struck with what may be the root of the church attendance problem today. If we tell the children that church is fun and games, they grow up expecting the church to compete with the entertainment industry for their time and attention.

For children, church then becomes a puppet show; for teens, it may be a rock concert. Worship services turn into stage productions. Records, t-shirts, and even doughnuts may be sold from the pulpit.

Do church attenders these days really know what it means to worship the Lord in spirit and truth, to bow humbly before the Creator and Lord of the universe?

LIFE RESPONSE:

I will seek to truly worship the Lord and not seek to be entertained.

THROUGH THE BIBLE

Joshua 5-7

INCALCULABLE RICHES

What determines the value of a gift? Is it simply the cost in dollars and cents? Obviously not, for there are some things very precious and meaningful to you that would bring little or nothing in the marketplace. When my oldest son was in the first or second grade, he made a gift for me. It was a baby food jar with his picture pasted on top. Inside, a little flower floated in water. You would not pay me anything for it. On the other hand, neither would I sell it to you, for it has value to me which cannot be calculated in monetary terms.

. . . enlightened
. . . tasted the
heavenly gift . . .
Hebrews 6:4 (NIV)

Ralph Waldo Emerson said in his essay on gifts, "Riches and jewels are not gifts, but apologies for gifts. The only gift is a portion of thyself."

A gift may be valued because it is unique or because it was given by someone special.

The gift of God is indescribably precious for all of these reasons. He gave His only begotten Son. He was giving of himself. His gift was unique.

LIFE RESPONSE:

I will praise God for the incalculable riches that He has given me.

LOVE IN ACTION

Sometimes God supplies our needs in miraculous ways, such as sending ravens to feed Elijah. Sometimes God provides for our necessities by giving us the privilege of working with our hands. Sometimes our needs are met through the generosity of others.

But we need more than physical necessities. Mother Teresa, whose entire life has been given ministering to the poor and starving of Calcutta, was awarded the Nobel Peace Prize in 1979. A large sum of money accompanied the prize and she said it would go to minister to the poor.

In her acceptance speech she said, "Today there is so much suffering, and I feel the suffering of Christ is being relieved not only in the poor countries but in the countries of the west as well. I have found the poverty of the west more difficult to remove."

Then she explained what she meant by the poverty of the west. She spoke of the elderly, the shut-ins, and those who feel unwanted and unloved.

People need to know they are loved, that someone cares. God uses His children to channel His love to those who have needs, whether physical, emotional or spiritual. Are we putting actions with our words of love?

> *Let us not love with words or tongue but with actions and in truth.*
>
> 1 John 3:18 (NIV)

LIFE RESPONSE:
"Lord, help me to put loving actions with my loving words."

TRUE TREASURES

"Money is not required to buy one necessity of the soul," said Henry David Thoreau. Think of the most precious memories you have. When were you the happiest? What were those times in your life that you would not exchange for any amount of money? The cry of your newborn baby? The touch of your spouse's hand on yours? The sunset over the mountains? The encouragement of a friend? The songs of praise in church? A walk through the woods in the fall?

Fill in from the reservoir of your memory the treasures that are dear to you and seldom will you count among your treasures the things that money has provided.

> *Do not store up for yourselves treasures on earth . . .*
>
> Matthew 6:19 (NIV)

Several years ago we bought a ten-year-old Volkswagen. Ten years later, it was time to sell it. As we watched that old friend go down our street for the last time, my wife began to cry. She was thinking of the memories connected with that old Volkswagen. The real treasure was not the car but the memories we value.

You won't need nearly as much money if you determine what is a true treasure and what is trash. One thing I have learned in all my traveling is to pack lightly, to carry with me only the essentials. Likewise, I want to wear the things of this earth lightly as I travel through life.

LIFE RESPONSE:

I am determined not to let earthly treasures become a burden.

WHEN CHRIST COMES CALLING

During eighteen years of pastoral ministry, I made thousands of calls in homes — visiting members and nonmembers, Christians and non-Christians. It was always amazing to see the effect the presence of the pastor had on the family relationships. I seldom had the feeling that I was seeing the family as they really lived. In many cases, I sensed tension. Sometimes I felt the parents were holding their breath, hoping the children would not say or do anything that would let the pastor know what their home life was really like.

During his call in a home, one pastor commented to the family how glad he was to be in their home and to see how well they lived. "Oh," they said, "Pastor, to see how we really live, you would have to visit us when you're not here."

Zacchaeus, come down immediately. I must stay at your house today.

Luke 19:5 (NIV)

When company comes, we are all on our best behavior. We mind our manners and are polite and kind. In one sense, we save our best for those who mean the least to us and give our beloved family members the short temper, the irritability and meanness.

I have thought many times, if the presence of the preacher makes a difference in a home, what a tremendous difference the presence of Christ ought to make!

LIFE RESPONSE:

I will give the Lord Jesus Christ a place of prominence in my home.

DON'T BE DEFEATED BY FEAR!

David Livingstone had been in Africa about sixteen years when he found himself one night surrounded by hostile natives. Knowing he was in danger of losing his life the next day, he considered fleeing into the night. He wrote in his diary of the turmoil of spirit he experienced, as he thought of having all his plans for the people of that region "knocked on the head by savages tomorrow." Then he read Jesus' words, "All power is given unto me . . . and lo, I am with you alway . . ." (Matt. 28:18, 20 KJV).

He thought, "It is the word of a gentleman." In his diary he wrote, "I will not cross furtively tonight as I intended."

Be of good cheer; it is I; be not afraid.

Matthew 14:27 (KJV)

The danger had not passed, but Livingstone's fear was gone. You, too, have "the word of a gentleman." Either you believe that word, or you doubt His word and allow fear to rule your heart. You can cure yourself of defeating, debilitating fear that brings torment and destroys your peace. "For he has heard my cry," the psalmist said (Ps. 28:6 NIV). And he will hear you, too.

Just like the shadows on the ceiling of a child's room have him convinced that a monster is creeping in, your fearful monsters will flee when you let the light of God's Word and His courage shine in your heart. Even when there is real danger, Jesus is there. He is with you and will keep you in His eternal purpose.

LIFE RESPONSE:
Am I defeating my fears or are my fears defeating me?

THROUGH THE BIBLE
Joshua 22-24

WHAT ARE WE PROJECTING?

O ur love for Christ is a response to His love for us. That works with other people as well. If you love them, they will respond with love. A little boy visited his grandfather who lived in the mountains. He enjoyed going to the edge of the valley and listening to his echo. "Hello," he would call, and back would come: "Hello," "Hello," "Hello." But one day his grandfather had to discipline him and the boy became very angry. He went off by himself and to vent his anger yelled out, "I hate you." To his surprise and dismay he heard repeated across the mountains: "I hate you," "I hate you," "I hate you."

Projecting hatred, we make enemies; projecting love, we make friends. Too often we refuse to take the initiative. We love only those who love us. That's easy. Jesus said that anyone can do that. We must love the one who doesn't love us, who in fact makes himself our enemy. Then, Jesus said, we can prove we are children of our Heavenly Father by demonstrating love for those who hate us.

> *We love him, because he first loved us.*
>
> *1 John 4:19 (KJV)*

Do you want to get rid of your enemies? Love them and turn your enemies into friends.

LIFE RESPONSE:

I am determined to try to turn my enemies into friends.

THE STORMS WILL COME

According to Jesus' parable of the wise man and the foolish man, the storms beat upon both their houses. Life is like that. Trouble comes to all of us. The question is, how do we handle it?

Years ago, our local newspaper carried a picture of a young woman sitting dejectedly on the front porch of a burned-out home. While she was asleep, the house had caught on fire. She awoke with only enough time to pick up her baby and escape with their lives. Nothing else had been saved. The same day, the mailman delivered the divorce papers her husband had served on her. "I've lost everything," she said.

The rain descended, and the floods came, and the winds blew, and beat upon that house . . .

Matthew 7:25-27 (KJV)

An African Christian wrote to me telling how rebels had come while he was away and burned his house to the ground. He and his family had lost everything they owned. But the man was praising God for protection and for wonderful neighbors who were helping to clothe and shelter the children.

Trouble can make us or break us. It all depends on how we react to it. During World War II, a devout Englishman looked at the gaping hole in the ground where his house had recently stood. A bomb had demolished his house and left a deep crater. "Well, I always did want a basement," he remarked.

LIFE RESPONSE:
What is my attitude when the storms come?

THROUGH THE BIBLE

Romans 4-7

UNWANTED CHILDREN

With ultrasound and other means of monitoring a baby's development, we now know that the baby's heart begins to beat between the fourteenth and twenty-fifth day after conception. The baby moves its arms and legs by six weeks of age, and by the forty-third day, its brain waves can be read. By eight weeks of age, the baby has fingerprints, can make a fist and feel pain. All body systems are functioning by twelve weeks of age.

That tiny package, nestled where it should be safe and secure beneath its mother's heart, is a distinct and individual person. "Before I formed you in the womb I knew you, before you were born I set you apart" (Jer. 1:5 NIV).

God had Jeremiah's life planned, just as He does every child's — even those born as the result of rape. A twelve-year-old became pregnant after being raped at knife-point — surely a good reason for an abortion, some would say! Yet the girl gave birth to a child who later became a star. The star helped many others get a chance in the entertainment industry, supported her mother all of her life, and raised over twenty girls. She sang at Billy Graham crusades and gave her testimony to millions. Ethel Waters may have been her mother's "unwanted one," but God used her in amazing ways.

> *For you created my inmost being; you knit me together in my mother's womb.*
>
> *Psalm 139:13 (NIV)*

There are no unwanted children as far as God is concerned.

LIFE RESPONSE:
I will praise God for who I am — His wonderful creation.

THROUGH THE BIBLE
Romans 8-10

DON'T START TOO SOON!

S omeone has suggested that there are two processes which should never be started prematurely: embalming and divorce. Both have a terrible ring of finality about them. To begin either one before its time would be a terrible tragedy.

I read a story about a man severely injured in an automobile accident. At the hospital, the doctors detected no vital signs and so sent him to the morgue. But the man could hear everything being said. His mind was working even though his body would not respond. "Why can't they see I'm still alive?" he thought. Miraculously, someone in the morgue finally did see a movement. The man was rushed back to the emergency room and resuscitation was accomplished.

I believe the process of divorce is started too soon in many cases. With a bit more effort, a closer scrutiny and a renewed commitment, many marriages could be saved. Evidence shows that a very high percentage of those who get divorced believe they could have worked out their problems and stayed married, if they had tried harder or waited longer.

For this reason a man will leave his father and mother and be united to his wife, and the two will become one flesh.

Ephesians 5:31 (NIV)

If someone wants a new spouse, it can be accomplished by becoming new people in Christ Jesus. He can make both brand new!

LIFE RESPONSE:

What steps can I take to bring healing to my home?

THROUGH THE BIBLE

Romans 11-13

ENJOY YOUR FREEDOM!

I've known people who have enslaved themselves to keeping the law. Their hope of salvation is in their careful observance of all the ordinances of their religion. Their life is a drudgery. There is no joy in their salvation. They go to church and pay their tithe out of a sense of duty. The law is their taskmaster.

But no one can keep the law perfectly enough to please God. We can never be good enough to meet God's standard. The righteousness which is by the law will always fail. But the righteousness which is of God by faith, is the righteousness of Christ — and that becomes ours when we trust Him completely. We no longer depend on our own works. We are set free from the bondage of legalism.

Those who enjoy this freedom go to church because they want to worship God. They do not give because it is demanded, but because of their love. Their hope is not in how carefully they perform the duties of their religion. Instead, *"My hope is built on nothing less/ than Jesus' blood and righteousness."*

In Christ we are set free from the slavery of the law.

> *It is for freedom that Christ has set us free. Stand firm, then, and do not let yourselves be burdened again by a yoke of slavery.*
>
> Galatians 5:1 (NIV)

LIFE RESPONSE:
Am I truly free to enjoy my salvation?

WHAT FRUIT ARE YOU PRODUCING?

I had several engagements in the lovely state of South Carolina one spring. As we drove along the highway, we came upon a fruit orchard in full bloom. Spring was at its peak and the color was an extravagant display of God's creative genius. I was not sure what kind of fruit trees they were, but I suspected they might be peach trees. It didn't matter since we were just enjoying their beautiful appearance. However, if I had gone back there and examined the trees after the fruit had formed, I would know with certainty what kind of trees they were.

> *A tree is recognized by its fruit.*
>
> Matthew 12:33 (NIV)

Jesus said, "A tree is recognized by its fruit." The proof that a Christian is filled with the Spirit and is walking in the Spirit, is the fruit being produced in his or her life. The fruit of the Spirit is evidence of the Spirit's presence.

Some people think the gifts of the Spirit are the sign of His residence. But the Apostle Paul made it clear that it is not *gifts* but *fruit* that identifies us. If we have all the gifts of the Spirit but not the fruit of the Spirit, which is love, we are nothing (1 Cor. 13).

LIFE RESPONSE:
Are there evidences of the Holy Spirit's presence in my life?

ACCORDING TO HIS LOVE

A man came upon a wrecked automobile with the driver trapped inside. Gasoline was leaking from the upside-down tank, and the car was on fire. It was obvious that the flames would soon reach the gas, and what was left of the car and anyone inside it, would be blown apart.

This man risked his own life to crawl inside the wreck and pull the injured driver out. Later he was asked, "Why did you do that? Why did you take such a risk?"

"I don't know," he said. "When I saw the man, helpless, and knew that he would die if I didn't get him out, something within me overcame my natural fear and made me do what I could to save him."

On a much higher plane, God saw you and me, lost, dead in our sins. He was compelled by His very nature to enter into the plight of the human family, to send His only begotten Son, so that through His death we might be saved.

> *But God demonstrates his own love for us in this: While we were still sinners, Christ died for us.*
>
> *Romans 5:8 (NIV)*

Paul said this was because God was rich in mercy, not because of righteous things we had done (Titus 3:5). It was not according to our worth but according to His love.

LIFE RESPONSE:

I will give praise to my Lord for His unconditional love for me.

HEAVEN IS MY HOME

Several years ago, I visited Rapid City, South Dakota, after a flood. Hundreds of people had been left homeless. Areas that had been lined with homes were just rubble and debris. We frequently see similar scenes on television after tornadoes and hurricanes have devastated an area..

Our earthly homes are, at best, only temporary. Even the most solid, palatial homes are but temporary shelters. The Bible says that this world and everything in it are passing away.

During my years as a pastor, I lived in many different homes. I remember one move in particular. We had loaded everything we owned on a moving van for a long-distance move. The house was empty, swept and clean. Our footsteps echoed as we walked one last time through those deserted rooms that had been our home. I watched forlornly as the truck pulled away with all of our earthly possessions on it. Once again I was smitten with that awful feeling of homesickness.

I will dwell in the house of the Lord forever.

Psalms 23:6 (KJV)

But heaven is an eternal home. We will never have to pack the van or say good-bye. One of the church fathers said, "God has made us for himself and we cannot find rest until we find it in Him."

Do you ever get homesick for heaven? It doesn't pay to get too attached to earth!

LIFE RESPONSE:

I will think more about my eternal home than my earthly dwelling.

LOVING THE UNLOVABLE

J esus' formula for getting rid of our enemies was to turn them into friends!

Frank Laubach believed in the power of sending out love thoughts to other people. If he boarded a bus and the driver was surly and grouchy, the whole atmosphere tense, Frank would sit near the back of the bus and send love thoughts toward the driver. He said that time and again he has had a driver turn around and — with a perplexed look on his face — smile; and the whole atmosphere would be different.

Too often we project angry feelings or negative thoughts toward other people, and they react in kind. If we extend love, love will come back to us.

When I was a pastor and someone would get upset with me, I would begin to pray with my wife for love to flow to and from that person. More than once we have seen people change and eventually come around with an entirely different attitude.

But I tell you: love your enemies and pray for those who persecute you . . .

Matthew 5:44 (NIV)

Loving those who love us is easy and natural. But the Christian goes beyond that and loves those who are unloving and unlovable, even as Jesus did.

LIFE RESPONSE:
  "Lord, help me to love that unlovable neighbor ."

GO HOME AND FIND THE TREASURE

I n the story "Acres of Diamonds" a farmer in South Africa decided to search for great wealth. Dissatisfied with what he possessed, he sold his farm and spent the money traveling the world over. At last, with money gone and health broken, he returned home to find that the man to whom he had sold his farm had discovered a rich diamond mine on that very location.

The prodigal son sloshed through the mud of a far country, but finally realized that what he wanted most had been at his father's house all along.

I will arise and go to my father . . .

Luke 15:18 (KJV)

People are on a universal quest, often without knowing what it is they really want. That restlessness of the soul can be satisfied only with the fullness of God himself.

Our consumer society does its best to create dissatisfaction in order to sell products. The wise Christian will realize this and stay away from the trap of materialism. Too many today are being drawn into thinking that "the good life" made possible by money is the real goal of life. Too late they discover it was a mirage. They are grasping what is passing away. "For what is seen is temporary, but what is unseen is eternal" (2 Cor. 4:18 NIV).

True treasure is found in our Father's house.

LIFE RESPONSE:

I will look for the diamond mines in my own backyard.

LOVE CAN'T BE LEGISLATED

President Lyndon Johnson said, "We have talked long enough in this country about equal rights . . . it is time now to write the next chapter and to write it in the books of law." But the breakdown of the relationships between people is not a breakdown of law.

Some time ago I was in an airport in a southern state. I noticed two little girls about three or four years old. One was black and one was white, and they were sharing a box of candy. Their sharing was not based on any law that insisted they must, nor do I believe any law could have kept them apart. They were simply two children, innocent, loving, accepting, who were willing to share with each other.

The relationships between people who should be "brothers" cannot be based on law. Law justifies us on the basis of what we do not do. For instance, if I don't commit a crime, I'm innocent.

Love the Lord your God . . . and, Love your neighbor as yourself.

Luke 10:27 (NIV)

Neither can relationships be based on religion. Religion justifies us on the basis of what we do and tends to make us self-righteous when we keep all our religious rules.

Relationships between people must be founded on something much deeper and stronger than law or religion. Jesus taught that the basis of human relationship is loving response to others' needs.

LIFE RESPONSE:
For my part, I will break down the barriers that separate people.

THROUGH THE BIBLE

Judges 16-18

"WELCOME, JESUS!"

I n my travels, I am often entertained by families with children. I can easily tell when Mom and Dad have coached the little ones on how to act in the presence of company. Their carefully practiced manners and polite conversations bring a smile of satisfaction to the faces of proud parents.

But with children, you cannot remain a guest for very long. In a matter of hours at best, they have grown accustomed to having someone share their home, and they get tired of being on their best behavior. Soon their guard is down and they return to normal. I've watched some parents get very uneasy and even a bit embarrassed as a child began to treat me like one of the family; but frankly, that's when I become most comfortable. It's much nicer to be treated as a member of the household than as an honored guest.

A woman named Martha opened her home to him.

Luke 10:38 (NIV)

What difference would it make if Jesus Christ were to reside at your house — not as a guest to be honored, but as a permanent resident — as a member of the family? What if He were sitting at the head of the table every time you gathered for a meal? Would you say the same things, tell the same stories? Would your relationships with family members change if He were there? But then . . . He *is* there!

LIFE RESPONSE:

Is Christ an "honored guest" in my home, or is He a "member of the family?"

No More Barriers

Turgenev, the Russian writer, said he met a beggar one day who asked him for money. The writer felt in his pockets but there was nothing there. The beggar waited and his outstretched hand twitched nervously. Embarrassed and confused, Turgenev seized the dirty hand and pressed it. "Don't be angry with me, brother," he said. "I have nothing with me."

The beggar raised his bloodshot eyes and smiled. "You called me brother," he said. "That is a gift indeed."

Barriers of all kinds separate people — differences of age, gender, race, social class, nationality, creed and education. For nearly two thousand years, those barriers have been broken down by Jesus Christ. But human beings keep raising them again.

It is true that we are not all brothers in Christ, in the sense of being adopted into His family. But we are fellow creatures, all equally loved by Him, and no difference is worth preventing God's love from flowing through us to another person. Jesus demonstrated it when He was here on earth and was criticized for being too friendly to sinners.

But that's how it is . . . God is love.

He . . . has destroyed the barrier, the dividing wall of hostility.

Ephesians 2:14 (NIV)

LIFE RESPONSE:

I am determined to demonstrate the love of God to *all* people.

A Song In The Night

A young boy named Jimmy became ill. By age eleven he was confined to a wheelchair. When he was twenty-four he became worse and was rushed to a hospital. For three days he was not aware of anything. Afterward, he was told he would live the rest of his life totally dependent upon a respirator. Weeks of depression followed. He had thought of himself as a good Christian, but in his desperation and despair he turned his back on God. For weeks, he did not want to go on living.

In the night his song shall be with me.

Psalms 42:8 (KJV)

But one day before dawn, a bird began singing outside his window. The clear, melodious music seemed to be right with him in the room. Peace and joy swept over him, and the depression diminished. For two weeks that bird returned at dawn every morning, singing even in the rain with a beauty that spoke of God's love.

Jimmy thought, if God loved this bird and it could sing even during the rain, why should he be so depressed? He began to improve. For eight more years, he was confined to his bed, dependent on a respirator, but knowing the joy of the Lord. Soon after the story appeared in a popular magazine, Jimmy went to be with the Lord.

God gives songs in the darkest night.

LIFE RESPONSE:
"Lord, teach me to sing during the dark nights of my life."

THROUGH THE BIBLE

1 Corinthians 1-4

IS YOUR LIFE A DRUDGERY?

In my early years of pastoring, I was anxious and troubled about some conditions in my church. I had heard of pastors who were unable to sleep at night when faced with similar problems. But my reaction was just the opposite. I couldn't wake up. Every morning, I was more tired than when I had gone to bed. I felt as if I could sleep all day. A doctor told me this was the result of mental strain. I was withdrawing from my work through this extreme weariness.

When he told me that, I determined that if anxiety, fear and tension could cause me to feel this way, then peace of mind, joy, faith and trust could result in energy and strength. Then I discovered this was a scriptural principle as well. "They that wait upon the Lord shall renew their strength" (Isa. 40:31 KJV).

Martha, Martha, you are worried and troubled about many things.
Luke 10:41 (NKJV)

Much of our weariness, as we face our tasks, is because we break God's laws concerning our mental health. Ill will is harbored, resentments seethe, quarrels rage, anger burns, and much of what we do becomes a drudgery because we do it to please men, not God.

Someone has suggested that if you can't do the work you love, learn to love the work you do. Good advice! Do it heartily as unto the Lord.

LIFE RESPONSE:
Am I troubled about many things or trusting God for *everything*?

LIFE'S UNCERTAINTY

Many people in eternity today were planning their future just yesterday. We have no promise of tomorrow.

A person with a terminal illness was asked how he could be so cheerful when he knew he was going to die. He responded, "We are all terminal. I am just more aware of it than most."

Even after the doctor gives his opinion as to how long you have to live, tomorrow is uncertain. I have a close friend whose mother was told many years ago she would not live very long. But she has outlived three or four of the doctors who predicted her death. On the other hand, I knew a man who went for a medical check-up and was given a clean bill of health. On the way out of the doctor's office, he suffered a heart attack and died.

> *. . . as a bird hasteth to the snare . . .*
>
> Proverbs 7:23 (KJV)

It is not morbid and depressing to think about how short life is on this earth. At least it should not be so for a Christian. For this world is not our home. Perhaps every Christian should live each day as though it is his last. That means keeping short accounts and being ready to meet the Lord. What a joyful and victorious way to live!

LIFE RESPONSE:

I will live this day as if it were my last.

DO OUR POSSESSIONS POSSESS US?

Some years ago, a conference for itinerant evangelists was held in Amsterdam. I thought about attending, but did not for several reasons. One consideration was whether I could afford the cost of the trip. Then I heard testimonies of some of those from third-world nations who had attended. One African, who raised pigs to support his family, sold everything to raise money for the conference. Some of these itinerants were asked what they needed most in their ministries, and they asked only for a complete Bible or a bicycle to speed their travel.

We are often so absorbed in our own needs that we forget about those who are serving the Lord sacrificially, without many of the essentials of life.

Much of our problem is that in our struggle to survive, we have become obsessed with possessions. The battle of life for many of us is not self-preservation any longer, but selfish profit. As someone has said, "Present-day necessities are luxuries that have become a habit."

A man's life does not consist in the abundance of his possessions.

Luke 12:15 (NIV)

According to Jesus, the first law of life is not self-preservation but self-giving. We need to look at "things" through Jesus' eyes.

LIFE RESPONSE:
Am I possessed by my possessions?

DON'T IGNORE
THE LITTLE FOXES!

Have you experienced the great pain or misery that grows from a very small irritation? One morning as I began my walk, I noticed something amiss in one shoe. It didn't seem important enough to stop and check it out. As I continued to walk, the irritation grew. Soon my foot was extremely uncomfortable. Then, I was limping in pain. When I finally stopped and removed my shoe, I found a very small pebble inside.

Catch for us the foxes, the little foxes that ruin the vineyards . . .

Song of Solomon 2:15 (NIV)

Seemingly insignificant annoyances can eventually rob you of your peace. Attitudes and sins long forgotten, hurts that fester, grudges that linger, anger that smolders, bitterness deep inside — these may seem harmless in the beginning. Often we rationalize these attitudes, justifying them in light of what has happened to us. But then we find the vineyard of our lives being destroyed by the little foxes which at first seemed inconsequential. Our fruitfulness is impaired, our joy diminished.

In my years of pastoring, I learned that many of the mental and emotional problems people face are really spiritual problems. No "little fox" is insignificant to God if it affects our relationship with Him and with others.

LIFE RESPONSE:

"Lord, help me to deal with 'little things' before they take over my heart."

THROUGH THE BIBLE

1 Samuel 1-3

HOMESICK FOR HEAVEN

Headed for Bible college, I was just seventeen when I left home for the first time. I will always remember my mother and father waving good-bye as my brother and I drove down the highway. When we turned the first corner and I looked back, I didn't really think much about the fact that I was leaving home for good. But it wasn't long before that universal disease, homesickness, began to affect me. From that day on, I have always been glad to go back home, even for a brief visit.

I have been at the bedside of many elderly people who knew the end was near. One of the most common reactions I have witnessed is that they all want to go home. One man lived many years in the same house and yet kept saying, "I want to go home." We tried to convince him he *was* home, but he insisted he wanted to go home. One cold winter night, he slipped out of the house and, in spite of weakness, walked barefoot through the snow trying "to get home."

> *Our citizenship is in heaven.*
>
> Philippians 3:20 (NIV)

Life on earth is a pilgrimage and we are all transients, wandering through a foreign land. Heaven is our homeland, our final destination. It will be our permanent home. Even the strongest castle can only hold us for a lifetime.

Do you ever get homesick for heaven?

LIFE RESPONSE:

I will not let my roots grow too deep in time. I am looking forward to a heavenly home.

THROUGH THE BIBLE

1 Samuel 4-7

GIVE WHAT YOU HAVE

O bviously, we can give only what we have. Yet, too many of us don't even realize what we have to give!

A business establishment in the Midwest was greatly changed, not because of new executives, but because of a new cleaning woman. Not only did she clean their offices at night, she cleansed their hearts as well.

She did it by writing notes after she had finished her work each night. Executives would come to work in the morning and find notes on their desks. "Dear Mr. So-and-So, It is beautiful outside. It has started to snow such large flakes and everything is still. It is going to be a lovely ride home. My heart is filled with peace on such a night." She told them about the elderly people she visited, how much she loved people and loved life, and how she enjoyed her work.

> *. . . such as I have give I thee.*
>
> Acts 3:6 (KJV)

Those business executives were invigorated by the notes which radiated love, warmth, joy and a zest for life. This cleaning woman did not have silver and gold, but she gave others a part of what she herself enjoyed — the true treasures of life.

Everyone has something to give others. Give your time, give a listening ear. Give a warm heart, give your love.

Give yourself.

LIFE RESPONSE:

What can I give someone that doesn't *cost* a lot but which will *mean* a lot?

THROUGH THE BIBLE

1 Samuel 8-10

ADMIT YOUR NEED!

When I was a college student in Pennsylvania, I worked at the Allentown State Hospital. Among the hundreds of patients there, we observed many who marvelously recovered. I thought one particular patient — who didn't seem terribly ill — would soon be discharged. But days turned into weeks and weeks into months, and still there was no sign of his release. In fact, he showed no change at all.

One day while talking with the doctor, I mentioned this man and inquired why he seemed to be at a standstill. The doctor said, "That man does not get well because he has never admitted he is ill."

What must I do to be saved?

Acts 16:30

What was true of that patient psychologically is true of all men spiritually. No man will seek to be saved until he recognizes that he is lost. A man may wander around a strange city for a long time, but if he doesn't admit he's lost and does not ask for help, he will never reach his destination.

In fact, God cannot help anyone unless that person admits a need. Many Christians deprive themselves of God's help because they do not bother — or are not willing — to confess their need.

LIFE RESPONSE:

Do I readily admit my spiritual needs?

THROUGH THE BIBLE

1 Samuel 11-13

KEEP WALKING!

A single-engine plane developed engine trouble and crashed high in the mountains. The plane was destroyed and the pilot critically injured. As a mountain storm raged, the pilot sheltered himself as best he could under one of the battered wings. When the storm subsided, he dragged himself slowly and painfully down the mountain. Hours passed before a rescue party found him and carried him to the hospital. Later, he was asked how he had managed to make his way down the mountain with his many injuries. He replied in part, "What saves a man is to take one step and then another."

Walking is a series of steps. The first step on the road to heaven is the step of salvation. The first and most important step you can take each day is to begin by talking to God. I have a friend who was, for a time, paralyzed from the waist down. In spite of some stiffness and pain, he now has the use of his legs again. I have heard him say, "Any day you can get out of bed in the morning and stand on your own feet, and those legs will work for you, it's a good day."

> *. . . Christ . . . leaving us an example, that ye should follow his steps.*
>
> *1 Peter 2:21 (KJV)*

Our God-given strength and abilities make walking possible, both physically and spiritually.

LIFE RESPONSE:

Am I taking steps that will draw me closer to God and, ultimately, to heaven?

LOST!

Some time ago, a little boy was lost in the southern part of our state. I think he was only about four years old and dressed for mild weather. But it was autumn in Indiana, a time when the temperatures heat up during the day and plunge below freezing at night.

At first the boy's parents and family members looked for him. Before long, neighbors, friends, state police, and various civic and community groups joined the search. Spreading out for several miles, the volunteers carefully examined every foot of ground.

When the boy was found alive the next day, he was lying on the cold ground next to his two dogs. Although the dogs had wandered away with him, they were never lost. They could have found their way out of the woods at any time. But if those faithful dogs had not stayed with the boy, sharing their body warmth during the cold night, the child would probably have died of hypothermia.

For this my son was dead, and is alive again; he was lost, and is found.

Luke 15:24 (KJV)

We can all understand the torment of that family during those long hours, and we can picture the rejoicing that took place at their house when the boy returned.

The difference between being lost and found is no small matter. It is the difference between life and death, between heaven and hell.

LIFE RESPONSE:

Am I really convinced that people without Christ are lost — convinced enough to lead them to Christ?

THE WIND OF THE SPIRIT

W hen I pastored in upstate New York, we enjoyed the seasonal winds that blew down from the Adirondack Mountains. With kites in hand, our children loved to climb a beautiful hill across the street from our parsonage. High into the heavens, the kites would soar, with very little effort on our part. All we had to do was let out the string, and the wind would do the work. The kites were limited only by the amount of string we released to the pull of the wind.

The wind blows . . . but you cannot tell where it comes from or where it is going. So it is with everyone born of the Spirit.

John 3:8 (NIV)

In order to fly, a kite must be well constructed — the tail must be the right length and there must be plenty of string to insure adequate altitude. There is a parallel here for the Christian. We cannot live a holy life on our own any more than we can fly a kite by blowing on it. The human side must be aligned according to God's Word.

The wind of God's Spirit made the dry bones of Ezekiel's vision become a mighty army. The wind of the Spirit blew into the Upper Room and propelled the infant church into evangelizing the world.

Let His Spirit be the wind under your wings!

LIFE RESPONSE:
I will give the Holy Spirit enough "string" and not hinder Him.

GOD DOES NOT WANT US IN HELL

Under an agreement between the United States and another nation, scores of prisoners were exchanged. The former American prisoners were then asked at a news conference to describe imprisonment in a foreign jail. No one gave a very high recommendation. One young lady told about the hardships she had endured, the physical abuse and the mental anguish.

"I can't describe it to you," she said. "It was . . . it was hell."

Hell is a common word in modern vocabularies. People use it freely, carelessly, as a comparison for anything unpleasant or miserable. Any hardship or misery may be referred to as "a living hell," or "hell on earth."

One of the peculiarities of this preoccupation with hell in our language is that so few people profess to believe in an actual hell. Satan is caricatured as a red imp with a long tail and a pitchfork, and hell is laughed off with little concern. Many people are convinced that a loving God will not send anyone to hell.

The wicked shall be turned into hell, and all the nations that forget God.

Psalms 9:17 (KJV)

God's Word reveals that hell is a real place but that God loves us too much to want us to go there. He has provided a way of escape. He is ". . . not willing that any should perish . . ." (2 Peter 3:9 NKJV).

LIFE RESPONSE:

"Lord, help me to treat the subject of hell seriously. And help me to do everything I can to keep people from going there."

THROUGH THE BIBLE

1 Samuel 21-24

THE NARROW WAY

A lively debate on religion broke out in a college class in which my wife was a student. Among the things discussed were the varieties of spiritual viewpoints, the differences of opinions, and the narrow-mindedness of some religious people. In the course of the debate, my wife mentioned that I was a preacher. Her professor replied, "But I'm sure that your husband is very broad-minded."

Now in the context of the class discussion, he assumed that I was open to other views, recognizing that other religions are also truth. In my opinion, however, what he meant by "broad-minded" I would interpret as "empty-headed."

I am the way, the truth and the life.

John 14:6 (KJV)

I asked my wife, "Did you tell him I'm not broad-minded? That I'm very dogmatic, even in his view, narrow-minded?"

So many people like to believe that there are a variety of paths to God. Their reasoning goes like this: the Mohammedans, the Buddhists and the Hindus are just taking a different way from the Christians, but we'll all end up in the same place.

That is not what Jesus said.

The apostles believed, "There is no other name under heaven given to men by which we must be saved" (Acts 4:12 NIV).

The narrow way is God's idea!

LIFE RESPONSE:

I am determined to actively point others to the "narrow way."

DOERS OR JUST HEARERS?

I once read that within 72 hours we forget nearly 95 percent of everything we hear. In that same length of time, we forget 70 percent of what we read. Of the information which comes to us simultaneously through the eye gate and the ear gate, however, we forget only about 50 percent. But if in that 72-hour period we assimilate information by simultaneously reading, hearing *and* doing, we will forget only ten percent.

A group of preachers was discussing favorite translations of the Bible. Some preferred the King James Version, others the *New International Version*, and so on. One preacher spoke up and said, "I like my mother's version best." The men were surprised that his mother had translated the Bible. "Oh, yes," he said, "my mother's version is translated into life and put into practice in our home."

Sunday school teachers are often told that the lesson is not taught until the life has been changed. Memorizing Scripture, quoting it, reading it — all this is fine and good. But these practices are totally inadequate if the examples of Scripture are not lived, if the warnings are not heeded, if the life is not changed.

Be ye doers of the word, and not hearers only . . .

James 1:22 (KJV)

LIFE RESPONSE:
Am I heeding what I am reading? Is God's Word lighting my path?

"COME, LORD JESUS!"

For many, the atmosphere in our world is heavy with pessimism. Economic instability, political uncertainty, the rise and fall of nations, strife between races and tribes, and the failures of peace talks do not present a basis for hope. Many look to the United Nations, and to elder statesmen and diplomats, to keep a civilized world from blasting itself into annihilation.

Still others speculate about a bright future. Robert Truax, former research chief at Aero General Corporation, said some years ago that "by the year 2060, means will be discovered to achieve earthly immortality." He also predicted a United States of the World, a world government of a free democratic type in which war will be forever eliminated.

> *Because of the increase of wickedness, the love of most will grow cold . . .*
>
> *Matthew 24:12 (NIV)*

God's Word says the consummation of all things will be the second coming of Jesus Christ. No Christian need wring his hands in fear. Jesus said that in the midst of persecution, confusion, wars and rumors of wars, we are to take comfort in the fact that He is preparing to come back to earth again.

The Bible says, "Behold I come quickly" (Rev. 22:12 KJV). And the heart of every Christian says, "Amen. Even so, come, Lord Jesus" (v.20).

LIFE RESPONSE:
I will be encouraged, and not discouraged, by the "signs of the times."

THROUGH THE BIBLE
2 Corinthians 1-4

GOD REVEALS HIS WILL

God reveals His will in several ways. He may call you by His Spirit. For example, I can take you to the very place where I was sitting when the Spirit of God called me to preach.

God also calls through spiritual counselors — godly, experienced people with discernment.

He sometimes calls through providence, through open or closed doors. A friend of mine once ran for the United States Congress. He is a fine Christian attorney and I felt he would make an outstanding legislator. I was disappointed when he lost the election. From a human standpoint it seemed that it should have been God's will for him to win. But my friend has had great opportunities for ministry since losing the election — opportunities he might never have known if he had won.

I delight to do thy will, O my God.

Psalms 40:8 (KJV)

God also leads through His Word. The Spirit of God will never lead you contrary to His Word. Check every prompting, leading, voice, or direction from the Spirit or from your spiritual counselors, even when doors of opportunity seem to appear. If it contradicts the Word, you know it is not from the Lord.

If we delight to do God's will, like the psalmist did, we can be sure He will let us know His will. Reluctance on our part can make it more difficult to discern His plan.

LIFE RESPONSE:

"Lord, help me to actively seek Your will for my life."

THROUGH THE BIBLE

2 Corinthians 5-8

HOW DO YOU KEEP THE LAW?

I remember when the 55 mile-per-hour speed limit was put into effect on our interstate highways. This was a highly unpopular law for the thousands of drivers who were accustomed to traveling at higher speeds. One day in protest, several truck drivers got together and drove side-by-side at 45 miles per hour, the minimum legal speed. They did this during rush hour, near one of our large cities. By blocking all four lanes of the highway with their huge rigs, they created unbelievable havoc, as the traffic clogged for miles behind them. They insisted they were keeping the letter of the law by driving the minimum legal speed. But in doing that, they thwarted the very purpose of the law and created a hazardous situation.

> *The letter kills, but the Spirit gives life.*
>
> *2 Corinthians 3:6 (NIV)*

The Pharisees kept the letter of the law, to the minutest detail, but they failed to realize the spirit which had prompted the law. They made the mistake of thinking that acceptance by God and entrance into the kingdom of heaven are based solely on the performance of duty and strict observance of religious codes.

In order to really keep the law, it is necessary to know the mind — the intent — of the lawmaker. The best way to truly keep God's laws is to know Him personally and do what pleases Him.

LIFE RESPONSE:

I am determined to be concerned with the *spirit* of the law as well as the *letter* of the law.

THROUGH THE BIBLE

2 Corinthians 9-13

HANG IN THERE!

I heard of a young lady who had perfect attendance through high school. She had not missed a single day in four years. Now I am sure that like any young person, there were days when she didn't really feel like going to school. There may have been mornings when she was tired or sick; but whatever she faced, nothing kept her from faithfully attending school every day. Finally, after four years, graduation arrived. The school officials held a ceremony to honor those students who had distinguished themselves in some way during high school. The young lady was called to receive her award for perfect attendance. To everyone's surprise, she was not there to receive it. Having not missed a single day in four years, she was absent the day the award was given!

Paul wondered if the Galatians had suffered so much for nothing . . . if they were going to turn away from their faith after they had suffered persecution for it.

Why would anyone who had been through so much to achieve a goal, want to turn away and miss the reward?

> *Have you suffered so much for nothing —*
> *if it really was for nothing?*
>
> *Galatians 3:4 (NIV)*

LIFE RESPONSE:

I plan to "hang in there" to the very end, no matter the obstacles.

BITTERNESS EXCHANGED FOR BLESSING

Abraham Lincoln said, "I am sorry for the man who can't feel the whip when it is laid on the other man's back."

I once visited with a fine, young black man from South Africa. I asked him about the feelings between blacks and whites. He said, "Many of our people are preaching hatred. And I myself once had bitterness and hatred in my heart. But no more. Jesus Christ has given me love for my fellow man, no matter what color their skin may be."

Which of these three do you think was a neighbor to the man who fell into the hands of robbers?

Luke 10:36 (NIV)

A man in Charlotte, North Carolina was filled with hatred of and prejudice toward people of another race. He had joined an extremist organization and was on the verge of engaging in violence. Out of curiosity he attended a Billy Graham crusade and was gloriously converted. He wrote to Billy Graham, "All bitterness, hatred, malice and prejudice immediately left me. I was in the counseling room seated next to a person of another race. Through my tears, I gripped the hand of this man who, a few hours before, I would have detested. I now find that I can love all men regardless of the color of their skin."

LIFE RESPONSE:

I will reach out to the needs of others — no matter who they are.

A ROAD MAP FOR THE 21ST CENTURY

John Naisbitt's best-selling book *Megatrends*, published in 1982, was called "a road map to the twenty-first century." It is reported that Naisbitt and his group continually monitored six thousand newspapers each month. By statistically analyzing what makes news, they discerned trends and thereby made predictions regarding the future. *Megatrends* was the most talked about book of the eighties and made Naisbitt perhaps the best known of all the social forecasters.

Undoubtedly, there is some validity to his method and, therefore, a certain degree of reliability in the conclusions he reached. That is why he was hired as a consultant by several leading corporations.

But in my opinion, the best road map to the twenty-first century is the one that has already proven itself accurate for more than two thousand years. It depends not upon rapidly changing events reported in newspapers, not upon speculative predictions that may be affected by a misinterpretation of the facts or subconsciously by personal bias, but upon the divine attribute of omniscience.

All Scripture is given by inspiration of God . . .

2 Timothy 3:16 (KJV)

The Word of God is the completely reliable road map to guide us through the unexplored regions of the third millennium.

LIFE RESPONSE:
Am I using God's Word as a road map?

THROUGH THE BIBLE
2 Samuel 8-11

How Much Do We Want Him?

W hat is the strongest desire in your life? How much would you give to attain it?

Some years ago, the sports world crowned a new heavyweight boxing champion, a young man no one had thought could defeat the older, more experienced champion.

"He doesn't have the skills, nor the experience," they said. But when he won, the experts explained by saying, "He had one thing — desire." He wanted the championship more than anything else in the world.

But what things were gain to me, these I have counted loss for Christ.

Philippians 3:7 (NKJV)

Paul gave up everything he had once held dear in order to gain a relationship with Christ.

The old story of the Indian's consecration illustrates the need for complete surrender. When the Indian Christian heard preaching on consecration he brought some of his possessions and put them on the altar, but felt that wasn't enough to please God. He placed his wallet there, then his jewelry. He even brought his horse and tied it to the altar. Finally he realized what was missing, and he lay down on the altar, saying, "Lord, you have all I have, and you have all of me."

LIFE RESPONSE:

What am I willing to lose in order to win Christ?

THROUGH THE BIBLE

2 Samuel 12-13

BURDEN-BEARING IS A TWO-WAY STREET

It is easier to reach out to someone else's need than it is to allow others to share in our need. When we are helped we feel obligated, perhaps embarrassed. It is difficult to admit our weakness, to confess our stumblings, to recognize that in this instance, I am the weaker brother and another is the stronger.

Many years ago, a great Christian gentleman taught me a good lesson. Someone whose circumstances were worse than mine had just offered me a gift. Thinking this person needed the gift more than I did, I tried to refuse it. My friend, who had witnessed the entire scene, insisted I accept the gift. When we had left he said, "Always receive a gift for the giver's sake. If you had refused that gift, you would have robbed him of the great blessing of giving, for Jesus said, 'It is more blessed to give than to receive.'"

Rise up and help us . . .

Psalms 44:26 (NIV)

Don't be too proud when you need help. We need each other. Are you quicker to give help than to receive it? It works both ways. "By love serve one another" (Gal. 5:13 KJV).

Burden-bearing is a two-way street for the Christian.

LIFE RESPONSE:

"Lord, help me to learn how to let another person share my burden."

RUN AND NOT BE WEARY

I was watching my oldest son run at the first high school track meet of the season. Prior to the race, young men were running, stretching, preparing. Then the participants lined up, the gun was fired and they were off. At first it looked as if any one of them could win. Then, one by one, they began to slow.

Four times around the track would complete the mile race. One young man continued at a steady pace while more of the others faded back. On the last lap, he actually picked up speed and won far ahead of the rest. The one who finished next to last fell to the ground, writhing in pain.

. . . they shall run and not be weary; and they shall walk, and not faint.

Isaiah 40:31 (KJV)

What could make such a difference? My son told me that the winner had been practicing all summer, running miles every day. Some of the others had just begun training, or had not trained at all.

Who "shall run and not be weary?" Who has that kind of energy? All of us? No, only those who have prepared, only those who have trained, only those who have waited upon the Lord. You cannot disregard God — ignoring His principles, breaking His laws — and expect to reap His benefits. The dynamic life principle is for those who wait upon the Lord.

LIFE RESPONSE:
I will work on my spiritual training regimen.

THROUGH THE BIBLE
2 Samuel 16-18

A REAL EXPERIENCE

Two Christians sat at lunch with some Harvard students. One was a Christian of long standing, the other a new Christian. The experienced Christian was sharing his faith, attempting to witness and win others to the Lord. One Harvard student who was an unbeliever began to raise philosophical questions and arguments against the Christian faith.

The experienced Christian did his best to answer the questions and refute the arguments but was getting nowhere. Just then, the new Christian spoke up.

"Recently I believed on the Lord Jesus and accepted Him as my Savior," he said. "He has given me a new life."

Immediately the unbelieving student was interested.

"Really?" he said. "Tell me about it. What happened? What did He do?" All the philosophical questions and arguments were forgotten as he learned firsthand about this great experience.

> *That which we have seen and heard declare we unto you . . .*
>
> *1 John 1:3 (KJV)*

It is not necessary to abandon sound reason in order to embrace faith. But when a person can tell what he has seen and heard, like the Apostle John, others want to hear about that experience. An actual experience is worth telling . . . and hearing about! As someone has said, "a man with an argument is no match for a man with an experience."

LIFE RESPONSE:

I am determined not to keep my faith to myself. I will share it with others.

THROUGH THE BIBLE

2 Samuel 19-20

EVERY PERSON IS IMPORTANT TO GOD

As a young man, I worked for a time in a ladies' shoe store. One day, an elderly lady entered the store. She didn't appear to have either money or good taste in clothing. The other salesmen avoided her, so the manager assigned me the task of waiting on her.

I began to show the lady the shoes she asked for. The pile on the floor grew, as I made trip after trip to the stockroom. I tried to get her to decide on one pair, but she kept asking to see more. The other salesmen were laughing at all my futile efforts.

Finally the lady said, "All right, young man, I'll take all of these." Since she had more shoes than she could carry, I helped take them to her car. To my surprise, her car was a very expensive model.

Waiting on that lady was not an act of virtue on my part. I didn't want to wait on her any more than the other salesmen. But this experience illustrates the spiritual principle of accepting every person as someone important in God's sight. We are incapable of judging between worthy and unworthy, between good and bad. Only God has that right.

> *Whoever welcomes a little child . . . in my name welcomes me.*
>
> *Matthew 18:5 (NIV)*

LIFE RESPONSE:

"Lord, help me to see others as precious in Your sight."

THROUGH THE BIBLE

2 Samuel 21-22

HATE BELONGS TO THE DARKNESS

B ooker T. Washington, the great black scientist and educator, was walking with a friend when he was roughly elbowed into the gutter by a passing pedestrian. His friend was furious. "How can you tolerate such an insult?" he shouted.

Washington quietly replied, "I defy any man to make me hate."

Hatred demonstrates itself in many different ways. It may be exhibited as contempt, racial prejudice, mistreatment or abuse. Someone has said that hate is a prolonged form of suicide. The man who hates another has the seed of destruction within his own heart.

Like the elder brother of the prodigal son, too many church people become angry, jealous, judgmental and unforgiving when they feel overlooked or think they have been treated unfairly. This is not the love Paul described in First Corinthians, chapter thirteen. Nor is it the love Jesus demonstrated to His enemies and critics.

Anyone who claims to be in the light but hates his brother is still in the darkness.

1 John 2:9 (NIV)

We may think we do not hate anyone, but an unloving spirit belongs to the darkness, not to the light.

LIFE RESPONSE:

I will not allow seeds of hatred to grow in my heart.

CAN I MAKE A DIFFERENCE?

When we see the overwhelming needs of people around the world, too many of us think, "What can I do?" What *can* one person do to make a difference?

In one experiment, a large piece of iron was suspended from a hook. Something lightweight, perhaps a cork, was suspended nearby and swung so it would strike the iron. At first nothing happened, but as the cork was swung again and again, the iron began to vibrate. Then, little by little, the iron began to move until it was swinging in rhythm with the cork.

Which . . . was neighbor unto him that fell among the thieves? . . . He that shewed mercy on him.

Luke 10:36-37 (KJV)

One woman, concerned for elderly poor people, prayed for a piece of land on which to raise a garden. God opened up a place at a state prison farm, complete with workers to help her. In time, she had vegetables to give to those in need. She couldn't feed all the hungry, but she was able to feed a few.

How do we feed the world's starving? As one relief organization says, "One person at a time." If several corks began swinging against the obstacle, it would move farther and faster!

What can one person do? He can do his part!

LIFE RESPONSE:

"Lord, help me to meet the needs of the world, one person at a time."

THROUGH THE BIBLE

Galatians 1-3

Overlook The Differences

Two men were sailing from America to England and were assigned to the same cabin. Shortly after boarding the ship, one man brought his valuables to the ship's steward to be placed in the safe. "My cabin mate looks like the criminal type," he said. "I don't trust him."

The steward began to laugh and said, "Isn't that strange? Just a few minutes ago, your cabin mate brought his valuables to me for safekeeping and said the same thing about you!"

When the two men became acquainted, they discovered one was a famous doctor, the other a well-known minister. They struck up a friendship on that voyage that lasted the rest of their lives.

It's difficult to understand the walls and barriers we build between one another. Why do we allow minor differences, such as the pigmentation of our skin, the accents of our tongue or the slant of our eyes, to cut us off from others? Why are we so anxious to make enemies of those who should be our friends?

> *Now you are the body of Christ, and each one of you is a part of it.*
>
> 1 Corinthians 12:27 (NIV)

It's amazing what companionship will do for us. When people band together, they can accomplish great things. Let's overlook our differences and pull together.

LIFE RESPONSE:

I will treat everyone in the church with the same compassion and courtesy.

THROUGH THE BIBLE
Galatians 4-6

LIVE PEACEABLY

When our oldest son was five, he was disciplined at the lunch table. Angry and upset, he packed a few toys in a suitcase and announced he was running away. I told him we wanted a picture so we could always remember him. So holding his suitcase, he posed at the front door, then started down the street.

A few minutes later, I got in my car to drive to the office. I caught up with him about a block from home.

"I'm going your way. You may ride along if you would like," I said.

He decided it would be better to ride than walk, so he got in the car. Finally I said, "As long as you're in the car, I could take you home, if you want to go." He agreed. Later that night, we talked about why he had run away and why he had come back home.

"It wasn't worth it over just a bowl of soup," he said.

As much as lieth in you, live peaceably with all men.

Romans 12:18 (KJV)

Most of the arguments and differences we have with others are not worth it. We human beings are strange creatures. We function far better in community than in solitude. Yet we make enemies of those who should be friends, and separate into camps rather than unite for a common cause.

Only issues of eternal significance should become a basis for disagreement. Even then we can, by God's grace, love those who disagree with us.

LIFE RESPONSE:

Is there a "bowl of soup" separating me from someone?

How Much Do We Care?

I saw a television program about a church in the Bedford Stuyvesant area of New York City. As scenes unfolded of the children and the slums in which they lived, I could not keep back the tears. All around them were the consequences of sin: drug addiction, alcoholism, crime, immorality. The suffering and disease that inevitably follow these sins were the playgrounds of these children. They slept in unheated apartments, huddled in front of open oven doors to keep from freezing. Most of them did not know who their fathers were. Many of them were sick, hungry, lonely and scared. Most will never escape the trap of the ghetto. A large percentage will either die young or will spend the majority of their lives in jail.

What does the saving gospel of the Lord Jesus say to them? Is it enough to offer them the hope of heaven when they die? Is there no salvation from the horror in which they are living here on earth?

If a brother or sister be naked, and destitute of daily food, and . . . ye give them not those things which are needful . . . what doth it profit?

James 2:15-16 (KJV)

James reminds us that it is not enough to preach salvation to the hungry and cold. Jesus showed us that we are to share both the gospel *and* our earthly goods.

LIFE RESPONSE:

Is there something I can do now to meet the needs of the hurting?

THROUGH THE BIBLE

1 Kings 3-5

AN IMPOSSIBLE WAY TO LIVE?

S omeone has said that after the first reading of the Sermon on the Mount, you feel that everything is turned upside down. But after the second reading, you discover that it turns everything right side up. The first time you read it, you think it is impossible. The second time, you feel that nothing else is possible.

We have become so accustomed to living life according to human philosophies that we have come to consider anything else as alien. One day, I sat for some time with my legs twisted under me in an unnatural position. When I got up and tried to walk, it was with great difficulty and pain. I had been in that position for so long that the natural function of my legs seemed unnatural for a short time.

> *. . . love your enemies, bless those who curse you. . . .*
>
> *Matthew 5:44 (NKJV)*

We have lived so long according to the human principles of selfishness, greed, competition, pettiness and strife, that at first reading, we find Christ's principles of love and kindness to be painfully unnatural.

E. Stanley Jones said, "The greatest need of modern Christianity is the rediscovery of the Sermon on the Mount as the only practical way to live." Someone may say that is not practical. No one can live that way. And they are right. Only human nature transformed by God's grace can live by the Sermon on the Mount.

LIFE RESPONSE:

I will seek to live the righteous life that is possible in the Lord Jesus Christ.

THROUGH THE BIBLE

1 Kings 6-7

LIFT THE FALLEN

Some years ago, a United States senator was asked by a mutual friend to help someone in a time of need. "I'm sorry," the senator said, "But I've become so busy lately, I can no longer concern myself with the troubles of individuals."

"That's quite remarkable," his friend replied. "Even God hasn't reached that point yet."

While many Christians may feel they are too busy to bother with the needs of others, Jesus does not have that attitude. He had time for others when He was here on earth, and He is still concerned for each of us.

What happens to many Christians when they fall or fail in some way? Are Christian brothers and sisters quick to help, to encourage? Or do they publish the mistake and see to it that he or she stays down? In Galatians 6:1 Paul said, "Restore such an one." That word "restore" in the original Greek means to set a dislocated bone. Bring them back to their place. Help them get up again.

For we have not an high priest which cannot be touched with the feeling of our infirmities.

Hebrews 4:15 (KJV)

Wouldn't it be wonderful if people held out a helping hand instead of a pointing finger? Someone has said, "He stands erect by bending over to help the fallen. He rises by lifting others."

LIFE RESPONSE:

With God's help, I will seek to extend a hand to those who have fallen, rather than point a finger at them.

THROUGH THE BIBLE

1 Kings 8-9

THE POWER OF GOD'S WORD

During the 1960s, every form of authority was challenged. Young people were convinced that nothing about the establishment, and absolutely no one over thirty, could be trusted. With so much of our faith in men destroyed, young people are once again searching for answers. Is there a final authority?

The holy . . . Scriptures are able to make you wise for salvation through faith in Christ Jesus.

2 Timothy 3:15 (NIV)

The Bible has come down to us through the ages, surviving attacks of barbaric vandalism and civilized scholarship. Neither the burning by fire nor the laughter of skepticism has annihilated it. It is the most enduring book the world has ever known. It remains the number one best seller of all time.

The French philosopher Voltaire declared in 1776, "One hundred years from today, there will not be a Bible on the earth except one that is looked upon by an antiquarian curiosity seeker." One hundred years after that declaration, Voltaire was long dead and his own house and press were being used to print and store Bibles by the Geneva Bible Society.

The Bible is more than good literature or interesting history. It is the power of God to bring us salvation. Millions of lives have been changed because of the transforming message of God's Word.

LIFE RESPONSE:

I will spend quality time in reading, studying and memorizing God's Word.

THROUGH THE BIBLE

1 Kings 10-12

WALKING WITH A FRIEND

When President Abraham Lincoln was carrying the heavy burden of the Civil War, an old friend who was a pharmacist from Springfield, Illinois, came to see him. They visited a while and then the president, accustomed to requests for help from former friends and associates, asked, "What do you want? Why did you come?"

"Oh, I don't want anything," the druggist said. "I just came to see an old friend and spin a few yarns with him the way we used to back home." The burdened President was so touched by this unselfish act of friendship, that he sat long into the night and poured out his heart to his companion.

Perhaps there is no greater treasure in all the world than a faithful companion, a friend to whom we can unburden our hearts.

Enoch was God's companion. They walked and talked together. And in their walk they became such good friends that God decided it was better for Enoch to walk with Him in heaven than to continue walking with Him here on earth.

> *Enoch walked with God; then he was no more, because God took him.*
>
> *Genesis 5:24 (NIV)*

To walk together, two people must be going in the same direction. "Can two walk together, except they be agreed?" (Amos 3:3 KJV).

LIFE RESPONSE:
Am I walking in agreement with God?

REAL "MEN"

Two young men were attending college. One served Christ. The other had an inflated opinion of himself. The young man who was serving the Lord was carrying his Bible across campus one day. The unbeliever, who considered himself a "he-man," approached the other student and accused him of being a sissy.

"You know, you're right," said the young man with the Bible. "I am rather small and weak. Someone as strong as you ought to carry the Bible. Perhaps you would carry it for me?"

At that, the criticizer turned and ran.

Be strong in the Lord, and in the power of his might.

Ephesians 6:10 (KJV)

You may have heard people describe Christians as weak people. They think Christianity is for women, little children and the elderly. Perhaps they picture Christians as those who sign a card or join a church. They do not know that being a Christian means taking up a cross and following Christ.

If you are going to truly live the life of Christ, if you will accept the challenge of this age, if you would grab hold of your cross and march forward with victory — you will need to have some of the internal strength of which real "men" are made.

LIFE RESPONSE:

I will live my life for Christ no matter what the critics may say.

Church: A Place To Be Healed

A noted doctor in New York City, recognizing that many of his patients were suffering physically because of emotional and mental problems, began to prescribe three months of regular church attendance. He explained, "In church, there is an atmosphere that contains the kind of healing power that will help men cure their mental, emotional, and even their physical troubles." He reported some amazing results from this prescription.

James pictures two extremes of emotion: grief and affliction on one hand, joy on the other. A funeral director once said, "Grief shared is grief diminished; joy shared is joy increased." This is the healing ministry of the church to which James refers.

A dynamic, Bible-believing church fellowship will offer the two most essential emotional ingredients of human existence: love and acceptance. If you are part of such a church you have the wonderful opportunity of both receiving and sharing these ingredients.

Is any among you afflicted? let him pray. Is any merry? let him sing psalms. Is any sick among you? let him call for the elders of the church . . .

James 5:13-14 (KJV)

Many do not receive love and acceptance at home, at school or on the job. But in the church, every person should be loved.

Life Response:

I will diligently look for hurting people in my fellowship, and love them with Christ's love.

Through the Bible

1 Kings 19-20

ARE YOU ROBBING GOD?

A faithful Christian man stopped by the church every week on payday to leave his tithe. One day the pastor said, "Brother, why do you come by on payday and leave your tithe? Why don't you just wait and put it in the offering on Sunday?"

The man replied, "If anything happens to me before Sunday, I don't want to die with the Lord's money in my pocket."

Bring ye all the tithes into the storehouse . . .

Malachi 3:10 (KJV)

This man may have been overly concerned, but you can't fault his motive. Too many people are not only going around with God's money in their pockets, but with God's money in their home, their car, their vacation cabin, their boat and in all the rest of their extravagance. Money that should have been given to the Lord's work has been kept for their own pleasure — and to their own hurt.

Will a man rob God? Malachi's message was as unpopular then as it is today. "Honour the Lord with thy substance," says the writer of Proverbs (3:9).

God's blessings rest on those who put Him first in their giving. The Lord does not have a person until He has his pocketbook. Stinginess in giving to God does not help our spiritual lives or bring glory to His name.

LIFE RESPONSE:
Does the Lord have first place in my finances?

WHY AM I FOLLOWING?

Many people look only for the benefits that Christ can bring into their lives. They don't really count the cost. In Jesus' day, some followed because He met their physical needs.

The ones who make an impact for God have a commitment that counts the cost.

Many years ago, Horace Pitkin, son of a wealthy merchant, was converted and called to be a missionary in China. He wrote to friends in America, "It will be but a short time till we know definitely whether we can serve him better above or here."

Not long after, a mob stormed the gate of the compound where Pitkin defended the women and children. He was beheaded. His head was offered at the shrine of a heathen god, while his body was thrown into a pit with the bodies of nine Chinese Christians. Someone said of him, "Pitkin won more men by his death than he could ever have won by his life."

The church under persecution has always been more convincing and powerful than the church at ease. When a few people are fully committed, they can affect their world. But an uncommitted majority will be powerless.

You are looking for me, not because you saw miraculous signs but because you ate the loaves and had your fill.

John 6:26 (NIV)

LIFE RESPONSE:

"Lord, help me to influence others by my personal commitment to Your cause."

THE CHURCH IS PEOPLE

Someone asked a pastor, "Where is your church?" He replied, "What time is it? Where my church is depends on what day of the week it is and what time of the day it happens to be. Right now, my church is in schools and factories, shops and stores, offices and homes all across the city. On Sunday morning, at about ten o'clock, my church will be gathered together in the building down on the corner of First and Main Streets."

Greet . . . the church that meets at their house.

Romans 16:5 (NIV)

The church is people, not buildings. In New Testament times there were no buildings used by the Christians exclusively for worship. The early Christians met in many places, in any place where they could gather in the name of Jesus. Sometimes they met in a house, sometimes in the Jewish temple, sometimes outdoors.

Later, during the times of persecution, Christians met in the dark underground cavern tombs known as the Catacombs.

When Jesus said He would build His church, He was not talking about buildings of wood or stone. He was speaking of people who would make up the "living stones" of a holy temple where God would dwell.

Are you part of the church, God's dwelling?

LIFE RESPONSE:

I will draw courage for each day from the fact that I am a part of the church — and all of hell cannot prevail against me.

THROUGH THE BIBLE

Ephesians 4-6

NO FOOTHOLD FOR THE DEVIL

S omeone wrote to a newspaper advice columnist asking if it was possible to foretell the future by looking at someone's palm. Her son, the writer said, had gone to a palm reader and been told he had a very short lifeline. "So he just lives for today," she wrote.

I am surprised that people in our so-called scientific age would be deceived by such things as fortune tellers, witchcraft, and psychics. It is now evident, however, that the doctrines of devils and deceiving spirits are not limited to the superstitions of the uncivilized.

I have never been one to see a demon behind every bush. Too many people are like the TV comic who said, "The devil made me do it." We must beware of being "devil conscious."

Jesus rebuked the devil . . .

Matthew 17:18 (KJV)

But it is just as much a mistake to write the devil off as it is to give him too much credit. As Christians, we need to be careful not to give the devil a foothold in our lives. Sometimes that happens unconsciously when we dabble with "new age" thinking or get drawn into the occult through horoscopes or transcendental meditation.

God, through His Holy Spirit, will lead you into the truth and satisfy the longing of your heart.

LIFE RESPONSE:

I will not make myself vulnerable to the teachings of worldly philosophers.

THROUGH THE BIBLE

2 Kings 1-3

WE NEED FELLOWSHIP

Chuck Swindoll tells of meeting an old Marine buddy who had been converted and in whom a complete change had taken place. The friend told Pastor Swindoll that the only thing he missed was the fellowship all the guys in their outfit used to have at the tavern. He enjoyed how they sat around, talked and "let their hair down." The converted Marine said, "I ain't got nobody to admit my faults to . . . to have 'em put their arms around me and tell me I'm still okay."

. . . the right hands of fellowship . . .

Galatians 2:9 (KJV)

Someone has written, "The neighborhood bar is possibly the best counterfeit there is to the fellowship Christ wants to give His church." Why should it be so difficult for new Christians to find the fellowship and acceptance they crave? Christ's body of believers ought to offer far greater and more satisfying fellowship than anything offered by the world. Yet too often churches are cliquish, cold and unfriendly. Newcomers find it nearly impossible to break into the fellowship.

Christians should be able to open up to one another, to confess faults when necessary, to sense the love and acceptance they need. Such fellowship is a place of healing.

LIFE RESPONSE:

Am I helping to make my church a place where everyone feels loved and accepted?

NEEDED: GODLY PREACHERS

The newspapers reported the story of a man divorcing his twenty-sixth wife. He was looking for number twenty-seven. He had no intention, he told reporters, of losing his place in *The Guinness Book of World Records*. The story also mentioned that he was an ordained minister in a certain denomination.

I recalled reading another newspaper account about that same man. A judge revoked his license to perform marriage ceremonies because he was such a bad example in his own life.

Is it any wonder people are scattered and faith is in confusion? If the preachers are not certain of their faith, if they are not established in their relationship with God, if they do not believe the Bible is the holy, inspired, infallible Word of the living God — our only faithful rule for faith and practice — what will the people believe?

> *Because you have rejected knowledge, I also reject you as my priests.*
>
> Hosea 4:6 (NIV)

Church leaders are held accountable for their own sins and for the influence they have on others. Thank God if your pastor lives the truth as well as preaches it. Hold his hands up and support him in his efforts to bring the church back to God.

Pastors and other church leaders who are leading their flocks astray will have much to answer for when they stand before God.

LIFE RESPONSE:

I will give a word of encouragement to my pastor this week.

You Can Be Comforted

Charles Shulz's cartoon strip "Peanuts" frequently features the character Linus, who is known for his faithful and familiar blanket. No matter what circumstance arises, Linus can face it if he has his blanket.

Many times adults also feel the need of a "security blanket." Christianity does not deny the stark realities of life. We don't close our eyes to trouble and sorrow. When we mourn we need to be comforted.

Blessed are those who mourn, for they will be comforted.

Matthew 5:4 (NIV)

But the Christian does not mourn without comfort. We know we are not alone. Trouble, pain and sorrow are not so hard to bear if someone is there with us.

When a little girl's playmate died, the child went to comfort the sorrowing mother. Later, her mother asked her what she had said.

"I didn't say anything. I just sat on her lap and cried with her," the little girl said. Sometimes we need someone to grieve and cry with us.

They who mourn can be happy, Jesus said, because they will be comforted. So many circumstances bring heartache and sorrow. You may be tempted to feel sorry for yourself. But happiness doesn't depend on sunny days and blue skies. When you mourn, that is when you can have the happiness of the Comforter's presence.

LIFE RESPONSE:

With God's help, I will learn not to depend on "sunny days" and "blue skies."

THROUGH THE BIBLE

2 Kings 9-11

IS YOUR LIFE MEANINGLESS?

The dean of a leading university was asked, "What is the greatest problem at this university?" He answered with one word, "Emptiness."

A young doctor at a leading medical center walked into a psychiatrist's office one day and said, "My life is a drag. You would think I have everything: a good position, unlimited access to laboratory and library facilities, medical journals that print my papers, grants from the government. I've got a great wife and nice kids. Why do I feel so empty inside?"

The Preacher in Ecclesiastes asked, "What profit hath a man of all his labour which he taketh under the sun? . . . the eye is not satisfied with seeing, nor the ear filled with hearing" (Eccles. 1:3, 8 KJV).

Meaningless! Meaningless! says the Teacher. Utterly meaningless! Everything is meaningless.

Ecclesiastes 1:2 (NIV)

In a world packed with some six billion souls, our individuality is easily lost in the press of the crowd. People fade anonymously into the great stream of humanity. They long for something that will make their lives significant. We sometimes feel that we are better known by our numbers than by our name — street number, zip code, area code, telephone number, social security number and credit card numbers.

Does your life have meaning? You are *not* a nobody! Let Jesus give your life real meaning.

LIFE RESPONSE:

I will discover my significance through my relationship with Jesus Christ.

THROUGH THE BIBLE
2 Kings 12-14

WE NEED THE POWER

Doctors report that their patients' most frequent complaint is, "I have no energy. I feel so tired and worn out all the time." There may be a physical basis for such symptoms, but often they are indicative of psychological, emotional and spiritual illness. This lack of energy is often caused by lack of purpose. Too many people lack the excitement of commitment.

You will receive power when the Holy Spirit comes on you . . .

Acts 1:8 (NIV)

The Holy Spirit provides power for committed Christians. He has authority over the spirit or attitude, and can help His children control themselves. He gives power over the tongue, making our speech wholesome and helpful. The Holy Spirit gives power over our human bodies. We need not be dominated by the desires of our flesh. Our bodies are the temple of the Holy Spirit.

The power of the Holy Spirit is an abiding power, giving continuous victory. I often ride on airplanes and I have felt the tremendous thrust of the giant jet engines. But if the power of that aircraft were let loose in one blast, it would blow the plane and everyone in it to pieces. The power is unleashed as it is needed. The dynamic life of real victory and blessing is for every child of God. It is the life in the Spirit.

LIFE RESPONSE:
Am I living a Spirit-empowered life?

Do The Roadwork

I heard a champion boxer say, "I love boxing but I hate the roadwork."

Every job has its roadwork. One man may earn his living cutting wood, and for him it is no pleasure. On the other hand, I enjoy cutting firewood. For me, it is recreational. Wouldn't it be great if the man who must do something and the man who enjoys doing it could be one and the same? But every job has its roadwork, the unpleasant but necessary part.

On one of my trips some years ago, I stopped to visit my parents. My brother drove me to the airport for my next flight. He said jokingly, "Now tell me again, this is your work? You do this for a living and call it work?" There are wonderful rewards and enjoyments in my work, but when I spend long, weary hours on the highway, lonely nights in motels and wait endlessly in airports, it's sometimes difficult to remember the adventure. Unless I remind myself, that is, that it's just a matter of doing your roadwork.

Let us run with perseverance the race marked out for us.

Hebrews 12:1 (NIV)

If we run the Christian race successfully, we must do our roadwork. We know what the cost of right living is. We know what it takes to be victorious. With the right attitude, we can learn to turn the roadwork into a joyful part of our lives.

LIFE RESPONSE:

Am I willing to lay aside every hindrance and make the race a priority?

NEEDED:
A FURROW SETTER

T he level land of much of the Midwest allows us a clear view of crops from the highway. Something that never ceases to amaze me are the straight furrows in acre after acre of corn and beans.

When I put out a garden, I carefully read the package. When it says to plant the seeds in rows six inches apart, I get out a ruler, measure the rows, stretch a string and keep the furrows straight. Many times my wife and I have different ideas about how to plant the garden. She likes to say, "Well, that looks like a good place for some beans," and then she just drops some seeds. Or, "I'll put some squash over there," and off she goes. Oddly enough, hers often grow better than mine!

Make straight in the wilderness a highway for our God.

Isaiah 40:3 (NIV)

In Isaiah's day, plowing was done with a mule or ox. Someone was called in who had what they referred to as a "dead eye." This furrow setter made the first perfectly straight furrow. Then the farmer just had to align the rest of the furrows with that perfect one. The furrow setter's purpose was to set the standard.

Straight furrows in life are much more important than those in a field or garden. A furrow setter is needed today to raise a standard of righteousness for the people to follow. When a nation loses its absolutes, the garden becomes a tangled wilderness.

LIFE RESPONSE:
Am I following a "straight furrow?"

THROUGH THE BIBLE
2 Kings 21-23

CHRISTIANS, UNITE!

I read about two small churches of different denominations, located across the road from each other in a rural community. Because they were both having a hard time meeting their obligations, maintaining their buildings and supporting a pastor, they decided to join their efforts and become one united congregation.

Everyone seemed to agree that it was the sensible thing to do. But they could not get together. It seems that when they recited the Lord's Prayer one congregation said, "Forgive us our trespasses" while the other said, "Forgive us our debts." Neither church would give in, and the merger talks broke down. The local newspaper reported that one church went back to its trespasses while the other returned to its debts. Unfortunately, it was probably true of both.

I heard of another proposed merger between a Christian Church and a Baptist Church. One of the Baptist deacons said, "I have been a Baptist all of my life and no one is going to make a Christian out of me!"

How good and pleasant it is when brothers live together in unity!

Psalms 133:1 (NIV)

Such stories would be humorous if they weren't so tragically typical. Where is the unity for which Jesus gave His life and for which He prayed so earnestly?

LIFE RESPONSE:

I will do everything in my power to live in unity with my brothers and sisters in the Lord.

Too Much Religion

George Washington Carver, an Afro-American who was many years ahead of his time, received citations and honors from many quarters, including the President. But he also had to endure racial prejudice. Although he seldom spoke out about it, he was once asked by a group of ministers how they could improve race relations.

"Your actions speak so loud that I cannot hear what you are saying," he told them. "You have too much religion and not enough Christianity. Too many creeds and not enough deeds. This world is perishing for kindness."

. . . having a form of godliness, but denying the power thereof . . .

2 Timothy 3:5 (KJV)

The ministers were caught off guard. They hadn't expected such frankness from Dr. Carver.

Too many people have too much religion and not enough demonstration of God. That is why religion can flourish — and right beside it, crime, wickedness, turmoil and trouble can also flourish. Religion, divorced from a life-changing faith in the living God, leaves men worse than heathen. When Paul visited Athens, he told the men on Mars Hill they were too religious.

Many very religious people know nothing of God's saving power. Is your hope in Christ or in your religion?

LIFE RESPONSE:

I will place my hope in Christ, not organized religion.

THROUGH THE BIBLE

Philippians 1-4

INSULATED, NOT ISOLATED

When I was a child, our family stayed for ten days each summer at our camp meeting cottage. The days were filled with Bible studies, prayer meetings, testimony times and preaching services. We lived with Christians, ate with Christians, played with Christians. We would often go for days — sometimes through the entire camp — without seeing a newspaper. It was easy to forget the things so troubling in the world around us.

Almost always, as we packed to go back home, someone would remark, "I wish we could stay at camp all year." There is something attractive about living in an atmosphere like that. It seems akin to heaven.

But while we are citizens of heaven, we are also citizens of earth. We cannot stay on the mountain like the Apostle Peter wanted to do. We must go back down into the valley where the needs are. Jesus prayed that we would be *in* the world, but not *of* the world. Not isolated from it, but insulated from its evil.

> *Master, it is good for us to be here: and let us make three tabernacles . . .*
>
> Luke 9:33 (NIV)

We need the "heavenly times" of being with other Christians. But the purpose of these times is to fortify us to live in and be a blessing to this present world.

LIFE RESPONSE:

"Lord, help me to be an influence for You right where I am."

ARE YOU FORGIVEN?

W hen Dwight L. Moody was only four, his father died. A month later, his mother gave birth to twins, the eighth and ninth children in the family. Then her oldest boy ran away from home. She placed a light for him in the window every night, and often her voice could be heard in prayer for her wandering boy.

Then one day, Mrs. Moody saw a stranger coming toward the house. With arms folded, he stood at the door, tears trickling down his face.

"Oh, it's my boy!" she cried, and asked him to come in.

"No, Mother, I will not come in until I hear first that you have forgiven me." Of course, she forgave him. She rushed to the door, threw her arms around her long-lost son and drew him back into her home.

. . . your sins have hidden His face from you . . .

Isaiah 59:2 (NIV)

What a picture of forgiveness. It cannot be bought or earned, nor can penance bring it. Guilt cannot be cured in any other way than through the forgiveness of God.

But forgiveness is blocked by lack of faith and by failure to forgive others.

LIFE RESPONSE:

I won't let anything keep me from experiencing God's forgiveness.

UNNAMED?

Like many today, Moses felt like a nobody. Often people have a sense of worthlessness because they see themselves as insignificant, unimportant. They think of themselves as pygmies in a land of giants. All around them they see heroes and rising stars destined for success.

But with God, there are no unnamed. He knew who the seven thousand were in Elijah's day who had not bowed the knee to Baal. Many unnamed people have had key roles in the success of others. (Who were the parents of Daniel who inspired and instructed their son to stand firm for God? Who was the elderly lady who prayed for Billy Graham for over twenty years? Who financed William Carey's ministry in India? Who taught Charles Wesley to write music? Who found the Dead Sea scrolls? Who was preaching the day Billy Sunday was saved?).

Who am I, that I should go unto Pharaoh . . .

Exodus 3:11 (KJV)

We know the names of the great heroes, the giants, but behind the scenes were countless hidden saints who helped them become heroes for God. In Hebrews, chapter eleven, many unnamed heroes are included in Faith's Hall of Fame. There were those who worked righteousness and obtained promises as well as those who stopped the mouths of lions! You may feel unnamed, but you are an important person in God's plan.

LIFE RESPONSE:
I will view my life as significant in God's master plan.

ARE WE ALL TALK?

An evangelist told of his mother-in-law's concern for his safety as he drove thousands of miles each year. She had read statistics which explained that, per passenger mile traveled, the airplane was the safest form of transportation. She told him of the comfort and speed of air travel and the time he would save. She sounded like the public relations officer of a major airline. Yet that lady had never been on an airplane — and refused to ride in one!

Faith without works is dead.

James 2:20 (KJV)

Some people say they believe in Jesus Christ, but they have never "gotten on board the plane." They know about His life and death, His parables and teachings. They are convinced that He is really who the Bible says He is. But they have never surrendered their personal lives to His claims.

Parents tell their children not to smoke, all the while puffing away on cigarettes. They often send their children to Sunday school while they sleep late, play golf or work in the yard. We can best influence others when our walk matches our talk.

LIFE RESPONSE:
"Lord, help me to put 'deeds' to my faith."

"HELP ME, GOD!"

A story in a religious magazine dramatically illustrates God's miracle power. It tells how a forty-year-old man, rough and wicked, came to know God. Profane, mean-spirited, this man loved to drink and fight. His pastor tried to convert him, to no avail. "God means nothing to me," the man would say. He went from bad to worse, from liquor to drugs. Finally, he got so low he couldn't handle himself. The pastor repeated the advice he had given so many times before, "Your only hope is God."

Beaten and humbled, the man asked, "How do I contact God?"

"Just talk to Him. Ask for His help."

The man looked up and said, "Help me, God. I can't help myself."

That was all, a simple prayer. But it must have been in real faith because the man was able to testify: "You told me there is a God. Now I know there is because He heard what I said. He came right close to me. I felt warm inside, I began to cry. I'm so happy. He set me free from alcohol and drugs and all that rotten stuff."

God be merciful to me a sinner.

Luke 18:13 (KJV)

How do you explain a miracle like that? Certainly it is not the work of religion. Only the power of God, unleashed by faith, can transform a sinner into a child of God.

We can all pray that prayer: "Help me, God. I can't help myself."

LIFE RESPONSE:

I will seek to live a God-sufficient life rather than a self-sufficient one.

CAESAR OR GOD?

Christians have dual citizenship — on earth and in heaven. Both kingdoms have authority over us. The question is, which has final authority?

In the nineteenth century some taught that man would eventually build his own heaven here on earth, a man-made utopia. But stark reality has crushed that dream. Power-crazed madmen, nuclear weapons, escalating crime and continued war are evidence that human beings do not know how to create a "brave new world."

Give to Caesar what is Caesar's, and to God what is God's.

Matthew 22:21 (NIV)

Too many Americans fail to distinguish between what is American and what is Christian. They have wrapped their Bibles in red, white and blue, and sung "God Bless America" until the line between Christ and Caesar has almost been obliterated.

We are commanded to honor those in authority, but our allegiance to Caesar should not be so complete that it violates our Christian conscience. When the laws of men and the commandments of God come into direct conflict, we must have the courage to say with Peter and the other apostles, "We must obey God rather than men!" (Acts 5:29 NIV).

LIFE RESPONSE:

Like the three Hebrew children, I refuse to bow down to the gods of the earth.

SOW SEEDS OF FORGIVENESS

World-famous engineer Peer Holm later came to failure and returned to the village of his childhood with his wife and little girl. His neighbor owned a fierce dog but was contemptuous of those who warned him that the dog was dangerous. One day, the dog killed Peer Holm's little daughter.

The sheriff shot the dog, but all the neighbors remained bitter against the owner. When spring came, no one would sell the man any seed for his fields. But Peer Holm, troubled by his neighbor's predicament, could not sleep at night.

On one of those sleepless nights, he finally arose and went to his shed. Taking his last half-bushel of barley, he climbed the fence and sowed the barley seed in his neighbor's field. When the seed germinated, it was obvious what Peer had done. His neighbor's field was green, while part of his own remained bare.

Be kind . . . to one another, forgiving each other, just as in Christ God forgave you.

Ephesians 4:32 (NIV)

Peer sowed seeds of kindness and forgiveness as well as seeds of barley.

Are there some seeds you need to sow? Can we afford to harbor unforgiveness in our hearts when we know that God's forgiveness is prevented by such thoughts? Nothing is worth the unutterable loss of God's forgiveness!

We hurt ourselves most when we do not forgive.

LIFE RESPONSE:
By my thoughts and actions, I will sow seeds of forgiveness.

THROUGH THE BIBLE
1 Chronicles 17-20

AN IMPROVED SOCIETY?

The dreams and fantasies of science fiction writers decades ago have become scientific realities. There are people alive today who witnessed the first automobiles to scare horses along deeply rutted dirt roads. They might have seen the first adventurous mail plane pilots circle a barn on which someone had painted a large arrow pointing north so the pilots could regain their bearings. Later, they attentively listened as news reports broadcast the first attempts of man to enter space, and sat glued to the TV screen as man walked on the moon for the first time.

The world and its desires pass away, but the man who does the will of God lives forever.

1 John 2:17 (NIV)

In one lifetime, we have transformed the lifestyle of our nation. But something is terribly wrong. Medical advances and technological inventions have not changed the basic sinful nature of human beings. Civilization, education, wealth and legislation have not, and cannot, make any nation a utopia.

Science can deal only with things of this world, which are passing away. Society is transformed only when individuals are changed from the inside out. People are going to live (or die) forever. What a difference it would make if the efforts spent on improving our lot in life were spent on doing the will of God.

LIFE RESPONSE:

I will concentrate more on doing God's will than on making temporal gains.

THROUGH THE BIBLE
1 Chronicles 21-23

HEAVENLY TREASURE

While living in an eastern city many years ago, I discovered one morning that someone had broken into my garage and gone through my car. Since nothing of value had been left in the car, nothing had been taken. But I soon learned that every garage on our street had been burglarized. Several of the neighbors had lost money, jewelry or other possessions which they had left in their cars.

We called the police and gave them the necessary information. We mentioned that not only had every garage been locked, but several of the cars inside the garages had also been locked. One policeman's comment shocked me.

"That makes no difference," he said. "Locks only keep out honest people. Anyone who wants to steal from you can."

If you set your heart on earthly treasure, Jesus says, someone will separate you from it. If you manage to keep robbers from stealing your treasure, the day will come when you will still be separated from it. Then where will your heart be?

> *Lay up for yourselves treasures in heaven . . . where thieves do not break in and steal.*
>
> Matthew 6:20 (NKJV)

Only treasure laid up in heaven is safe. Gifts of time and effort, as well as money, contributed to God's work — these are treasures that endure.

LIFE RESPONSE:

Am I investing my time, talent, and treasure in the things that are eternal?

USE YOUR SENSES

Helen Keller was one of the most remarkable people this world has ever known. Blind and deaf from infancy, she was able — through the untiring love and discipline of her teacher, Anne Sullivan — to learn to understand the world around her. Through smell, touch and taste, she became aware of the beauty around her that many sighted people never observe.

"What did you see?" Miss Keller asked a friend who had just returned from a long walk in the woods.

Her friend responded, "Oh, nothing much."

Helen Keller later said, "I might have been incredulous, had I not been accustomed to such responses, for long ago, I became convinced that the seeing see very little."

He that hath an ear, let him hear . . .

Revelation 2:7 (KJV)

Helen Keller suggested that people use their eyes as if they would be blind tomorrow, and their ears as if they would be deaf tomorrow. Make the most of every sense! Such attention to the world around us can give us a greater appreciation of our Creator. It can make us more sensitive to other people and more attentive to their needs.

We need to use our God-given abilities while we have them.

LIFE RESPONSE:

"Lord, help me to use my senses to enjoy your creation."

LIGHTEN THE LOAD!

There is a parable about a man who carried a heavy load of sticks on his back as he walked along a country road. A farmer in a horse-drawn wagon stopped and offered the man a ride. The man gratefully accepted, climbed into the wagon and sat down, but kept the heavy load of sticks on his back.

"Why don't you take that load off your back and leave it in the wagon?" asked the farmer.

"Oh, no! It is enough that you would give me a lift. I couldn't ask you to carry my heavy load besides."

Do you look for ways to help people with their burdens? People carry many kinds of loads. Although sometimes not as obvious as a bundle of sticks, these loads can be very heavy and even overwhelming. The load may be a physical handicap, a financial burden or a difficult home situation. There is also the load of sin borne by so many.

Charles Dickens said, "No one is useless in this world who lightens the burden of it to anyone else."

As we have opportunity, let us do good to all people.

Galatians 6:10 (NIV)

All of us know someone whose load we can lighten. In fact, nothing lightens one's own burdens so quickly, it has been said, as helping others carry theirs. We can help others because Jesus has lifted our load!

LIFE RESPONSE:

I will ask the Lord to bring someone into my life whose burden I can share.

DRESS FOR SUCCESS

Years ago the popular book, *Dress For Success*, made an impact on the business community. It describes how dressing effectively can aid in climbing the corporate ladder. According to this book, every item of attire should be chosen and coordinated carefully to impress people and project the proper image. No matter what your calling in life, the author said, you can be more successful if you dress for it.

But the true principles of "dressing for success" were written many years before this book was published. Given centuries ago, they have been adapted to every society and culture since. What's more, they involve success in the areas of life that are really important.

> *Put on the full armor of God.*
>
> Ephesians 6:13 (NIV)

The Apostle Paul described the well dressed man in Ephesians, chapter six. Each item has an important function. For success in Christian living we must put on truth, righteousness, peace, faith, salvation and the Word of God. God has provided the attire necessary to be successful as a Christian soldier.

A person dressed like this may not make the "best-dressed list" but he will be able to fight the good fight of faith and live victoriously.

LIFE RESPONSE:
Am I dressed for success?

THROUGH THE BIBLE

2 Chronicles 1-4

A Gift
For Everyone

The first church I pastored was a little frame building in a patch of woods at the end of a dirt road. We began with just a handful of common, hard-working folk. I'll never forget those precious people, and I'll always be indebted to them. What I lacked in experience, I tried to make up in enthusiasm — and they put up with my youthful exuberance.

One man in this group was talented in playing stringed instruments. He could pick up a guitar or banjo and play any song in the hymnal. Since his wife could play the piano, it seemed natural to put them in charge of the music. Another woman was a good bookkeeper, so she became the treasurer. Each person was given some responsibility, determined primarily by a gift or talent.

But one man seemed to be talentless. He couldn't sing or teach or keep books. But he faithfully attended church. I soon discovered that he was also punctual. I could never get to the church ahead of him. I realized the natural position for him to hold was that of janitor.

> *We have different gifts, according to the grace given us.*
> Romans 12:6 (NIV)

God gives His believers gifts to use in building up the church, for edifying the body. Each has a part to play. No one should say, "I don't have any gifts!" God sees to it that you do!

LIFE RESPONSE:
"Lord, show me the interest or ability that might be used for You."

FACT OR FICTION?

I read somewhere that fifty million adults in America profess to be born-again Christians. The obvious question is, where are they? Are they visible on the streets and in the stores? Can they be seen in the school rooms and shops? Are they recognizable along the assembly lines and in the marketplace?

The image of Christ should be seen in every Christian. The world took note of the early Christians that they had been with Jesus (Acts 4:13). Are modern Christians walking the highway of holiness with Christ long enough, and often enough, to be recognized as His disciples?

. . . you have taken off your old self . . . and have put on the new self . . .

Colossians 3:9-10 (NIV)

I heard about a clergyman whose friend was an actor. The actor was drawing large crowds of people while the clergyman was preaching to just a few in his church. He said to his actor friend, "Why is it that you draw great crowds and I have practically no audience at all? Your words are sheer fiction and mine are the unchangeable truth."

The actor said, "I present my fiction as though it were fact, and you present your truth as though it were fiction."

Are we as Christians demonstrating in our lives a denial of what we profess in our testimony?

LIFE RESPONSE:

"Lord, help me to demonstrate my testimony."

THROUGH THE BIBLE

2 Chronicles 8-11

Win The Inner War!

Two little boys were fighting in the school yard. One boy finally got on top of the other and was holding him down. But at the same time, he was yelling loudly for help. A passerby stopped and asked, "Why are you the one calling for help? You've got him down."

"Yes, but I can feel him starting to get up."

Do you ever feel that way in your spiritual struggles? You have done your best. You're living for the Lord. You have been holding down the "old man of sin" with his deeds. You seem to be winning over the old habits and sins. But sometimes you feel a stirring in your heart that tells you the "old man" is starting to get up again.

Who will win this inner war? Those who have crucified the old man, the sinful nature, those who live and walk in the Spirit. Lay down the arms of rebellion and let the Spirit of God take over. The battle has already been won. Just as forgiveness for sin was provided by Jesus' death on the cross, so deliverance from the sinful nature has been provided in the same way. "We have been made holy by the sacrifice of the body of Jesus Christ once for all" (Heb. 10:10 NIV).

> *What causes fights and quarrels among you? Don't they come from your desires that battle within you?*
>
> James 4:1 (NIV)

LIFE RESPONSE:

I will surrender myself to the cleansing and empowering work of the Holy Spirit for victory over my sinful nature.

THROUGH THE BIBLE

2 Chronicles 12–16

ADMIT IT!

A woman came to the hotel where a well-known pastor was to speak and asked if he could help her husband. The man was weak, sick and depressed. The pastor invited the man to his hotel room to talk with him. After he listened to the man tell about his physical ailments, he said, "All right, now tell me all of the mean, dirty, sinful things you've been doing." At first the man was irate. But when he calmed down he asked, "How did you know?"

"From what you were telling me, I perceived that your problem was the load of guilt you are carrying for the way you've been living," the pastor replied.

Then the man poured out his awful tale. While maintaining an image of respectability, even church membership, he was living a low-down life of sin. The pastor got the man onto his knees, praying and confessing to God.

If we claim we have not sinned, we make him out to be a liar . . .

1 John 1:10 (NIV)

When they went to the lobby to meet his wife, she said, "What did you do to my husband? He even looks different." The pastor said, "I didn't do anything; Jesus took care of his guilt."

Guilt does terrible things to people. Denying our sins will not help us. Only when we confess our sins and find forgiveness will God make us new people.

LIFE RESPONSE:

I will make sure my guilt is confessed and my conscience clear.

Are You Communicating?

The most frequent complaint heard by marriage counselors is "my spouse won't talk to me." As one pastor was counseling a married couple, the wife kept shouting at the husband and he kept shouting back — with neither one listening to the other.

The pastor took the husband aside and told him that if he wanted effective counsel he would have to do as the pastor said. The husband agreed, and the pastor said, "Every time I nod my head at you, say, 'You may be right.'"

Back together again, the couple resumed their argument. The pastor nodded his head, and the husband said, "You may be right." A few minutes later, this happened again. After several occurrences the woman stopped yelling and said, "That's the first time you ever suggested I might be right about anything."

From that point on, they began to communicate.

Most of our differences would be mediated quickly if we would simply be willing to talk face-to-face and really listen to each other. James has some good advice: "Everyone should be quick to listen, slow to speak and slow to become angry" (James 1:19 NIV).

> *I hope to visit you and talk with you face to face, so that our joy may be complete.*
>
> 2 John 12 (NIV)

LIFE RESPONSE:

I will take time to listen and talk to the significant others in my life.

THE MEASURE OF SUCCESS

T he keynote speaker was being introduced at a pastors' luncheon I attended some time ago. A well-known television preacher, he was described in glowing terms as one highly qualified to bring the message. The introduction included references to the preacher's large church membership, his television ministry to millions, and the many books he had authored.

When the preacher rose to speak, he said that the most important things had been left out of the introduction. He explained that anyone can gather a crowd, anyone with enough money can get on TV, and almost anyone can write a book. These are not the things by which he measured success. He said that the most important things in his life were these: He has been married to the same woman for over thirty years, his children love the Lord, his son is in the ministry and his daughter was preparing for ministry. He said that the love and happiness of his family were the crowning achievement of his life.

> *Do not love the world or anything in the world.*
>
> *1 John 2:15 (NIV)*

How do you measure success? If you want to be counted a success by the world, you will need to be a lover of the world and the things that are in it. But you cannot be successful in God's eyes at the same time. He has a different measure of success, and it has something to do with selflessness and servanthood.

LIFE RESPONSE:

"Lord, help me to measure my success by Your standards and not the standards set by the world."

THROUGH THE BIBLE

2 Chronicles 23-25

Keep Your Eye On The Prize!

In the midst of a heavy travel schedule some years ago, I was trying to keep up with several engagements, flying to one appointment after another. One day I rushed to the airport, boarded the plane and immediately began reading some materials I needed to go over. Another man boarded and sat next to me. He smiled and asked, "Where are you going?"

When I tried to answer, my mind went blank. Sitting in embarrassed silence, my thoughts raced frantically. Where *am* I going? What is my next meeting? Who is expecting me? Finally I asked him, "Where is this plane going?" All I could conclude was, wherever the plane was going, I was going as well.

Some people live their entire lives that way. They don't know where they are going, but they are rushing around trying to get there.

> *. . . the prize of the High Calling of God in Christ Jesus.*
>
> Philippians 3:14 (KJV)

The Apostle Paul was pressing toward the mark. He had a goal in mind and wasn't looking to the right or to the left. His eye was on the goal, the mark, the prize. Nothing could turn him away. It is total concentration on the goal that brings success.

LIFE RESPONSE:

I will concentrate on eternal rewards and not earth's awards.

TAKING A RISK

When I was a boy, my friends and I often played "Follow the Leader." We formed a line and everyone had to do what the leader did — run, jump, swing from a limb, balance on a ledge, jump over the creek. I remember sometimes hesitating before some particularly daring feat, while those who had already accomplished it would call, "Come on! It's easy!" Finally, gathering all my courage I would "follow," only to discover that it was as easy as my friends had said. Then I would stand with them and taunt those behind me. How quickly we forgot the risk once we had accomplished our goal!

Whatever was to my profit I now consider loss for the sake of Christ.

Philippians 3:7 (NIV)

The Apostle Paul found he had to let go of the old in order to have the new. He had to give up his former treasures in order to experience the treasure found in Jesus. Nothing was worth anything, compared to the riches found in Christ. People who are considering "taking the plunge" and becoming a Christian may think it too risky. They cannot imagine giving up their bad habits and shady practices to make the leap over to God's side.

But Jesus promises abundant life. Anything given up for Him will be repaid many times over — if not in this life, then in the life to come. He is the "pearl of great price" (Matt. 12:46 KJV).

LIFE RESPONSE:

What earthly losses am I willing to suffer in order to make heavenly gains?

WHO WERE YOUR ANCESTORS?

If you're looking for exciting reading, the first chapter of the first book of the New Testament is about as exciting as reading a telephone directory. But the genealogy recorded by Matthew is very important, for it traces the history of the human family into which Jesus Christ was born. Luke's account also lists the family tree, beginning with Joseph and going back through his forefathers.

I met a college student who remained at school during a vacation break. She explained that she had no place to go. "I was raised in an orphanage," she said. "I have no home." To better appreciate your heritage, you may have traced the roots of your family. It is a blessing to be able to feel that you "know" your forebears. However, illustrious ancestors do not insure that all descendants will be noble!

The Bible is painfully honest about the ancestors of Jesus. Included with noble Abraham and Boaz are people like Rahab, the harlot; Ruth, a Moabite; Bathsheba, with whom David committed adultery; and Manasseh, a wicked king. Yet from this motley array of ancestors, God brought the promised Messiah. He works with what He has in all of our lives.

Descendants eventually become ancestors!

A record of the genealogy of Jesus Christ the son of David, the son of Abraham.

Matthew 1:1 (NIV)

LIFE RESPONSE:

I will glory in the fact that I am a child of God through faith in the Lord Jesus Christ.

THROUGH THE BIBLE

2 Chronicles 33-34

STAY LITTLE!

Like many still do today, my college senior class voted on the "best" person in a variety of categories. One of the votes was for "most likely to succeed." Our choice for that honor was very deserving. Talented, personable and capable, he had many characteristics necessary for success. Immediately after graduation, he started out in his chosen career in a way that reinforced our vote. For him, success was just around the corner.

When you were little in your own eyes, were you not head of the tribes of Israel?

1 Samuel 15:17 (NKJV)

In a very few years, however, his career was over, his home destroyed, his life entangled in sin and disgrace. One of our mutual friends said, "I don't understand it. He was voted 'most likely to succeed.'"

I answered, "The most likely to succeed may be the most likely to fail. He trusted himself instead of relying upon God."

Like King Saul, too many people become self-confident and fail to stay "little" in their own eyes. True success comes to those whose confidence is in God. Don't let your gifts and talents become a stumbling-block!

LIFE RESPONSE:

"Lord, help me to understand that my real worth is in my relationship with You."

You Are Special

I t was the custom when I was a boy to "choose up sides" for a ball game. Some boys would be picked quickly because they had a special gift. One might be a good pitcher, one a reliable hitter, one a fast runner. (I remember a certain boy being chosen because he was the only one with a catcher's mask and shin guards!) then one by one the rest of us would be selected in descending order of talent.

Men tend to choose the talented, the rich, the beautiful, the young, the desirable, or the influential. These are chosen because they are special. But God' didn't choose you because you are special. You are special because He has chosen you!

You are special to God because you are His creation, because you are an object of His concern. We need to teach children that they are special because God made them. He has a purpose in mind for each human being.

I have never liked receiving mail addressed "Current Occupant." That certainly is not the way God thinks about you or me. He knows each of us by name and cares about us individually. Jesus tells us the very hairs of our heads are numbered (Luke 12:7).

What is man that you are mindful of him . . .

Psalms 8:4 (NIV)

You are unique and God has a plan for you to do something worthwhile with your life.

LIFE RESPONSE:

I will meditate on the fact that I am God-created, God-redeemed, and God-blessed.

THE CHURCH: ALIVE AND WELL

In the late 1800s the Methodist Church was opening one new church a day. One Methodist pastor, Rev. C. C. McCabe, read a newspaper account of a speech delivered in Chicago by the famous infidel, Robert Ingersoll. Ingersoll said the church was dying and in another generation few, if any, churches would be left.

McCabe sent a telegram to Ingersoll which said, "In the Methodist Church, we are starting more than one new church a day and propose to make it two." He added a P.S.: "All hail the power of Jesus' name."

Word of the telegram spread and someone wrote a song about it:

I will build my church; and the gates of hell shall not prevail against it.

Matthew 16:18 (KJV)

The infidels, a motley band, in counsel met and said / Churches are dying across the land, and soon they'll all be dead / When suddenly a message came and caught them with dismay / All hail the power of Jesus' name, we're building two a day.

In spite of all its enemies have done, the church has never been destroyed. It has sometimes been driven underground but it has not died. One reason for that is the nature of the church: it is God's church! Another reason is that sinful humanity desperately needs the Savior of the church.

LIFE RESPONSE:

I will praise the Lord for the fellowship and overcoming power of His church.

THROUGH THE BIBLE

Ezra 1-4

LOVING OTHERS

When I began pastoring, my father would often write me letters of encouragement (and sometimes of advice), sharing from his years of wisdom and experience. One line I remember, because he repeated it often was, "Norman, love your people. Everyone needs love."

Sometimes we are tempted to think that the greatest human needs are food, shelter and clothing — the necessities of life. But nothing is more necessary than love. Some people are starving, that's true, but others who are well fed are starving for love.

Some time ago, the morning newspaper published the photograph of a murder scene not far from where I lived. A millionaire's residence, the house looked like a castle. There was no love in that mansion, however, for the owner had shot and killed his wife.

As I have loved you, so you must love one another.

John 13:34b (NIV)

Too often, we build walls to separate us instead of bridges to unite us. We withhold our love because we don't approve of the conduct of others.

But how did God love us? While we were yet sinners. When we love unconditionally, we love like Jesus loves. If we do this, we will be amazed at the love that flows back to us in return.

LIFE RESPONSE:

I will offer unconditional love to my relatives, friends and associates.

FORGET · THE PAST

Every summer when I was a boy, my family vacationed at my grandmother's house in the Adirondack Mountains of upstate New York. My memories of those pleasant times seemed to grow through the years, achieving monumental proportions. Memories of swinging on Grandma's porch swing, playing ball in wide-open fields, hearing the crack of the bat echo thunderously, fishing treacherous mountain brooks and catching huge trout.

But then I began to work summer jobs. Years passed. Grandma died and I had a family of my own. Finally, we decided to take a trip to New York and show the children a bit of their heritage. At first excited, I pointed out every favorite place along the way. But when we arrived, I was disappointed. Somehow, nothing was quite as I remembered it. The house and porch were so small! The "ball field" was a patch of grass, the brooks so shallow and narrow.

Forgetting those things which are behind . . .

Philippians 3:13 (KJV)

As we drove back home, my excitement was gone. Bright memories of the past were somehow tarnished by the stark reality of the present.

That may be why the Apostle Paul admonishes us to forget those things that are behind. Attempting to live in the past is not only disappointing, it is impossible.

Someone said, "This place isn't as nice as it used to be." Another responded, "It never was."

Remembering our heritage is one thing, but living in the past is nonproductive.

LIFE RESPONSE:
I will set personal, spiritual goals, and move toward them by God's grace.

TALENT OR HARD WORK?

A famous pianist had just completed his concert. The audience was loud and long in its applause. At the reception which followed, a woman remarked to him, "What talent! What genius! I wish that God had gifted me like that."

The great pianist replied, "Madam, that is not genius, nor am I especially gifted. If you would simply practice eight hours every day for forty years, you could play the piano as well as I!"

That is not entirely true, of course, for talent *is* necessary. But he is correct in asserting that some accomplishments are simply the results of hard work and faithful practice. Too many people sit around waiting for the talented, the gifted, or the inspired to do what needs to be done, when what is really needed is for someone to just roll up his sleeves and go to work.

The whole body . . . grows and builds itself up in love, as each part does its work.

Ephesians 4:16 (NIV)

Thomas Edison said, "Genius is one percent inspiration and ninety-nine percent perspiration."

Those who have been involved in the church know that much of what is accomplished is not done by those with the greatest abilities — but by those with a willing spirit.

If the talent is possessed by a lazy person, hard work will accomplish more than talent. Your availability is far more important than your ability.

LIFE RESPONSE:

"Lord, help me to use the *abilities* You have given me for the *work* You have given me."

THROUGH THE BIBLE
Nehemiah 1-4

DEAD SEA
OR LIVING WATER?

W hen we were in Jerusalem for a conference, we took a trip down to the Dead Sea. Someone suggested that we dip our finger in the water and put a drop on our tongue. (I knew better because I had done it before.) It is extremely salty and bitter. Only one person was swimming in the water at the time, a tourist curious about the buoyancy of the dense water. The only boats allowed in the Dead Sea are military boats, which must be treated to withstand corrosion. No fish live in that water and all around is dry, barren land.

Although water pours into the Dead Sea, it has no outlet. Rich minerals rush in and are deposited, but go nowhere after that.

That is the picture of the empty lives of many people. Rich blessings from God flow into their lives. They have health, prosperity, ability and talent. But all around them is dryness. Their lives are barren, unable to flow out to bless the world that touches them from day to day.

Whoever believes in me, as the Scripture has said, streams of living water will flow from within him.

John 7:38 (NIV)

Are you asking: Why am I so empty? It may be because you are so full of yourself, no room is left for the satisfying, refreshing water of life which only God can give.

LIFE RESPONSE:

Is my life a dead sea or a flowing well?

GOD MAKES A DIFFERENCE

*T*he *Guinness Book of World Records* tells of a man named Joe who is the world's greatest automobile salesman. He didn't start out that way. Joe was raised in a poor family. His father was mean to him and told Joe he was no good. Joe joined a gang and got into trouble. Finally, he married a girl who stuck with him through everything. But he was still a failure.

One night, he came home and had to climb over the backyard fence because there was a court representative at the front door. His wife told him they had no money and no food for the children. In despair, Joe fell on his knees in the living room. "Dear Lord, are you going to tell me I'm no good, too?" That night, he turned his life over completely to God.

Then Joe had the idea that he was to go to a certain place and ask the man to let him sell cars. He did this, was given a job and, at first, had no success. But God told him to be patient and shortly afterward, he made his first sale. He went on to become the world's greatest car salesman!

He is able to save completely those who come to God through him . . .

Hebrews 7:25 (NIV)

God doesn't always give a person such dramatic success. But He does transform people, and He works in the lives of His children.

LIFE RESPONSE:
I will turn every area of my life over to God.

ARE YOU COUNTING YOUR TROPHIES?

Several years ago, I heard former Senator Harold Hughes explain in a speech why he was giving up a distinguished career. Living an empty life that was lived only for the praise of men, he told of going into the room that contained all of his trophies, memorials, awards and plaques — the recognition given him by men.

He said it seemed so hollow and empty. He felt like taking them all and making a big bonfire of them. They were meaningless.

Then he discovered the real meaning of a life lived for Jesus Christ and decided to devote his full time and attention to the ministry of prayer fellowships. Accomplishment is not worldly recognition. The greatest rewards come from life lived for eternity.

What will a man give in exchange for his soul?

Mark 8:37 (NKJV)

Albert Einstein said, "Try not to become a man of success but rather try to become a man of value." The only way to become a person of value is to become a child of the King.

Abel, one of earth's earliest inhabitants, did not perform great achievements. But he was pleasing to God and his name is still remembered for that. "He being dead yet speaketh" (Heb. 11:4 KJV).

LIFE RESPONSE:
What will I be remembered for?

MEANS TO THE RIGHT END!

O ver a hundred years ago, Henry David Thoreau sat in his haven at Walden Pond watching linemen put up wires along the railway track. Inquiring, he learned that this new thing was called a telegraph and that it would link states from Maine to Texas. It would now be possible for people to talk to each other across the continent.

Thoreau was unimpressed and asked, "But what if the people of Maine have nothing to say to the people of Texas, and what if the people of Texas have nothing to answer the people of Maine?" He concluded, "We are improving the means for reaching unimproved ends."

We have become good at that in our technological age. In almost every area, our means are improved. Transportation is faster and more efficient. Communication improves almost by the minute — satellite transmission, high definition television, fiber optics, etc. And yet, what goals are we reaching?

The way of the righteous is made plain.
Proverbs 15:19 (KJV)

How foolish to keep improving the means when the end is all wrong! Jesus is not only the *Means*, He is also the *End*. He is the *Way* and He is the *Goal*.

LIFE RESPONSE:
I am determined to point others to the real way by my deeds and my conversation.

A
Transformation

One of the nice things about being a grandparent is having a good reason to play with toys. I grew up in the good 'ol days of Lionel trains, Erector sets, wind-up cars and homemade rubber-band guns. It is almost overwhelming to see the toys children have today — battery-powered, remote controlled objects, as complicated as the computer technology that devised them.

. . . be transformed by the renewing of your mind . . .

Romans 12:2 (NIV)

While visiting a home, I was being entertained by a young boy with an intriguing toy. I believe he called it a 'transformer." It looked like some sort of futuristic all-terrain vehicle for use by the military. But then the boy began to twist and turn some of its parts. Suddenly the vehicle was gone and a mechanical robot had taken its place. I had to study the robot carefully to find even a resemblance to the vehicle I had seen earlier. It had literally been transformed before my eyes.

When God transforms people, He does more than shift parts and pieces around to make a different looking creature. He begins with our minds and hearts, renewing us from the inside out. Then He can use us as He sees best — sometimes in surprising ways!

LIFE RESPONSE:
Has the mind of Christ replaced the "mind" of the world in my life?

THROUGH THE BIBLE
Esther 1-4

THE INVISIBLE WORLD

I saw a fascinating program on TV some years ago. First, the camera focused on a man lying on a blanket in a Chicago park. Then, the camera moved away from him, seemingly traveling at phenomenal speed. It moved vertically into the heavens. Through the complexity of special effects, the man was very quickly lost as he merged into the park, then the park was lost in the city, the city soon lost in the globe. The "camera" then passed beyond the moon and stars, until our universe converged into one tiny light, millions of light years away.

Then the process was reversed as the camera sped rapidly toward earth. Our world was distinguishable again, then the western hemisphere, the city of Chicago, the park and the man on the blanket. The figurative camera did not stop, however, but zoomed in on the man's arm, into his flesh, into a cell, through the molecules, the genes and the smallest particles known to man.

> *Elisha prayed, and said, 'Lord, I pray thee, open his eyes, that he may see.'*
>
> 2 Kings 6:17 (KJV)

A scientist on the broadcast said, "We have just explored all of man's knowledge about his world. And at both ends we reach unexplainable mystery." What the scientist should have admitted was they had explored the present limits of our *visible* world. The Christian knows something about the *invisible* world. This world, too, was made by Him. We need to have our spiritual eyes open to see it!

LIFE RESPONSE:
Are my eyes open to God's world?

THROUGH THE BIBLE
Esther 5–10

CALLED
TO BE SAINTS

To the question — "What is a saint?" — a little boy in Sunday school replied, "A saint is a dead Christian."

Many people believe that saints are only those who have been canonized. Long after they are dead, their piety and holiness are rewarded by the church when it declares them to be saints.

Some think of saints as older members of the congregation, the white-haired men and kindly grandmothers.

To all in Rome who are loved by God and called to be saints.

Romans 1:7 (NIV)

Your idea of a saint may be someone who displays an air of superior piety, someone with a holier-than-thou attitude — a person so heavenly-minded he or she is of no earthly good.

It's amazing how few people want to be saints. Some say, "I don't mind having some religion, but I don't want to go too far with it. I'm no saint."

But the Apostle Paul addressed the Christians of Rome as saints. They lived in a sinful city, but they were called to be saints — just as Christians today, surrounded by evil on every side, are called to faithfully walk the way of holiness.

We do not need to wait until we are called to heaven in order to be saints. God calls His people now to be His holy people, faithful saints.

LIFE RESPONSE:
Do I live like a "saint" in my "Rome?"

HEARTS THAT SING

A man was riding in an airplane next to a machinery manufacturer. "How do you know," the man asked, "when you have produced a perfect machine?"

"Oh, that's easy," the manufacturer said. "When a machine is perfect, when it is running just the way it should, it sings. Listen to the great engines on this plane. Can't you hear them singing?"

The next time you hear a piece of machinery running, listen carefully and see if you can hear its melody!

I don't know much about machinery, but I do know something about people. And I know that when a person is running right — in tune with God, with neighbors, and with self — that person will sing.

Many people don't find much in life to sing about. If you are one of those who looks for reasons to be unhappy, you will find them easily enough. Abraham Lincoln said most people were about as happy as they made up their minds to be. And I believe some are as unhappy as they make up their minds to be.

When our hearts are in tune, they will sing!

> *Speak to one another with psalms, hymns and spiritual songs. Sing and make music in your heart to the Lord . . .*
>
> *Ephesians 5:19 (NIV)*

LIFE RESPONSE:

Is there heavenly music in my heart?

FAULTY AND BLAMELESS?

How can we faulty people ever be blameless before God? Consider a hypothetical situation. Suppose your young children are fussing with each other at the table. You would reprimand them, warning them to be careful not to spill their milk or break something. In their disobedience, one of them knocks over a glass, breaking it and spilling the milk. You would have quite a mess on your hands.

Then suppose that at another time, they were behaving very well. Desiring to help, they offer to set the table. But in their eagerness one knocks over a glass of milk, breaking it and spilling the milk. The same mess would result.

In both cases, whoever knocked over the glass was at fault. In the first instance, however, there is not only fault, there is blame. The deliberate, disruptive, disobedient action of the children caused the mess. And with the blame comes punishment. In the second instance, the child cannot be blamed because the motivation of his heart was right.

May he strengthen your hearts so that you will be blameless and holy in the presence of our God . . .

1 Thessalonians 3:13 (NIV)

Many times we "spill the milk." We have missed the mark and made a mess. But in God's sight, we are blameless.

LIFE RESPONSE:

I will praise the Lord for His acceptance and understanding.

IN GOD'S TIME

They needed wine, and wine takes time. Grapes must be grown, harvested and pressed. The juice must be carefully processed and stored. But they didn't have time. So Jesus compacted time and completed in a matter of seconds what otherwise might have taken years.

The Bible says a thousand years in God's sight are but as yesterday when it is past (Ps. 90:4 KJV). God can use time or He can ignore time, for He is eternal. When I was conducting meetings in the state of Wyoming, I was awed by the vast stretches of prairie that seemed so dry and desolate. Geologists, I was told, claim that the entire area was once the bottom of a great salt sea. Beneath the barren surface lie vast resources of minerals. For example, there is a vein of coal in that area that is seventy-five feet thick and stretches for miles.

How did that thick vein of coal get there? Scientists tell us it takes millions of years for the earth's pressure to compact decaying materials into coal. But God, who created this world in six days, could easily have compacted those millions of years into a single day. God's workings may seem slow to us, but remember: He transcends time. Someone once said "God is never in a hurry, but He is always on time."

When the wine was gone, Jesus' mother said to him, 'They have no more wine.'

John 2:3 (NIV)

LIFE RESPONSE:
I will learn to live by God's clock.

How Can I Be Happy?

W hat would it take to make you happy (blessed)? Many say it would take enough money to live comfortably, or perhaps the right marriage partner, or a lovely new house, or a car. Does happiness come from an external source? Or does it rise from within us?

Jesus began His great Sermon On The Mount with a lesson about happiness (the Beatitudes). He mentions none of the external, temporal things that many people equate with happiness. We are often like the child on Christmas morning who rushes to open his presents with glee. But in a matter of minutes he sits sadly amid the discarded wrappings and cries, "Is that all there is?"

Blessed are the poor in spirit . . . blessed are they that mourn . . . blessed are the meek.

Matthew 5:3-5 *(KJV)*

Like the prodigal son, many people think money, friends and excitement will make them happy. Perhaps temporary happiness does come as the result of having these things. But lasting, meaningful happiness is not dependent upon outward circumstances nor should it be sought as an end in itself.

Jesus said happy people have right relationships — with God and with other people. Happy people have a wholesome attitude about themselves and they desire to do right things. Happy people find forgiveness for their sins.

Is your happiness external or internal?

LIFE RESPONSE:

What kind of happiness am I seeking?

AMAZING SACRIFICE

On a cold winter day a few years ago, my wife and I flew into Washington, D.C. As we came in low over the Potomac, I remembered the jet that had crashed into the bridge on take-off and landed in the icy waters of that very river below me. News cameras captured dramatic pictures of the rescue attempts, and of the brave man who had passed a life preserver to one person after another. But when the rescuers finally went back for him, it was too late. He had succumbed to the cold, slipping under the water to his death.

I looked down at the Potomac and asked myself, "Could I have done that?" Frankly, I don't know. None of us can know until we are actually faced with the situation.

But God gave His only begotten Son. To risk your own life for that of another is one thing, but to sacrifice the life of your only son is quite another. Let's take this to another level: To offer your son's life to save someone dear and precious to you would be difficult enough, but to sacrifice him for sinful, unlovable people would be nearly unthinkable!

He was delivered over to death for our sins . . .

Romans 4:25 (NIV)

Yet, God's love did just that, for while we were yet sinners Jesus died for us. God sacrificed the very Prince of Peace in order to save the rebels of earth. An amazing sacrifice!

Let it not be a sacrifice made in vain.

LIFE RESPONSE:
"Lord, I praise You for the Greatest Sacrifice.'"

THE TWO-MINUTE OFFENSE

In professional football, every team has what is called a two-minute offense. When there are just two minutes left to play, the clock is stopped and the referee informs each coach how much time remains. From that moment on the strategy of the game changes. Certain plays have been prearranged so that no time is wasted in the huddle. Each team member knows exactly what is expected of him.

> *Therefore keep watch, because you do not know on what day your Lord will come.*
>
> Matthew 24:42 (NIV)

Some have called this the "hurry-up offense." But a well-coached and carefully prepared team doesn't seem to be hurrying. They are simply making every movement count, doing only those things that are absolutely essential to the success of their team.

It occurs to me that with time running out for our world, we as Christians need to have a two-minute drill, a hurry-up offense. We ought to have a strategy for the most efficient use of whatever time we have left. The Apostle Paul called it "redeeming the time" (Col. 4:5 KJV). J.B. Phillips translates it, "Make the best possible use of your time."

Jesus warned His disciples to take heed lest "that day come upon you unawares," the day of His second coming (Luke 21:34b). Will you be ready?

LIFE RESPONSE:

I will make every moment count for Christ, especially as His return nears.

THROUGH THE BIBLE

Job 27-30

FREE FROM SIN

I once heard someone say, "The difference between being a Christian and a non-Christian is now that I'm a Christian, I still sin but I no longer enjoy it."

But God's Word says you not only no longer enjoy it, you no longer do it. Jesus did not say to the woman taken in adultery, "Go on sinning, but don't enjoy it." He said, "Go and sin no more."

To fallen men, sin is almost a trifling matter. We often hear people joke about sinful things. We watch television programs that make light of sin. But sin is no laughing matter. It was sin that sent Jesus to the cross. It is sin that dooms people to hell.

Sin is a merciless taskmaster. A person who continues to sin is a slave to sin. But when Jesus rules in our hearts, sin is no longer our master. Jesus came to destroy the works of the devil (1 John 3:8). The New Testament refers often to the experience of being set free from sin. "How shall we who died to sin live any longer in it?" (Rom. 6:2 NKJV).

> *No one who is born of God will continue to sin . . .*
>
> *1 John 3:9 (NIV)*

The good news of the gospel is that we do not have to be slaves of sin and unrighteousness. "If the Son makes you free, you shall be free indeed" (John 8:36 NKJV).

LIFE RESPONSE:
Am I enjoying the freedom of God's forgiveness?

GOD KEEPS HIS PROMISES

Dinny Malone was an old, retired sea captain with a reputation for integrity. He told his minister that he had been trying for six years to get God to forgive him and He wouldn't.

"Have you repented and trusted God?" the minister asked.

"Yes," replied Dinny. "But I never feel in my heart that He has forgiven me."

The minister read 1 John 1:9 to the old man and then asked, "Dinny, when you give your word, don't you keep it?"

If we confess our sins, he is faithful and just to forgive us our sins . . .

1 John 1:9 (KJV)

"I sure do!" he thundered. "I'm a gentleman, and I have never gone back on my word."

The minister looked straight at Dinny. "Don't you consider God to be as trustworthy as you? Don't you think He will keep *His* word?"

Suddenly the light broke through. "Why, of course!" Dinny shouted. "God would not lie. He has said He would forgive me, so He must forgive me. Now I know I'm forgiven!"

Many people struggle to know they are saved. To question that God has saved you after you have met His conditions and done what the Word tells you to do, is to deny that God is eternal truth and cannot lie. "In hope of eternal life, which God, who cannot lie, promised before time began" (Titus 1:2 NKJV).

LIFE RESPONSE:

I will trust God for a glorious future because He always keeps His word.

PEOPLE ARE LOST!

It is a frightening thing to be lost. I was hunting with a friend in the mountains of north central Pennsylvania. He had been born and raised in those mountains. I was new to the area, so I followed him closely. We walked for miles, crossing streams, up one slope and down another. Chilled to the bone, I finally asked, "Where are we?"

"I don't know," he said. "I've been lost for about an hour or two and I'm trying to find a way out of here."

My heart sank and fear began to grip me. I had been all right as long as I thought he knew where we were going.

Perhaps there is no better way to describe man's condition than the word LOST. Politically, the world is lost in confusion. Morally, we have lost our bearings. Socially, we are in a wilderness. And worst of all, spiritually, most of the billions of people in this world are lost in sin.

What is most frightening, though, is that few seem concerned about our lost condition. We have learned to trust the government, the United Nations, the preachers, the church, anyone we think *should* know. But we are learning that no one has the answers. Thank God for a Savior who came to seek the lost! He is the Way!

For the Son of Man came to seek and to save what was lost.

Luke 19:10 (NIV)

LIFE RESPONSE:
I pledge myself to help lost people find Christ.

AFTER YOUR DREAM DIES

Who else but Moses could lead the Israelites into the Promised Land? Was this the end of their dream? Not as far as God was concerned. The death of a dream does not have to mean the end.

You may be like the young man who loved to climb the rugged cliffs of the Colorado Rockies. Every summer he hiked the trails and scaled the peaks. The mountains seemed almost like an extension of himself. His dream all year long was of summer in the mountains.

Moses my servant is dead . . . get ready to cross the Jordan River into the land I am about to give to them.

Joshua 1:2 (NIV)

But in the summer of his eighteenth birthday, something went wrong. A rope broke and he fell to the rocks below. Flown to a hospital, he was told he would never walk again. It was devastating news and he became angry and bitter, turning against God.

Then one day, the bitterness subsided and he decided he would make something of his life. God was telling him to go on, to move ahead. He began working at moving his toes and then his feet, persisting until he graduated to braces and crutches. Today he is able to get around on his own. He finished college and found employment. His dream may have died but he found he could still go forward.

God challenges each of us to do the same.

LIFE RESPONSE:

I will move ahead in spite of adversity.

THROUGH THE BIBLE

1 Timothy 1-6

YOU CAN'T IGNORE GOD'S LAWS

A man went deep-sea fishing with his employer. As they were making their way back toward shore late that night, the employer grew weary and decided to get some sleep. He turned the helm of the boat over to the employee, pointed out the North Star and said, "Keep your eye on that star and steer a straight course by it."

No sooner had the ship's owner fallen asleep, than the employee did, too. In a little while he woke up, looked for the bright star but couldn't find it. Trying to steer the boat, he was totally confused. Finally he shook his boss awake.

"You'll have to show me another star," he said. "We've already sailed clear past that one."

Many people in our sophisticated, educated, advanced society feel that they have run past the law of God. The result is confusion, discouragement and despair. Searching desperately for life, they have ignored the law of life.

> *You have laid down precepts that are to be fully obeyed.*
>
> Psalms 119:4 (NIV)

But you can no more bypass the law of God and find life, than you can get beyond the North Star. Albert Einstein didn't need to recite the multiplication tables every morning in order to check out his formulas, but neither could he ignore the fact that two times two equals four.

LIFE RESPONSE:

I will praise the Lord for the safety of His boundaries.

THROUGH THE BIBLE

2 Timothy 1-4

A MARKED PERSON

I read about a man who claimed he could listen to the speech of any person living in America, and tell within a one-hundred-mile radius the place he came from. People are marked by their speech.

Some people and things are marked in more obvious ways. A policeman is identified by his uniform and badge. In the West, cattle are marked with a brand of ownership, an identifying mark burned into the hide of the animal.

Christians are also marked. They can be recognized as God's children. Even without uniforms, badges, or crosses on their lapels, God's children should *still* be identifiable. Paul said, "If anyone does not have the Spirit of Christ, he does not belong to Christ" (Rom. 8:9).

Having believed, you were marked in him with a seal, the promised Holy Spirit . . .

Ephesians 1:13b (NIV)

In the New Testament, the word for "church" means "the called out ones." Christians should stand out from the crowd. They have been redeemed from sin, and that sets them apart from the pollution around them.

Are you a marked person? Do those around you know you as a separated one, someone who is different? Do you have a different attitude and spirit from the unsaved?

When you wear the mark of the Holy Spirit, you will be recognized as His possession.

LIFE RESPONSE:

Do others recognize that I am a follower of the Lord Jesus Christ?

THROUGH THE BIBLE

Psalm 1-7

OUR CREATOR KNOWS OUR NEED

God pronounced His creation "good" — complete. But when sin entered the world, man lost something and became incomplete. It took God's redemptive work to make it possible for us to be complete again. It makes sense that the One who created us in the first place can recreate us and complete His work.

If your watch stopped working, you wouldn't take it to the blacksmith for repair. If your car needed an overhaul, you wouldn't go to a jewelry store.

Many years ago, a man was driving along in his Ford when suddenly the car stopped. He couldn't get it to start again. He got out and looked at the engine but he didn't know what was wrong.

A man driving a brand-new Lincoln stopped to help. The tall, friendly stranger looked under the hood and did something to the engine. "Now start it," he said. When the engine started, the grateful owner introduced himself and asked the man his name. "My name is Henry Ford," replied the helpful stranger.

Know that the Lord is God. It is he who made us, and we are his.

Psalms 100:3 (NIV)

The one who made the Ford in the first place, knew how to make it run again. God made you and He knows what is lacking in your life.

LIFE RESPONSE:

I will praise the Lord for His constant consideration of me.

THROUGH THE BIBLE

Psalm 8-14

KEEP YOUR EYES ON THE GOAL

Three boys were playing in the snow. A neighbor happened by and said, "How would you boys like to have a race? I'll give a surprise to the winner." The boys agreed, and the man explained, "The winner will not be the one who runs fastest, but the one who runs the straightest line. I'll go to the other side of the field. When I give the signal, you race toward me."

. . . I press on toward the goal . . .

Philippians 3:13-14 (NIV)

When the signal was given, the boys began to run. The first boy kept looking down at his feet to be sure they were pointing straight ahead. The second boy kept looking to either side to line himself up with the other boys. But the third boy looked straight at the man on the other side of the field, keeping his eyes on the goal. Of course he won.

The other two boys were victims of the problems common to most losers. There are those self-conscious individuals who constantly worry about themselves: their weaknesses, mistakes and difficulties. The second group worries too much about other people: What will they think? How do I measure up? Is someone getting ahead of me?

The winners are those who have a goal and never lose sight of it.

LIFE RESPONSE:
I will set some spiritual goals and keep my eyes on them, no matter what happens around me.

WHICH WAY?

There is an interesting incident in the story *Alice in Wonderland*. Alice comes to the cat and asks, "Can you tell me which way I should go?" The cat says, "That depends on where you wish to go."

"Oh," Alice comments. "It doesn't matter where I go."

"Well then, neither does it matter which way you take," replies the cat.

Alice then says, "Oh, but I do want to get somewhere."

"Well, you are sure to do that," the cat answers.

We are all sure to arrive somewhere. That destination is determined the moment we choose the path. Many people seem to believe that you can follow one road all of your life and then arrive at a different destination. That is impossible. We cannot travel the broad road and reach the destination of life, any more than we can travel the narrow road and reach the destination of death.

> *. . . broad is the road that leads to destruction . . . narrow the road that leads to life . . .*
>
> Matthew 7:13-14 (NIV)

You may have chosen your destination and decided you want to go to heaven someday. But have you chosen to walk the road that leads to heaven?

LIFE RESPONSE:

I will set the course of my life toward Heaven.

A NEW START

O ne of the major events that takes place in our city every May is the Indianapolis 500. For weeks, the city is buzzing with the activities that surround this race. Several years ago, just after the start of the race, a terrible accident occurred. Several cars collided, smashing some of them against the wall. Pieces of race cars were strewn all over the track. The race had to be stopped and the track cleared of debris. Those cars still able to run were then lined up for a new start.

Have you ever felt your life was something like that? You made a wreck of things almost before you got started. You wish you could call a halt, clean up the mess of your past failures and start all over again.

The vessel . . . was marred in the hand of the potter: so he made it again.

Jeremiah 18:4 (NKJV)

When our children were small, it was a joy to teach them to walk. My wife and I would get just a few feet apart and hold the little toddlers by the fingertips to get them started. Then, gently, we removed our hold until they were taking steps on their own. Each one took many falls. But they were not failures. We would pick them up, comfort them and start them all over again.

The idea of a new start has a divine origin. We can't go back and live our lives over again. But we can go forward, accepting God's forgiveness and abounding grace.

LIFE RESPONSE:
I will praise the Lord for the opportunity to "start over."

GOD'S KIND OF SUCCESS

Nothing succeeds like success." That appears to be true. Human beings are fascinated by success. We are interested in winners, not losers.

A man ordered lobster in a restaurant but was disappointed when the lobster presented to him on a platter didn't have claws. He asked the waiter, "What happened to those claws he was supposed to have?"

The waiter said, "I don't know, maybe he lost them in a fight with another lobster."

The man pushed his plate away and said, "In that case, take this one back and bring me the one that won."

Whosoever will be chief among you, let him be your servant.

Matthew 20:27 (KJV)

Success is the name of the game today — not only in the world, but in the church. Humility is out. Self-depreciation is out. Servants' robes are for the timid souls who haven't learned the techniques of management by intimidation. All that matters now is that you succeed and feel good about yourself.

But success in God's eyes is very different. Setting the example, Jesus humbled himself to be a servant, ministering to others and giving His life as a ransom for many. God's rewards will not go to those who shine the brightest and make it big by this world's standards, but to those who faithfully serve, walking with Jesus in obedience and trust.

LIFE RESPONSE:
By whose standard of success am I living?

HOPE AND HEALTH

I read of a man who had suffered many illnesses and endured many troubles, but lived to be eighty-nine. Even then, he didn't die of old age, but was killed in an automobile accident. After performing an autopsy, the doctor said to the man's wife, "Your husband must have been an amazing man. I found enough evidence in his body to indicate that he should have died twenty years ago from one illness or another. How did he live so long against the odds?"

"My husband had great faith in God," the wife replied. "And every morning I remember him saying to me, no matter what difficulty lay before us, no matter how hard the times were, 'Honey, don't let anything worry you. I have hope. I have hope.'"

O my soul . . . hope in God . . . the health of my countenance . . .

Psalms 42:11 (KJV)

Here was a man who lived possibly twenty years longer than he should have because he had faith in God — and he had hope. When people lose the ability to hope, they lose their desire for living. Despair and despondency overwhelm many people, who then try to drown their hopelessness in drink or drugs. Some even take their own lives.

Cling to hope in the midst of trouble and you will yet praise Him who is the health of your countenance.

LIFE RESPONSE:

"Lord, help me to hope in You and not be consumed by earthly concerns."

SECONDHAND RELIGION

M any times when my family and my brother's family got together over the years, the children would play church. One would be the organist, one the soloist, and one the preacher.

Too many people in churches today are playing church. Their faith is not real, personal or meaningful. Their religion is secondhand, something they've heard about or had passed on by their parents.

Walt Whitman once attended a lecture about astronomy. The hall was stuffy, the air stale, the lecture dull and the charts were even more so. He later wrote, "I could bear it no longer. I rose and wandered out into the night and looked up at the stars themselves."

Many people are reciting songs and creeds and prayers about Christ, but they have never come to see Him and know Him for themselves. "Are you speaking for yourself about this, or did others tell you this concerning Me?" Jesus asked Pilate.

Are you speaking for yourself about this, or did others tell you this concerning Me?

John 18:34 (NKJV)

Are you taking someone else's word about Jesus or have you experienced Him yourself? "Oh, taste and see that the Lord is good" (Ps. 34:8 KJV).

Secondhand religion is not only tasteless, it is useless.

LIFE RESPONSE:
I will experience Christ and His Word firsthand.

WHAT DO YOU SEE?

While I was in college, our choir toured throughout Virginia. We stopped to sightsee at some caverns in the Blue Ridge Mountains. In one large room called The Cathedral, we viewed indescribably beautiful formations and sang "How Great Thou Art." Then the guide turned off the lights. We stood in total darkness, unable to see our hands before our faces. Although we stood in the midst of some of the most unusual beauty in the world, we were totally blind to it all.

If you were blind, you would have no sin; but now you say, 'We see.' Therefore your sin remains.

John 9:41 (NKJV)

The person who has not been born again is in darkness. All around him are beauty and splendor. But he cannot see the reality of the kingdom of God and may even deny that it exists. A buzzard flying over fields of flowers sees only the dead animal he wants for food. What we are determines what we see.

We also see what we are interested in. The Pharisees were blind to Jesus and His wonderful teachings and miraculous works. They were interested only in themselves.

When the blind man was healed by Jesus, he saw much better than the blind Pharisees who criticized the miracle. Spiritual blindness is a lot more serious than physical blindness.

LIFE RESPONSE:

I will allow the Holy Spirit to open my "spiritual eyes" to the things that have eternal beauty.

THROUGH THE BIBLE

Psalm 43-48

A CHILD OF THE KING

My dad was an identical twin. He and my uncle had the kind of fun that identical twins have in bewildering people who meet one or the other for the first time. Even I was once fooled by their similarity to one another. We were at a camp, and I thought I saw my dad standing by a store where candy was sold. Excited about an opportunity to get a treat, I didn't look carefully enough to see that it was not my dad but my uncle standing there. I pulled at his trouser leg and said, "Dad, can I have a nickel?" In a mocking kind of sternness my uncle said, "Why should I give you a nickel? Go ask your own father." Of course he was just teasing. But my father would not have answered me that way. I knew that because I had absolute confidence in my father.

You received the Spirit of sonship. And by him we cry, 'Abba, Father.'

Romans 8:15 (NIV)

We have been adopted into God's family and He knows our needs. We are invited to come boldly to the throne of grace and receive grace to help in time of need. Some people would have great difficulty getting into the White House or into Buckingham Palace. But a child of the President or the Queen could walk through those doors without any difficulty. Likewise, a child of God has courage to come before His presence with great boldness.

LIFE RESPONSE:
"Thank you, Lord, for the courage that comes from my relationship with You."

❈

HELP
LIFT BURDENS

E very day brings opportunities to lift and encourage someone else. Too many of us are busy feeding our own egos and do not notice the needs of others. A sure way to make our own load lighter, however, is to help someone else with his.

A depressed, unhappy and unhealthy man came to his pastor. The man had been passed over by his company for promotion to the position of president. He had become so jealous and angry that he was miserable. The pastor asked him if he had gone to the new president and congratulated him. The man yelled, "Congratulate him! I won't even speak to him."

Bear one another's burdens . . .

Galatians 6:2 (NKJV)

The wise pastor suggested, "Go to the new president, congratulate him, tell him you will work with him and do anything he needs done to make him the most successful president ever."

After prayer, the man agreed. He followed the pastor's advice and became a valuable source of advice and help to the president. When his superior was promoted to chairman of the board, the previously overlooked man became the natural successor and was chosen as president.

We can make lives better by helping people get rid of burdens that make them miserable.

LIFE RESPONSE:

I will look for someone who seems to need help bearing their burden and I will help them bear it.

It Can Happen Fast!

One New Year's Day, I was on a flight home. For part of the trip I was seated next to a tall, young black woman who was a model and an aspiring actress. We talked about her life, her plans and ambitions. She brought up the subject of the brevity of life. I asked her, "If you were to die, what would happen to you?"

She confessed she didn't know. Then I shared with her from God's Word that we could know that we have eternal life. She indicated a genuine desire to know Jesus Christ, to know what it is to be born again, to have a meaningful life here and the satisfaction of knowing she had eternal life.

I talked with her about the need and possibility of being born again. "You can pray right now and ask Christ to come into your heart, and you can be born again before this plane ever touches the ground."

Already you have become rich!

1 Corinthians 4:8 (NIV)

In surprise, she asked, "Can it happen that fast? Can God do that for me right now?"

"He certainly can," I told her. The young woman prayed a simple prayer, confessed her sins and received Christ into her heart. As we deplaned, she said, "I can't wait to call my mom and tell her: 'It's New Year's Day and I have become a new person!'"

That's what Christ's promise means today. All who will, may take of the water of life freely.

LIFE RESPONSE:
"Thank you, Lord, for the eternal life you have given me."

THROUGH THE BIBLE
Psalm 61-67

DO YOU PRAY FOR PATIENCE?

I got up one Saturday at 4:30 a.m. to catch a plane. Long lines were already waiting at the airport. One line was marked for passengers needing to purchase tickets. The other was the express baggage check-in for those who already had their ticket. I got in the express line but it didn't seem to move. Our flight was announced. People were getting nervous.

Behind me was a young woman burdened down with a baby, a diaper bag, a stroller, her luggage and other items. When she heard the flight announcement, she headed for the front of the line and almost shouted at the clerk, "That's my flight!" He calmly assured her that it was the flight of everyone in the line and it wouldn't go without us. But for the next fifteen minutes, she fussed and fumed and added to the ulcers that, I'm sure, were already beginning to develop.

> *The fruit of the Spirit is love . . . patience . . .*
>
> Galatians 5:22-23 (NIV)

Another time, my wife and I almost missed a flight on an international trip. The relaxed clerk told me there was another flight the next day and that it would be good enough.

Life continually offers opportunities for us to develop the fruit of the Spirit called patience. No doubt we would prefer to have a package of it delivered to us, but the reality is that it comes bit by bit, as our "tribulation worketh patience" (Rom. 5:3 KJV).

LIFE RESPONSE:
"Lord, help me to be patient when things don't go 'as scheduled.'"

THROUGH THE BIBLE
Psalm 68-71

GUILTY CONSCIENCE?

The United States Government receives thousands of dollars every year — unsolicited. That seems strange, given the hostile attitude of many citizens toward taxes and excessive government spending. But this money comes from people who have a guilty conscience. Some is from those who have cheated on their income tax returns. Some comes from government employees who have stolen from the government. Some is from those who have stolen from other people and don't know how to repay them.

Much of the money comes in anonymously. Occasionally, the money is accompanied by a letter of explanation. One man makes regular contributions to this fund. Is it because he is a habitual thief? Or does making restitution make him feel so good he wants to repeat the experience? The government doesn't know. Maybe he experienced what Benjamin Franklin meant when he said, "A good conscience is a continual Christmas."

. . . the work of the law written in their hearts, their conscience also bearing witness . . .

Romans 2:15 (KJV)

The Bible teaches that Jesus Christ can cleanse the conscience and deliver us from the nagging dread of guilt. Restitution is the logical action to *make right* the *wrongs* that we have done.

LIFE RESPONSE:
If I "owe an apology" to someone, I will "pay my debts."

THROUGH THE BIBLE
Psalm 72-75

GET RID OF YOUR BURDENS

At the close of my message one Saturday evening, a young man came and knelt at the altar. He was only nineteen years old. Just that week he had been released from prison, after serving two years. On Wednesday night, he had been walking past the church when he saw the lights on, went in and was invited to the youth meeting.

The following Saturday night, he again saw the lighted church and came to our revival service. That night at the altar, he found what he had been searching for. Drugs, alcohol, crime — all that his life had been to that point — were only indications of the emptiness, the longing and the guilt that plagued his soul.

. . . casting all your care upon Him . . .

1 Peter 5:7 (KJV)

That young man came to church on Sunday morning with a different look. He was clearly a new creature!

Many troubled, sin-burdened hearts are longing for freedom from guilt and condemnation. Many children of God carry burdens of worry and care as well.

Jesus invites all burden-bearers to come to Him and find rest for their souls.

Leave your heavy burden at the cross!

LIFE RESPONSE:
What am I carrying today that I could lay at the cross?

IS HELL NECESSARY?

One winter day, I was attempting to get home from a preaching engagement and was caught in a snowstorm. For sixteen hours I drove through wind and blinding snow. I had a citizens' band radio in my car for just such emergencies. Each time the road was blocked, I was forewarned by the radio.

But I also heard foul language and filth over that radio. When I got home, I told my wife that I felt like I'd been in a tavern all day. Many of us are subjected to the same kind of barrage — whether on the job, in school or in a public place. Sin, it seems, is present everywhere.

But a day of final separation is coming. Righteousness will be forever in heaven, and sin and wickedness will be forever in hell. God is a just God. He will balance the books and punish sin some day. Without a hell for the punishment of sin, God could not be just.

Jesus himself warned of the danger of hell. He came to earth for the specific purpose of offering a way of escape. God is merciful as well as just, and His mercy is extended today. Have you accepted that mercy?

All sinners will be destroyed; the future of the wicked will be cut off.

Psalms 37:38 (NIV)

LIFE RESPONSE:
I will "rest my case" in the One who has the final word.

CITIZENS OF THE HEAVENLY CANAAN

In *Pilgrim's Progress*, Christian arrives at Vanity Fair and finds he doesn't fit in. His clothes, his conversation and his conduct are out of place there. Today, unfortunately, many church members *would* fit in.

J. B. Phillips wrote of the early Christians that they trained themselves "not to be taken in by this world nor to give their hearts to it, nor to conform to its values." They reminded themselves that they were citizens of another world. "We may find ourselves saying a little wistfully, perhaps these men were right."

Their mind is on earthly things. But our citizenship is in heaven.

Philippians 3:19b-20 (NIV)

I'm not sure the average Christian today would agree that the early Christians were right. Vance Havner said, "We have feathered our nest so well that we have no desire to fly." Congregations seldom sing of the "Sweet By and By" because they are too contented with the saccharin *sweet here and now*. They have listened to those who ridicule our "pie-in-the-sky" and have decided they would rather have an earthly reward. Who needs eternal security when social security is right at hand?

Matthew Henry said, "This world is our passage and not our portion."

LIFE RESPONSE:

Am I willing to settle for my portion here, or am I anticipating the portion I will have in the heavenly Canaan?

THROUGH THE BIBLE

Psalm 85-89

MURDER IN THE HEART

The photograph was of a basketball coach courtside during a championship game. Glaring at the referee, he was obviously unhappy with the decision of an official and was protesting the call. Anger, bitterness and frustration were written all over his face. The caption under the photo read: "If looks could kill!"

Many people would say the worst crime is murder. But where does murder begin? Not with the hand that takes up the knife or gun. It begins with hatred or anger in the heart.

Henry Ward Beecher had a clock in his church that did not keep correct time. One day Beecher put a sign over the clock, "Don't blame my hands. The problem lies deeper." The sinful actions of our hands come from a deeper source, our hearts.

People talk about stopping crime. But it will never be done through laws, courts or punishments. These have their place, of course. To stop crime, we must get at the

> *Anyone who is angry with his brother will be subject to judgment.*
>
> Matthew 5:22 (NIV)

source. Murder in the heart makes us unfit to enter the kingdom of heaven.

Do you have something against someone? Are you harboring bitterness, resentment and anger? Your life can only be as clean as your heart is pure.

And only God can deal with the murder within our hearts.

LIFE RESPONSE:
"Lord, please rid my heart of any bitterness or anger."

THROUGH THE BIBLE

Psalm 90-95

STILL ONLY ONE WAY

Have you been in a secular bookstore recently? Visit one and ask to see the section on New Age literature. Well-known authors have popularized some ancient beliefs, and now many people in America believe in such things as reincarnation and channeling. New Age concepts are accepted in many businesses as necessary for success.

To make matters worse, various aspects of New Age thought are infiltrating a shallow and biblically illiterate church under the guise of psychology, the science of the mind and inner healing.

There is no other name under heaven given among men by which we must be saved.

Acts 4:12 (NKJV)

Radical and liberal theologians argue that all religions, including Christianity, are basically human in origin. They believe that each religion has some valid insights into the meaning of life, but that each, including Christianity, is encrusted with superstition and error. One team of authors has written a book promoting the "plurality" of religion. When asked if a person can be saved by some other name than Jesus, they reply, "Yes, there are other ways . . . you can still be a Christian and believe that."

But God's Word has not changed, and we must understand that Jesus *alone* can bring salvation.

LIFE RESPONSE:

I will preach and practice the truth of "one way."

THROUGH THE BIBLE

Psalm 96-102

LOST?
DON'T RUN FASTER!

T homas Huxley, famous disciple of Darwin, was in a hurry to catch the train to his next speaking engagement. He took a horse-drawn taxi and told the driver, "Hurry, I'm almost late! Drive as fast as you can!" He assumed the hotel doorman had told the driver the destination.

The horses lurched forward and galloped at breakneck speed. After a time, Huxley realized they were going in the wrong direction. Leaning forward, he shouted to the driver, "Do you know where you're going?" Without looking back or slacking the pace, the driver answered, "No, Your Honor, but I'm going as fast as I can."

. . . for this thy brother was dead, and is alive again; and was lost, and is found.

Luke 15:32 (KJV)

Sadly, that story is not only an illustration of Huxley and his misguided followers, it portrays the predicament of many today. Great speed toward an unknown destination!

I can recall two times when I was lost — once in a mountain wilderness and once in a large city. Both times, I experienced a sensation of panic and a desire to run. I had no idea of where I was or which way to go, but I wanted to go as fast as I could.

In the hurry of modern living, do you know where you are and where you are going? Or are you running fast toward an unknown destination?

LIFE RESPONSE:

I will be sure that my destination is Heaven.

THE TIME OF PRAYER

When the disciples asked Jesus to teach them to pray, He underscored the importance of prayer by answering, "When you pray." By putting it this way, Jesus is telling us the time to pray is anytime. In fact, He used a parable to teach that men ought always to pray and not faint (Luke 18).

But prayer time should be prearranged. Make an appointment with God and keep that appointment.

> *Lord, teach us to pray . . . He said to them, 'When you pray . . .'*
> Luke 11:1-2 (NIV)

When I was a teenager, my sister and I were invited to go ice skating. A friend arranged to pick us up at seven o'clock. The appointed hour came, but our friend did not. Finally, around nine o'clock we decided he was not coming. He did, however, arrive the *next* evening at seven o'clock. He was there at the appointed hour, but he was a day late!

Do we ever treat God like that? The time for prayer comes and passes. God waits to hear from us, but we miss the appointment. It may be the next day, or several days later before we get around to prayer. Pressures and distractions of business and pleasure sidetrack our minds — and God gets pushed aside.

We cannot afford to miss the appointed time of prayer. God is waiting to meet us.

LIFE RESPONSE:

I will set a daily appointment with God...and keep it.

THROUGH THE BIBLE

Psalm 106-108

YOU CAN RELY ON GOD'S LAW

W hen the 55-mile-an-hour speed limit became law, a slogan appeared on bumper stickers and billboards which said, "55, it's a law we can live with."

While driving on a superhighway one day at the legal speed, I was passed by a car going much faster. Ironically, it was a government vehicle with the same bumper sticker: "55, it's a law we can live with."

I was reminded of the inequity of human law. It was as if the government said to me, "Fifty-five is a law you can live with, but a law I can ignore." We know that the laws of our land or any land — whether traffic laws or criminal codes — are not applied with universal equality. There are favored classes, privileged rich, powerful ruling parties, superior majorities and downtrodden minorities. Inequity, injustice and inhumanity are quite evident.

Some organizations claim as their goal equal treatment under the law for everyone. Although that is a noble goal, men are fallible, courts are imperfect, and judges have human weaknesses and prejudices. Only God's law is perfect, God's judgments infallible and God's justice universal. Whoever you are, wherever you are, you can rely on God's law.

> *The judgments of the Lord are true and righteous altogether.*
>
> *Psalms 19:9 (KJV)*

LIFE RESPONSE:

I will RESPECT the laws of the land but I will LOVE the laws of God.

❊

FOR WHOM ARE YOU WORKING?

With the exception of sleeping, you will probably spend more of your life at work than at any other activity. Is there a connection between your work and your Christian witness? Too many Christians leave their witness in the sanctuary, instead of taking it with them to the shop.

Every legitimate, honorable means of earning a living should be approached as a calling from God. When you think of it as a divine calling, your entire attitude toward your job will change

Whatever you do, work at it with all your heart, as working for the Lord, not for men . . .

Colossians 3:23 (NIV)

I heard of a man who felt God had called him to the assembly line of a particular factory. When he took the job, he quickly realized that his was the only Christian witness in that section of the plant. He accepted the challenge as from the Lord. In time, he was offered advancement, a better position, a higher salary — many of the things men work for. But he refused them all.

"God called me to this position," he said, "and I'll stay here and do my best until God calls me to something else." He was working for the Lord and not for men.

For whom are you working? "Live a life worthy of the calling you have received" (Eph. 4:1)

LIFE RESPONSE:

"Lord, help me to serve You with my work."

THROUGH THE BIBLE

Psalm 116-119:64

MANY WAYS OR ONE WAY?

When I was a young ministerial student, I worked my way through college by serving as a night attendant at the state mental hospital. It was there I met Jack. I attempted several times to witness to him about the Lord Jesus Christ. On one occasion, we had a lengthy conversation about heaven, hell, and where we would spend eternity.

Jack was waiting for me the next day with a sheet of paper. In the center he had colored a bright red circle. A number of lines, drawn at different angles, were sketched from the edge of the paper to the red circle. Jack explained that the red circle represented heaven and the lines were what he believed to be the different ways to get to heaven.

"This line may be your way," he said, "through faith in Jesus Christ. But this may be my way, and this other line the Jewish way or the Muslim way. I really don't think it matters which way you take if you are sincere."

There is a way that seems right to a man. But it's end is the way of death.
Proverbs 14:12 (NKJV)

A short time later, Jack was transferred to a state prison. I never saw him again, but heard that one day he hanged himself in his cell. I wondered if he had found his way to heaven adequate.

Don't make that mistake! Jesus is the only way. It is a good way, a sure way.

LIFE RESPONSE:

I will praise the Lord for providing a true way to Himself.

THROUGH THE BIBLE

Psalm 119:65-119

SOW THE RIGHT SEED!

While still in junior high school, another trumpet player and I were good enough to play in the high school band. I felt at the time that I was the better player of the two. But when we entered high school the following year, the other boy was moved to a higher chair. Disappointed, I began to feel sorry for myself. I thought surely the band director liked him better than he liked me. But then I heard the other boy play, and had to admit that he was now the better player. During the summer months he had practiced trumpet while I played baseball. His promotion was not because the director liked him better, but because he had worked hard and was now reaping the benefits.

Do not be deceived: God cannot be mocked. A man reaps what he sows.

Galatians 6:7 (NIV)

Seed determines the harvest. You can't change the harvest after the seed is in the ground. Vice and virtue are their own paymasters.

"For the wages of sin is death, but the gift of God is eternal life" (Rom. 6:23). Too many people live as servants of sin and then expect to collect a saint's reward.

If you want to reap the benefits of righteousness and holiness, you must sow seeds of righteousness and holiness in your life. That is a simple but profound law of God.

LIFE RESPONSE:
I will consider the harvest as I sow the seeds of this life.

THROUGH THE BIBLE
Psalm 120-131

PEACE IN THE STORMS

Far out in the Pacific, a young sailor sat in the radio shack of a ship during World War II. On that particular night, the sailor was feeling the loneliness, tension and fear of the long and terrible war. Suddenly it occurred to him that other wireless operators on other ships might be just as lonely as he.

He had just read Psalm 23 and felt peace in his heart. He decided to send the psalm out over the ocean by means of the wireless. When he finished tapping out the last word, sixteen operators answered him with a wireless "Amen."

A man in South Africa wrote to me telling how rioters had burned his home while he and his family were out. He lost all he owned and felt like Job on the ash heap. But he thanked God his family had been spared. Christian friends soon provided the family with clothing and basic needs, while God provided another place to live. He wrote, "Thank God, I could look to the cross of Calvary where all my problems were solved."

> *I will fear no evil: for Thou art with me . . .*
>
> Psalms 23:4 (KJV)

Jesus gives peace in the midst of storms. Countless numbers of Christians have testified that He gives songs through nights of sorrow and suffering. His presence is with us and He gives us rest.

LIFE RESPONSE:

Do I have my eyes on my *Captain* or on my *calamity*?

YOU ARE CHOSEN

D r. Norman Vincent Peale told of meeting a young lady who considered herself a nobody.

"Who made you?" he asked her.

"You mean, do I realize that God made me?" she asked.

"Yes," said Dr. Peale. "Are you a Christian, a child of God?" When she said she was, he continued, "Did God ever do a bad job? When He made you He didn't make a nobody. You don't believe in yourself as much as God believes in you."

. . . chosen by God and precious to Him . . .

1 Peter 2:4 (NIV)

Then he asked her to stand up and say out loud, "I am a child of God. I have talents and abilities that God has given me, and I can do all things through Christ who strengthens me."

That young lady became a different person.

The only nobodies in this world are the followers of Satan. Every child of God is precious and important in His sight. He has chosen each of us for a purpose. No matter what your age, God still has something for you to do in His kingdom. He ordains that you live a fruitful life.

We can't go back and change what life has been, but we can begin now to change what life will be.

LIFE RESPONSE:

I will not just live, I will live to make a difference.

THROUGH THE BIBLE

Psalm 139-144

A BIG MISTAKE

Have you ever made a mistake?

Someone said, "The man who makes no mistakes does not usually make anything." You probably know someone who feels his calling in life is to uncover the mistakes in everything. One editor explained away the mistakes that crept into his publication with this notice: "If you find any mistakes, please consider that they appear for the benefit of those readers who always look for them. We try to print something for everyone."

Most of our mistakes are unimportant and easily corrected. Some of our mistakes, however, have long-lasting and tragic results.

The worst mistake anyone can make is to neglect the salvation of his or her soul. People first make the mistake of disregarding their conscience. Then they make the mistake of discounting the consequences of sin. Then they find it easy to discard their salvation.

How shall we escape if we ignore such a great salvation?

Hebrews 2:3 (NIV)

This salvation is a great salvation because it is the *only* salvation. It is also great because of its tremendous price — it took the life of God's only Son. This salvation is great because it reaches to the lowest, is open to the least, and leaves no one out. It is great because it saves us from sin and prepares us for heaven.

Don't make the mistake of neglecting it!

LIFE RESPONSE:

I will pay careful attention to the way of salvation.

THROUGH THE BIBLE

Psalm 145-150

CHILDREN OF GOD

I have one daughter and two sons. I fully believe the three of them are glad to have me as their father. And I am pleased to call them my children. They have not always pleased me with their actions. In fact, there have been times when they have disobeyed me. But they didn't become my children through a merit system. They became my children by birth. I expect now that, as the children of Norman and Nancy Wilson, they will live exemplary lives in keeping with our love for and relationship with them.

As many as received Him, to them he gave the right to become children of God . . .

John 1:12 (NKJV)

You do not become a child of God because you are worthy. But when you have become a child of God, He has high expectations of you. We should strive to live a life worthy of a child of the Most High God.

Absolute dependency and absolute submission are the conditions of becoming God's child. We must admit we are poor before we can be made rich. We must admit we are destitute before we can be adopted. We must recognize that we are lost before we can find the way. When we realize that all of our own goodness is as filthy rags in God's sight; when we become aware of the destructive power of our stubborn will; when we realize our absolute dependence upon the grace of God through faith and nothing more — then we begin to understand what it means to become a child of God.

LIFE RESPONSE:

I will live my life as a witness of my relationship with my Heavenly Father.

ALIVE OR HALF DEAD?

M y uncle preached the gospel for more than forty years and enjoyed his work as an evangelist. Even when age, infirmity and a lifetime of rigorous travel had taken their toll, Uncle Dave still loved to preach, and would take any preaching opportunity offered.

One day my brother was driving him to a preaching assignment. After a while, Uncle Dave grew quiet. My brother saw him holding his wrist, taking his pulse. When my brother asked him what he was doing, he replied with a mixture of humor and sadness, "Oh, I'm just checking to see if I'm still alive."

People exhibit life in varying degrees. When you see a child scampering around, climbing, jumping and laughing, no one checks his pulse to see if he is alive. But as a pastor, I have entered a hospital room and not been sure, at first glance, if the patient was alive or dead.

He who has the Son has life . . .

1 John 5:12 (NIV)

No doubt you have times when you feel very much alive. At other times, you may feel like the old man who said, "My get-up-and-go got up and went!"

The one who has Jesus, the Son of God, living within has a continuous source of life. Even when our bodies feel worn out, the life of Jesus can still be springing up within us!

LIFE RESPONSE:
Have I checked my spiritual "vital signs" lately?

THE PROBLEM OF RICHES

I didn't know we were poor when I was a child. I thought all little boys wore clothing handed down from their older brothers. It never occurred to me that parents could actually go to a store and buy shirts and trousers in sizes small enough to fit younger children. We were poor, but only in financial terms. We were rich in other ways.

Prosperity has its peculiar difficulties. I visited a very wealthy lady in the hospital. At one time, she and her family had been poor, but circumstances had changed. Money didn't appear to be one of her problems, but in a sense it was. With tears on her cheeks she said to me, "Pastor, it's so hard to be rich."

How hard it is for the rich to enter the kingdom of God!

Luke 18:24 (NIV)

Money tends to distort people's vision, corrupt their judgments, color their relationships and destroy their peace. Of course, the real problem is not money — the lack of it or the abundance of it. The real problem is our attitude toward money. Money seems to take people's minds off God. They begin to rely upon their own resources and ingenuity instead of on Him.

It is important to remember that we are but stewards of all we possess, whether we have much or little.

LIFE RESPONSE:

I will live so that I can give a good account of my stewardship when I stand before Christ.

THROUGH THE BIBLE

Proverbs 8-10

RECOGNIZE THE ENEMY

One of warfare's key problems is how to recognize the enemy. During the Vietnam war, American soldiers sometimes came upon villagers working in rice paddies and going about their daily business. Mingling with them, however, were enemy soldiers dressed like civilians.

Christians sometimes do not recognize their spiritual enemy. If the devil came as he is often pictured, with horns and a tail, we wouldn't be deceived. Although he does sometimes come as a roaring lion, he also frequently comes disguised as an angel of light. His suggestions meet with the approval of our inner nature, and may be offered by people who are our friends. He tries to catch us off guard. He appeals to reason, to common sense.

James gives a plan for victory. "Submit yourselves, then, to God. Resist the devil, and he will flee from you. Come near to God and He will come near to you" (4:7-8). Submit to God in obedience, giving Him first place. Offering Him only leftovers makes victory impossible.

> *Satan himself masquerades as an angel of light.*
> 2 Corinthians 11:14 (NIV)

Remember that the outcome of this war is never in doubt. Satan is already defeated. The victory is ultimately God's, and because God's power is in us, victory is also ours!

LIFE RESPONSE:
"Lord, help me to be sensitive to the clever devices of the Enemy."

THROUGH THE BIBLE
Proverbs 11-13

A WORLDLY CHRISTIAN?

Duuring World War I, Teddy Roosevelt spoke critically of "hyphenated Americans." He referred to German-Americans who maintained a divided loyalty. He said, "If you are an American and something else, you are not an American."

The fiery old evangelist Billy Sunday said, "There is no such thing as a worldly Christian. You may as well try to talk about a heavenly hell."

> *Come out from them and be separate, says the Lord.*
>
> *2 Corinthians 6:17 (NIV)*

Perhaps never before in history has the church made so many attempts to yoke itself to this world's affairs. Some people try to work both sides of the street at the same time. They want to run with the foxes and still hunt with the hounds. "No one can serve two masters," Jesus said (Matt. 6:24). The Bible says whoever is the friend of the world is the enemy of God (James 4:4).

I met a peddler of a false religion who tried to sell me some literature in an airport. I refused, but gave her some of my Wesleyan Hour sermons. When she saw my material she responded, "Oh, we love Jesus, too." In other words, she thought she could have a false god and Jesus, too. But according to God's Word, she cannot. You can't love this world and still love Christ. Our God demands absolute allegiance. It's for our own protection and good!

LIFE RESPONSE:
I will not be a "hyphenated Christian."

THROUGH THE BIBLE
Proverbs 14-16

Grow Through Your Temptations

I overheard two Christian women talking in the restaurant booth next to mine. Referring to a third party, one said, "Do you know what her biggest battle was? She couldn't give up . . ." I could not hear the sin she mentioned.

"Isn't that silly?" the woman continued. "To think someone would struggle over such a little thing!" Then she said, "My hardest battle was to give up going out on weekends for dancing and a few drinks."

Now that would seem silly to me! But whatever the sin that may tempt us, God provides strength and power to live victoriously. Temptation is universal. All Christians are tempted, but no Christian has to yield to the temptation. Temptation is an opportunity to grow stronger and to be more like Jesus.

Too many Christians begin each day with the predisposition that they cannot resist temptation and are, thus, bound to fail. But if you approach each temptation as a new challenge, an opportunity for growth, a development of your character, an expression of your faith, you can be more than conquerors through Christ! You are able . . . you can bear it. There is always a way of escape. Look for it! God is faithful.

> *God is faithful; he will not let you be tempted beyond what you can bear.*
>
> *1 Corinthians 10:13 (NIV)*

LIFE RESPONSE:

"Thank you, Lord, for your faithfulness in the face of my temptations."

WE NEED REGULAR REST

Jesus said the Sabbath was made for man, not man for the Sabbath (Mark 2:27). God did not hallow and sanctify a day just to force us into submission and obedience. Rather, He set one day apart from the rest for our benefit because He knows how much we need it. We have been created in such a way that we need periods of rest between our activities.

The human heart is an example. It beats regularly at about 72 beats a minute all of our lives. That is more than 4000 beats every hour, more than 100,000 a day and nearly 38 million beats per year — close to 3 billion beats in the average life span. How can it continue to work like that? Because it is the most efficient and long-lasting pump ever devised. Between each of those beats, the heart rests.

Six days you shall labor . . . but the seventh day is a Sabbath to the Lord. . . .

Exodus 20:9-10 (NIV)

Out of every seven days, God's plan is six days of labor and one day of rest. You can ignore that pattern, but you will do it to your own hurt and detriment.

A cartoon portrays a disheveled, pajama-clad man getting up and mumbling, "On Monday mornings I don't know if I'm live or on tape." People often forget that weekends are a time for rest and worship.

LIFE RESPONSE:

I will replenish my soul and my body by observing a day of rest.

THROUGH THE BIBLE

Proverbs 20-22

TRADING PRAYERS

I've never visited Wall Street or observed the New York Stock Exchange firsthand. I have seen glimpses of it on television. To anyone as uninitiated as I, it appears to be total chaos. Thousands of issues of stock are traded daily and millions of dollars change hands. Fortunes are made and lost in the bidding and buying. The workers seem almost frenzied, with no appearance of concern for others or even common courtesy. Their only concern seems to be the investor's gain. But that is the nature of the stock exchange.

I would like to suggest a different kind of exchange — a prayer exchange. One day as a friend and I were saying good-bye, he said, "Let's agree to trade prayers." The more I thought about it, the better I liked the idea. He was saying what the Apostle Paul said to the Colossians, "I pray for you, you pray for me." Paul began his letter by emphasizing his prayers on their behalf; he ended it by requesting their prayers for him.

. . . we pray for you . . . pray for us, too.

Colossians 1:3; 4:3 (NIV)

One of the reasons I like his suggestion is that in trading prayers, we avoid one of the greatest hindrances to our prayers, selfishness.

Is there someone you can trade prayers with this week? If you do not have a prayer partner, do your best to find one.

LIFE RESPONSE:

I will ask the Lord to give me a prayer partner this week.

A TIME
TO LAUGH

I believe God created us to have a sense of humor. The great preacher Charles Spurgeon loved to laugh. Late one afternoon, he and a friend went out to the country. They had spent a hard day in serious discussions and now walked the fields in high spirits — like schoolboys freed from school. The friend told a funny story and Dr. Spurgeon laughed heartily. Then suddenly he turned to his friend and said, "Let's kneel down and thank God for laughter."

> *A time to weep, and a time to laugh . . .*
>
> Ecclesiastes 3:4 (KJV)

There is a time to laugh. In fact, laughter is a gift from God. It is good for our emotional health and our physical health. I read of one man who, with laughter, literally cured himself of a dreaded disease. After the doctors had told him his chances of recovery were slim, he decided he would not allow this thing to defeat him. He checked into a hotel, ordered some funny films and kept himself amused for weeks. He walked out of the hotel cured, saying he had laughed his way back to health.

Not every disease can be cured by laughter, but certainly the opposite effect is true. Hospitals are full of people whose despondent spirits and dreary outlooks destroy their health.

Granted, some things are no laughing matter. But it is also true that laughter makes burdens grow lighter and makes many troubles melt away.

LIFE RESPONSE:
I will take time to laugh . . . to enjoy God's gift of joy.

THROUGH THE BIBLE
Proverbs 26-28

BEYOND THE SORROW

I n order to learn the secret of coping with life, we must recognize the inevitability of death. "It is appointed unto men once to die," the Bible says (Heb. 9:27 KJV). And the universal testimony of all men confirms that as unalterable fact.

One man said, "Sorrows are visitors that come without invitation." Sometimes, when we seem least prepared to handle them, sorrows come. Longfellow put it poetically, "Into each life some rain must fall . . ." We all must face the sorrow, trouble and heartache that are common to the human family.

But there must be a reality, an assurance, a hope which can see *beyond* the sorrow.

We fix our eyes not on what is seen, but on what is unseen.

2 Corinthians 4:18 (NIV)

Some years ago I met Virgil Brock, known for composing the touching song, "Beyond the Sunset." He explained how he came to write that song. He was attempting to describe a spectacular sunset over Winona Lake, Indiana, to his blind wife.

"Oh, I just wish you could see this beautiful sunset," he said. And she responded, "My dear, I can see beyond the sunset."

We can all do that. With eyes more sensitive than human vision we can, by faith, see beyond the sunset of the present moment and learn to cope with sorrow.

LIFE RESPONSE:

"Lord, help me to fix my 'spiritual eyes' on the hope that lies beyond these times."

THROUGH THE BIBLE

Proverbs 29-31

IS YOUR SOUL WELL?

S atan almost spoke the truth, for people generally go to great lengths to preserve life and health. The health and physical fitness "craze" of recent years almost borders on a new religion. Many of us are more conscious than ever about cholesterol, salt, caffeine, additives, preservatives, refined sugar, whole grains, fruits and vegetables. Jogging and other forms of exercise have become common. Millions of dollars are spent yearly on health supplements, exercise equipment, personal trainers, therapists and other health professionals.

> *Satan . . . said . . . all that a man hath will he give for his life.*
>
> Job 2:4 (KJV)

When Job became physically afflicted, he naturally became quite upset — even to the point of cursing the day of his birth. He had already lost all his possessions and all ten of his children. Depression must have been his constant companion. All he had left was his faith in God, and that was being sorely tested.

Some years ago a television commercial said, "If you have your health, you have just about everything." Yet, death is the worst that can happen *physically*. The health of our souls should be of much greater concern than bodily health.

How healthy would you be if you spent as much time and thought on your spiritual health as you do on your physical well-being?

LIFE RESPONSE:

I will give attention to my spiritual diet and my spiritual exercise.

THROUGH THE BIBLE
Titus & Philemon

LOVE IS STRONGER THAN HATE

J esus showed this greater love when He laid down His life for His enemies. He proved that love is stronger than hate.

Many are struggling with ill will, hard feelings — even hatred. Much of it occurs within families. Maybe you have been wronged; you're hurt. Love seems to have died.

During a weekend revival at a church, we met a young couple with a small child. They seemed so happy together. But they told us they had been separated and had only recently reunited. Their love had turned to bitterness and hatred. She had filed for divorce. Then they met Jesus Christ. They told us, "We have just renewed our marriage vows. We are so much in love." Love had triumphed over the tragedy of hatred.

Out of the ugliness and cruelty and hatred of this world, Jesus Christ is the demonstration of the triumph of love. No matter what your life has been, no matter how deep the scars of sin or how ugly the results of your life, no matter how much you have felt alone and unloved — Jesus Christ laid down His life for you because He loved you. Love triumphs where the tragedy of hatred and sin have failed.

Have you discovered the triumph of life, the way of victory, the way of love?

Greater love has no one than this, that one lay down his life for his friends.

John 15:13 (NIV)

LIFE RESPONSE:

I will let love triumph over my anger at the actions of others.

THROUGH THE BIBLE

Ecclesiastes 1-4

DO I REALLY BELIEVE?

The story is told of an acrobat who rolled a wheelbarrow across the Niagara River on a tightrope. Thousands shouted encouragement and urged him on. He put a two-hundred-pound sack of dirt in the wheelbarrow and rolled it over and back again.

"How many of you believe I can roll a man across in the wheelbarrow?" he asked. The crowd shouted its approval, its belief in the acrobat's ability. One man in the front row seemed especially supportive. The acrobat pointed to this excited spectator and said, "All right, sir, you be first." According to the report, you couldn't see the man for his dust as he ran away from there.

. . . he was afraid and, beginning to sink, cried out, 'Lord, save me!' . . . Why do you doubt?

Matthew 14:30-31 (NIV)

Why? He just *thought* he believed it. But he was not willing to trust himself to his belief.

The Apostle Peter, like the excited spectator, had faith in Christ and believed He could keep him from drowning. He even got out of the boat and started to walk on the water toward Jesus. But his faith failed when he saw the stormy sea. "You of little faith, why did you doubt?" Jesus asked. If Peter had only continued to trust as he did when he stepped out of the boat, he would not have gone under.

Many people profess to have faith in Jesus Christ, but do not demonstrate their faith in obedient trust.

LIFE RESPONSE:
Do I trust the Lord with my actions, as well as my attitude?

THROUGH THE BIBLE
Ecclesiastes 5-8

GOOD OUT OF BAD?

Chocolate cake is one of my favorite desserts. Suppose my wife said to me, "Honey, I want to give you a special treat. I've brought you the ingredients of a chocolate cake: flour, baking powder, raw eggs, bitter chocolate, vanilla and all the rest."

How much of a treat would it be if I tried to eat those ingredients? I would probably say, "Why don't you take all of those things, mix them together, put them in the oven and when it is done, give me the finished product."

Any one ingredient in life, taken alone, may be bitter, painful — even unbearable. But God says He can make them work together. Dave Dravecky, the major league pitcher who lost his pitching arm to cancer, says, "Everybody is going to have adversity. The only way to handle it is to take our eyes off our own circumstances and put them on the Lord."

And we know that in all things God works for the good of those who love him . . .

Romans 8:28 (NIV)

A cathedral in Milan, Italy, has inscribed around its entrance these words: "All that pleases us is only for a moment. All that troubles us is only for a moment. Nothing is important but that which is eternal."

In His great love, God takes the bad and the good of our lives and creates something beneficial for each of His children.

LIFE RESPONSE:

I will trust the Lord to make something "tasty" out of my trials.

CHOOSE YOUR THOUGHTS

Someone has said, "You are not always what you think you are, but always, what you THINK, you are." Jesus said, "Out of the overflow of the heart the mouth speaks. The good man brings good things out of the good stored up in him, and the evil man brings evil things out of the evil stored up in him" (Matt. 12:34-35 NIV).

In Noah's day, God saw into man's heart and "every inclination of the thoughts of his heart was only evil all the time" (Gen. 6:5 NIV).

As he thinketh in his heart, so is he.

Proverbs 23:7 (KJV)

We can choose what we put into our minds. The television programs we watch, the music we hear, the books and magazines we read — all these feed our thought life. And our thoughts prompt our actions.

We are responsible for our thoughts. "Take captive every thought to make it obedient to Christ," the Apostle Paul said (2 Cor. 10:5 NIV). Take charge of your mind. Direct your thoughts toward those things that are good, noble and pure. You will become what you think about. "Be transformed by the renewing of your mind" (Rom. 12:2 NIV).

Someone has said, "As you think, you travel." Today you are where your thoughts have brought you. Tomorrow you will be where your thoughts take you.

LIFE RESPONSE:
I choose to travel with godly thoughts.

THROUGH THE BIBLE
Song of Solomon 1-4

THE ORIGINAL PURPOSE

While driving through a small town on my way to a meeting, I noticed a building that had originally been constructed as a church. It had high arched windows and door casings, and a bell tower on top. But it was no longer a church. The stained glass windows had been replaced with ordinary glass, the bell was missing from the tower and the cross had been removed from the roof. A sign in front advertised antiques.

I was saddened at the sight of that old church. I wondered if the congregation had simply outgrown the building and relocated. Maybe there were no longer enough people to keep the church going. Were there sharp disagreements that divided and destroyed the congregation? That stately old building, built for worship, was now just a warehouse for relics of the past.

Sadly, many people are like that old church. Although they may keep up appearances, they have lost their original purpose, lost what they once had in their lives as Christians.

Guard your heart! Don't let your salvation fade away!

> *I am astonished that you are so quickly deserting the one who called you . . .*
>
> Galatians 1:6 (NIV)

LIFE RESPONSE:
"Lord, help me to concentrate on my 'original purpose.'"

THE TRAP OF SIN

I have had people challenge me about my Christian lifestyle saying, "Oh, you are a Christian, so you can't do this or that." I usually respond, "Oh, but you are wrong. Christians are the only ones who are free to choose. I can do the things you name. I have the same ability and the same opportunity as you have to do those things. The difference is, I can choose not to, but you have no choice. You are bound by the power of sin."

The evil I do not want to do — this I keep on doing.

Romans 7:19 (NIV)

The alcoholic, the drug addict, the liar, and other sinners may wish to stop their evil deeds, but they are slaves to sin. Only Christians are free. We could do sinful things, but choose not to.

Many people fail to reckon with the dominating power of sin. It begins as an exciting adventure, but soon sucks the person in. The camouflaged trap gradually closes on the unsuspecting victim. Satan is a master of deceit, luring people with glitter and excitement. What he conceals, however, is that the end is death.

The way to avoid the trap of addiction is to never take the first drink or drug. But what about sins like lying or pride? These are more subtle, yet just as entrapping. The only way out is God's way of deliverance. He can set the captive free.

LIFE RESPONSE:
I will praise God for the freedom NOT to sin.

HARVEST TIME IS COMING

My wife and I enjoy having a small garden in our yard. One year, however, we got ambitious and planted a large garden in a friend's field. At first, I tended the garden faithfully, pulling weeds and hoeing the corn and beans.

But my summer was busy and travel schedules kept me away much of the time. When I got back to the garden, the weeds had gotten out of control. Although I tried, I finally got discouraged and stopped working at it. The garden was too big, the weeds too far ahead of me, my time and energy too short, and I just gave up.

Although I had planted much good seed, I harvested very little from that garden. I abandoned it and the harvest failed.

I've seen some Christians like that. They start out well, but there are so many temptations, so many difficulties, they get discouraged and faint by the wayside. Don't get discouraged doing good. There is a harvest coming. You can count on it. "He that soweth to the Spirit shall of the Spirit reap life everlasting" (Gal. 6:8 KJV).

Let us not become weary in doing good, for at the proper time we will reap a harvest if we do not give up.

Galatians 6:9 (NIV)

What will the harvest of your life be? You are responsible for your harvest — just as I am responsible for mine.

LIFE RESPONSE:

I will reject thoughts of "giving up." I will concentrate on the harvest.

THROUGH THE BIBLE

Hebrews 5-7

EARN . . . SAVE . . . GIVE

John Wesley had a threefold bit of financial advice for his followers: "Earn all you can. Save all you can. Give all you can."

His advice is scriptural and practical. Christian workers should be the best workers on any job. They should be industrious, punctual, diligent and honest. *Earn all you can.*

Save all you can. Wesley was not advocating miserliness but frugality. Even Jesus encouraged frugality, telling the disciples to gather up the fragments when the multitude was fed. The world may be impressed with extravagance. But it is neither wise nor scriptural to waste the blessings God has given.

. . . work . . . that he may have something to share with those in need.

Ephesians 4:28 (NIV)

Give all you can. One reason some people have so little to give is because they do not save. And one reason some people cannot save is because they do not give. Self-preservation may be the first principle of nature, but it contradicts the first law of Christ. The first law of Christ's kingdom is self-giving.

John Wesley's advice may seem incongruous at first. But if you put it into practice, it will work and God will bless you.

LIFE RESPONSE:

I will strive for financial balance . . . earning, saving, and giving.

DO WE HATE SIN?

Turn-of-the-century evangelist Billy Sunday was known for his colorful illustrations. He said, "The reason sin flourishes is because we have treated it like a cream puff instead of treating it like a deadly rattlesnake."

I think he's right. Sin is taken too lightly. We have analyzed it, defined it and redefined it. We have called it sickness or maladjustment or predisposition. We have made excuses for it, rather than recognize and admit that it is a deadly evil.

A dying man was asked if he had made his peace with God. He said, "I never knew I was at war with Him." But the natural man is always at war with God. The carnal, sinful mind is contrary to the spiritual life. Anyone who has tried to live for God has found himself in the midst of a battle.

The mind of sinful man is death . . . hostile to God.

Romans 8:6-7 (NIV)

No compromise with sin is possible. Jesus made it clear that there are only two alternatives. "He who is not with me is against me," He said (Luke 11:23). We are either on the narrow way or the broad way; we cannot walk with one foot on each path.

Neither can we afford to give the devil any place in our lives. "Do not give the devil a foothold," Paul advises (Eph. 4:27).

Do we hate sin like God hates it?

LIFE RESPONSE:

I will seek "peace with God" by agreeing with Him about the seriousness of sin.

Why Do The Righteous Suffer?

G od's economy seems to be all mixed up. If I were in charge, good
people would always be healthy, wealthy and happy. Prizes would
be passed out every Sunday morning in church to those who had lived
right all week. Every kind word, good deed and thoughtful act would be
properly recognized and rewarded. And every evil deed would be
properly punished! Sinfulness and wicked living would feel the
immediate sting of judgment! Bad things would happen only to bad
people. Everyone would recognize that God is in His heaven and that all
is right with the world.

Shall we accept good from God, and not trouble?

Job 2:10b (NIV)

But God just doesn't run His world the
way we think He should. And in our
misunderstanding and confusion, we are
always asking Him why.

Suffering came to a righteous man
named Job, who was pleasing to God. Job
did not suffer because he had sinned or
because he needed to be disciplined. He
suffered because God permitted Satan to test
him. Job has become the example of patience and faith in a time of severe
suffering. God knew He could trust Job and gave him an opportunity to
prove it.

LIFE RESPONSE:
"Lord, I trust You to balance the books of judgment or reward."

SPIRITUAL HOUSECLEANING

I read of a man who was so filled with life and joy that he infected everyone around him with his enthusiasm. Someone asked him how he came to be such a happy person. He said, "I wasn't always this way. I was a sick man, tired and gloomy. My doctor sent me to a specialist who said nothing was wrong with me except I was low and listless in my thoughts and mental attitudes. 'You need to get in touch with creative power, in other words, with God,' the specialist said. So I sought the Lord and life took on new meaning. I began to really live. I have new energy and new spiritual power. I have a happy life."

Maybe you need to take a look at your life and attitudes. Some people are so negative in their thinking they have negated every positive good in their lives.

Rejoice in the Lord always.

Philippians 4:4 (NIV)

What about old resentments you have been harboring? What about those petty jealousies, the small injuries you have kept alive in your mind? What about your attitude toward those you refuse to forgive? Are you ready for a positive and dramatic change?

Do some spiritual housecleaning. Dig into the closets of your mind and heart and, with the help of God's Spirit, throw out the old negative attitudes. Forgive and forget. Rejoice and be at peace.

LIFE RESPONSE:

I will "take out the trash" and allow the Holy Spirit to fill the empty spaces with His joy and peace.

THROUGH THE BIBLE

Isaiah 4-6

THE WAY TO HEAVEN

The old spiritual says, "Everybody talkin' 'bout heav'n ain't goin' there." It may be that deep in every man's heart is the desire to go to heaven. But not everyone is going to get there.

Dr. D. James Kennedy, pastor of the Coral Ridge Presbyterian Church in Fort Lauderdale, Florida, is a former classmate of mine. I have often heard him tell of his conversion. He was awakened one Sunday morning by his clock radio, which was broadcasting a man preaching the gospel.

> *Not every one that saith unto me, Lord, Lord, shall enter into the kingdom of heaven . . .*
>
> *Matthew 7:21 (KJV)*

Dr. Kennedy was about to reach over and turn off the radio when the preacher asked a question that gripped his heart and mind and changed his life. "If you were to die today and stand before God, and God were to ask you, 'Why should I let you into my heaven?' what would you say?"

That's a good question, isn't it? Would you answer that you belonged to the church, had been baptized, had tried to be good, had done your best? All those things are commendable and good as far as they go. They just don't go far enough. The only sure way into heaven is through repentance and faith in Christ.

LIFE RESPONSE:
"Lord, I have no hope for eternal life but You."

THROUGH THE BIBLE

Isaiah 7-9

A CLEAR CONSCIENCE

Some people think they can make up for wronging someone by being especially nice to the one they have wronged. Years ago in one of our pastorates, someone did something that was not only unpleasant, but wrong and injurious. Surmising that it was done by a certain woman, I said to my wife, "If it was that lady, we'll have a loaf of bread by Thursday."

Sure enough, on Thursday she came to the parsonage with two loaves of freshly baked bread. Now, I enjoyed that bread. But if she had done wrong, confession and repentance would have accomplished more than bread to make things right.

Wrong and guilt are not wiped out by good works. A clear conscience can be gained only by dealing with sin according to God's instructions.

Are there people and places you avoid because of past sins that have not been made right? Have you rationalized and tried to lessen

. . . first be reconciled to thy brother.

Matthew 5:24 (KJV)

the guilt by giving more money to the church or by doing good deeds? If you want a clear conscience and a clean slate before God, confess your sins and make the needed restitution.

"He that covereth his sin shall not prosper: but whoso confesseth and forsaketh them shall have mercy" (Prov. 28:13 KJV).

LIFE RESPONSE:
Are there any barriers between "my brother" and me?

THROUGH THE BIBLE
Isaiah 10-13

UNSELFISH SERVICE

O n my desk I have a set of brass bookends made from a model of the painting by Albrecht Dürer, "The Praying Hands." As a young man, Durer was trying to earn a living and study art at the same time. He lived with a friend, an older man, who was trying to do the same. He told Durer, "If one of us worked to support both, the other could study and paint." Durer agreed and offered to work while the older man studied; then he could work while Durer studied.

The older man persuaded Durer to let him work first. Day after day he worked hard in a restaurant, doing anything and everything to earn enough money for the two of them to live. Finally the day came when Durer sold a wood carving and brought home plenty of money. It was now his friend's turn to study.

> *He had . . .
> nothing in his
> appearance that
> we should
> desire him.*
>
> Isaiah 53:2b (NIV)

But when the friend took up his art, he discovered his hands had been ruined by the hard labor and he could no longer use them for painting and carving. Durer was so sorry it had happened, he knew he would always provide for his friend. When he saw his friend praying with hands folded one day, he painted the workworn hands as a memorial of unselfish service.

Jesus, too, was marred and broken in service and sacrifice for others.

LIFE RESPONSE:

I will praise the Lord Jesus Christ for the ugly scars that evidence His unselfish and saving sacrifice.

THROUGH THE BIBLE

Isaiah 14-16

PLAYING CHURCH?

I drove past an old church one night and noticed the parking lot was full of cars. But the people were not there for a religious service. The old building was no longer a church. It had been converted into a community theater.

What happens there now is all pretend, make-believe, a place for the fantasy world of acting. The church sign, which once announced the titles of pastors' sermons, now serves as the theater marquee, advertising the latest play.

When I saw that church-turned-theater I thought about some other churches I've known. Services are conducted there every Sunday. The choir sings, the pastor goes through his assigned duties. But the reality is gone. It's as if they are only pretending — just playing church.

The worshipers are like actors, going through the motions. Sin is no longer confronted and rebuked. Darkness is not dispelled by the light of the Word. Lives are not challenged and changed. The services have become an empty ritual, a dull routine, the fulfillment of some kind of religious duty.

Keep watch over yourselves and all the flock of which the Holy Spirit has made you overseers.

Acts 20:28 (NIV)

Why does a church die? It may be because it loses its love or because it loses its purpose. But a church only reflects the spirituality of its members.

LIFE RESPONSE:
Is my life helping or hindering my church?

A CRUMBLING BODY — OUR SOUL'S HOUSE

When Oliver Wendell Holmes was eighty, he was greeted one day by a friend with the usual inquiry, "How are you?"

"I'm fine," Holmes said. "The house I live in is tottering and crumbling, but Oliver Wendell Holmes is fine, thank you."

We all need to be reminded that there is a vast difference between the house of clay, which is our body, and the soul which lives forever. The real, lasting part of us — that which is eternal — is not the visible, but the invisible.

Dust thou art.

Genesis 3:19

Thou hast made him a little lower than the angels . . .

Psalms 8:5 (KJV)

Yes, we are fearfully and wonderfully made. True men of science admit that they have not even begun to probe the depths of the mysteries of the human body. Yet when God breathed into man the breath of life, man became a living soul, clothed with intelligence, a conscience and a free will. He was made for the lofty purpose of fellowship with the Almighty.

Much of modern society's time, money and energy is expended in an attempt to perpetuate the physical part of us. We spend billions of dollars on medicine, doctors, beauty, diet and cosmetics. What kind of people would we be if we were equally concerned about spiritual health?

LIFE RESPONSE:

"Lord, help me to give earnest attention to the part of me that will last forever."

WE NEED PARDON

I once visited a man who told me he was an alcoholic. He described the many places he had been, trying to find a cure. Then he leaned forward, looked into my face and asked me, "What do you think, Reverend? Is there any hope for me?"

I replied, "Is there any hope for me?" He looked startled and said, "What do you mean, is there any hope for you? You're a Christian, a preacher."

"The only difference between you and me is not that I am a preacher and you're not," I told him. "Or that I'm in the church and you're not. The only difference between us is the grace of God. I am a sinner saved by God's grace, and you are a sinner in need of God's grace. The grace of God is your only hope, and the grace of God is my only hope."

God has promised not to reward us according to our iniquities. That is why we need to be pardoned. A mother begged President Lincoln to have mercy on her boy and grant him a pardon.. The President looked at the young man's record and said, "According to the evidence, your son is guilty. This is a just punishment."

Our God . . . will abundantly pardon.

Isaiah 55:7 (KJV)

The mother cried out, "But I'm not asking for justice. I'm asking for mercy."

It is all any of us can ask for!

LIFE RESPONSE:

I will praise God for the grace that pardoned me even though I deserved punishment.

DON'T BE BLINDED BY MONEY!

A rich man was talking to his pastor about the difficulty of being a faithful Christian. The pastor told him to look out the window and tell him what he saw.

"I see the city — people."

"Now look into this mirror and tell me what you see," said the pastor.

"I see only myself."

"Exactly! The window is glass, and through it you can see others. The mirror is also glass, but when the glass is covered with silver, you can see only yourself."

The love of money is a root of all kinds of evil.

1 Timothy 6:10 (NIV)

Money tends to blind our eyes to the needs of others. The Apostle Paul said that the love of money is a root of all kinds of evil. People who love money are susceptible to every other sin. When money becomes the driving passion of a man's life, he is apt to lose sight of everything else.

Contrary to popular preaching today, wealth and prosperity are not necessarily an indication of God's blessings. Such preaching does not come from the Word of God but from the same greed that motivates the spirit of the world. Material and financial prosperity may actually be an instrument Satan uses against you.

Don't let money blind you!

LIFE RESPONSE:

"Lord, help me to concentrate on living rather than just making a living."

THROUGH THE BIBLE

Isaiah 29-31

CIRCUMSTANCES CANNOT CRUSH US

Ed Gibson failed the first and fourth grades. Yet he distinguished himself as one of our sky lab astronauts, competing with 1,500 other applicants for the job. Abraham Lincoln ran for office and was defeated seven times. The famous Babe Ruth, struck out about as many times as he hit home runs. Benjamin Franklin was a third-grade dropout, the fifteenth child of a poor candlemaker. Through diligent effort, Franklin became one of the best-educated men in the colonies. He was an inventor, publisher, educator, diplomat and a signer of the Declaration of Independence.

Circumstances of life need not overwhelm and defeat us. The eighth chapter of Romans reminds us that no earthly situation, no matter how difficult or depressing, can affect our relationship with God.

When my wife and I visited Rome, we saw the dungeon tradition says was the Apostle Paul's prison. We made our way down into the damp, dark confinement of stone. What a desperate situation life had handed him! Yet from that cell he wrote, "Rejoice in the Lord always: and again I say Rejoice" (Phil. 4:4).

> *If God be for us, who can be against us?*
>
> Romans 8:31 (KJV)

LIFE RESPONSE:

I will defeat my circumstances by not letting them defeat me.

❈

The Good News

The first job I ever had was delivering newspapers. When I was only nine years old, I began helping my brother with his paper route. Every day, we delivered the *Knickerbocker News* out of Albany, New York. Some days we delivered good news. More often than not, it was bad news. We delivered news of trouble, war, death, heartache, accidents and strife. This bad news wasn't the newspaper's fault — the paper simply printed the activities of men as they happened.

For many years, I have been delivering the good news of the Lord Jesus Christ. To those who find life empty and meaningless, the gospel comes with the message of Christ, who offers abundant life.

These things write we unto you, that your joy may be full

1 John 1:4 (KJV)

A discouraged, hopeless man drove from Canada to New York City, thinking he would get a job on a ship and sail as far away as possible. He arrived late on a Saturday night, stayed at a hotel and took a walk the next morning. Coming to a church, he went in and sat down. He noticed happy smiles and an atmosphere he had not known before. One person sitting near him leaned over and said, "God loves you." Because of that experience, he turned to the Lord and his life was transformed.

The good news made the difference.

LIFE RESPONSE:

"Lord, help me to deliver the 'good news' to those around me."

WHICH GOD DO YOU SERVE?

Several years ago, a widow in Indianapolis was brutally murdered and her luxurious home set on fire in an attempt to conceal the crime. Investigators discovered that the murderers had robbed the woman of hundreds of thousands of dollars. This widow had inherited a large fortune, but because she did not trust banks, she had kept all of the money in her home. She had stuffed her life savings in every conceivable hiding place. The unfortunate woman lived in constant fear, a prisoner to her wealth, until the day when both her money and her life were taken from her.

A heart set on material things cannot live worry-free. It is not possible to make earthly treasure absolutely secure. But no one worries about treasure laid up in heaven.

Riches often make people lonely and afraid. When man makes wealth his god, it leaves him empty and alone. Jesus warns us that if our treasure is on earth, our hearts will be on earth as well. But if our treasure is in heaven, our hearts will be set on heaven.

. . . the deceitfulness of wealth and the desires for other things come in and choke the word . . .

Mark 4:19 (NIV)

If we are trusting in earthly riches, then money is our god. But that god will utterly fail us in our hour of need.

It's better to trust in God who richly gives us all things to enjoy! He never fails.

LIFE RESPONSE:

I will examine my "heavenly bank account" to be sure I have invested wisely.

THROUGH THE BIBLE

Isaiah 38-40

HE IS LORD

National Geographic once published a fascinating article titled "A Pacific Island Awaits Its Messiah." The "christ" referred to is not the Lord Jesus, however, but a legendary figure called John Frum. The author, Dr. Kal Miller, points out that the islanders think this person will be a "beneficent spirit," a "god come to earth," or "king of America."

That latter description originated from U.S. troops occupying the area during World War II. Their presence was accompanied by many material benefits and the people concluded that John Frum had finally arrived. Although the islanders were disappointed when the soldiers left, their hopes did not die. To this day, they frequently march with bamboo rifles over their shoulders and the letters "USA" painted on their bodies.

That at the name of Jesus every knee should bow . . .

Philippians 2:10 (KJV)

That is the kind of messiah many people are looking for today. Some try to portray Jesus as a kind of Santa Claus. But Jesus did not come to give material blessings. He is King of Kings and Lord of Lords, to be worshiped and adored. As Savior of sinners, He is worthy of our praise, whether we lack material benefits or have them in abundance.

LIFE RESPONSE:

I will acknowledge that Jesus Christ is Lord whether I prosper or suffer loss.

WE HAVE AN INHERITANCE!

I once conducted the funeral for an eighty-year-old lady, a member of my church. Her seventy-nine-year-old husband was blind. He told me that after his wife's death, relatives came to visit and helped themselves to his wife's possessions. "They can't even wait until I'm dead to get hold of what little I have," he said. I have heard of the same kind of greed and selfishness at the reading of wills.

Jesus spoke about a group of people who will someday enjoy a great inheritance. The meek are happy, Jesus said, because they know the books haven't been balanced yet. The inheritance is coming, and they can wait for it! They will not inherit a corrupt, defiled and depleted earth, however. Their inheritance is incorruptible, undefiled and will not fade away (1 Peter 1:4).

> *. . . an inheritance among all those who are sanctified.*
>
> Acts 20:32 (NIV)

Andrew Carnegie, after trying to distribute 300 million dollars for charitable causes, told a friend, "You have no idea the strain I have been under." He finally set up a foundation to manage his philanthropy. But not even 300 million dollars is inexhaustible. The Christian's inheritance will not fade away. It is being preserved in heaven and is not in danger of being stolen like treasures on earth.

LIFE RESPONSE:

I will not spend my life yearning and earning for the things that fade away.

THROUGH THE BIBLE

Isaiah 43-44

WITHOUT GUILE

W hen we moved into our present home, we bought a new piece of furniture for our dining room. Now, my wife is a good housekeeper — neat almost to a fault — who faithfully dusts, cleans and waxes. But the other day, the sun was shining through the dining room window striking that piece in such a way as to highlight previously unseen dust. In fact, we even found a flaw in the finish which we had not noticed before. When viewed in the sunlight, it was not as clean nor as perfect as we had thought it to be.

The Apostle Paul told the Philippians that he prayed for them that they would be "sincere and without offense." The word *sincere* as used here means that which, when viewed in the sunlight, is found clear and pure. We need to get rid of dirt and defects that show up in the light of the Son.

. . . that ye may be sincere and without offense till the day of Christ.

Philippians 1:10 (KJV)

Peter said of Jesus, "Who did no sin, neither was guile found in his mouth" (1 Peter 2:22 KJV). Jesus had nothing to hide. Guile is fraud or deception. It is a picture word, meaning bait or a trap. No deception was in Jesus' mouth because there was none in His character.

Walking in His light makes it possible for us to deal with whatever is unlike Him. When we see it like He sees it, we can take steps to correct the places where we fall short.

LIFE RESPONSE:
Are my attitudes and my words fee from deception?

GOD'S PEOPLE WILL DO YOU GOOD

After a great victory on Mount Carmel, Elijah was threatened with death by Queen Jezebel. Discouragement and depression invaded the man of God.

Often, I arrive home from my travels late at night. My wife brings me up to date on what has happened at home. But she saves the problems and difficulties for the next day, after I have rested.

God let Elijah sleep and eat before giving him more work to do. Elijah thought he was the only one left serving God, but God showed him there were seven thousand faithful souls in Israel. As soon as Elijah got out from under the juniper tree of self-pity, he began to look for others who would serve the Lord with him. He found Elisha, who remained with Elijah until the day he was translated.

[Elijah] requested for himself that he might die; . . . And as he lay and slept under a juniper tree, behold, then an angel touched him . . .

1 Kings 19:4-5 (KJV)

If you are discouraged today, look for men and women who are serving God, going to church, worshiping in faith, praising God in victory, and serving the Lord with gladness. God has His people. The entire church is not backslidden, and the devil has not taken over everywhere. Join with God's people and they will do you good.

LIFE RESPONSE:

I will seek refreshment and fellowship with God's people.

ABOUNDING LOVE

We used to live near the shore of Lake Huron. Often, the children would go down to the shoreline and build castles and forts in the sand. It was easy to find enough stones, sticks and sand to build a strong fortress. But upon returning to that spot a day or two later, there would be no sign of their construction project at all. The washing of wave after wave quickly broke down and carried away whatever had been there previously.

> *This is my prayer: that your love may abound more and more in knowledge and depth of insight.*
>
> *Philippians 1:9 (NIV)*

That is the kind of experience the Apostle Paul prays the Philippian Christians will have in the love of God — wave upon wave of love washing over their souls, until every hindrance to the Kingdom of God in their lives is gone.

Paul also prayed that their love would develop in "knowledge and depth of insight." False prophets and teachers abound. Don't be led astray by every wind of doctrine that blows, but mature in the love of God. Test every teaching by the Word of God, so that you are not led into error and false doctrine.

Every Christian needs that kind of experience in the love of God. It will wash away all bitterness and resentment — giving discernment and understanding in their place.

LIFE RESPONSE:
"Lord, let your 'waves' of mercy flow over me unhindered."

LET HIM CHANGE YOU

A hopeless alcoholic attended a Billy Graham crusade in England. He was under the care of a psychiatrist but was getting no better. As he listened to the sermon, he wondered if there might be hope for his situation. He went forward, Christ saved him and a new power came into his life. He poured all his liquor down the drain.

In the morning, from force of habit, he reached for the bottle, but it was not there. Yet, there was no feeling of disappointment. He phoned his psychiatrist and said, "You have lost a patient. Christ has saved me and delivered me from drink."

The psychiatrist, deciding he too needed help, went to the crusade and was saved. Later, the psychiatrist and the former alcoholic testified together of the saving power of Christ.

Not every conversion is so dramatic. I was converted in my teens. I had never experimented with drugs or tasted alcohol. I lived at home and obeyed my parents, at least reasonably well. I was probably regarded as a good boy. When I was saved, my outward lifestyle changed very little — but it was no less real in terms of the change in my heart. I have been changing from that day on.

> *Repent, then and turn to God, so that your sins may be wiped out . . .*
>
> *Acts 3:19 (NIV)*

LIFE RESPONSE:
"Thank You, Lord, that you changed me and that You are still changing me."

GENEROSITY

I t is a paradox that poor people are often more generous than the rich.

When the war in Vietnam ended, refugees were transplanted to nations around the world. Thousands of them came to America. How two towns responded to requests to take in refugees was reported in two contrasting news reports. One article described an oceanside resort which did not welcome the refugees. The town was dependent on its tourist trade, which was attracted by the clean, white beaches. Town members feared an influx of refugees would spoil their beaches.

The second article described another community, which accepted hundreds of these victims of war. The townspeople contributed anything they could to help, especially toys, which were high on the request list. One girl brought a doll, obviously not new. A news reporter noticed this little girl with the worn and tattered doll, and asked why she had brought it.

Their overflowing joy and their extreme poverty welled up in rich generosity.

2 Corinthians 8:2 (NIV)

"Because they told me these children don't have any toys, and I wanted to give them one of mine," she said.

"But why did you bring this one? This looks like it might be your favorite. Why did you bring this one instead of one of your other dolls?"

"Oh," the little girl said matter-of-factly, "because it's the only one I've got."

God blesses that kind of generosity!

LIFE RESPONSE:
I will discover the joy of generosity.

GETTING IN SHAPE FOR HEAVEN

During the Great Depression, a man lost everything he had — his job, his fortune, his wife and his home, but he tenaciously held onto his faith. It was the one thing he had left. One day, he stopped along the street to watch some men doing stone work on a church. One of the workers was chiseling a stone into a strange shape.

The man asked, "What are you going to do with that odd-shaped stone?"

"You see that little opening way up near the top of the steeple?" the worker answered. "I'm shaping this down here so it will fit up there."

Tears filled the man's eyes as he walked on down the sidewalk. It seemed God was saying to him, "Through all these trials, the suffering and loss, I'm shaping you down there so you'll fit up here."

Come . . . take your inheritance, the kingdom prepared for you . . .

Matthew 25:34 (NIV)

You may be tempted to ask, "Is this the best of all possible worlds? This life is so filled with trouble and heartache, is this the best that God can do?" Just remember, God is shaping you down here on earth so you will fit up there in heaven.

Someone has said, "Heaven is a prepared place for a prepared people." God is shaping us into holy people so someday we will enjoy being with Him forever in a holy heaven. Suffering is one of the tools He uses.

LIFE RESPONSE:

I will let the Creator use earthly trials to prepare me for heavenly triumphs.

THROUGH THE BIBLE

Isaiah 61-64

THE VALUE OF ONE SOUL

Among the many fine people I have pastored over the years was a woman who had been saved in a revival meeting when she was a girl. In the entire ten-day meeting, she had been the only person who sought the Lord. At the close of the meeting, some of the people spoke critically, saying it hadn't been much of a meeting, since only one little girl had been saved.

What can a man give in exchange for his soul?

Matthew 16:26b (NIV)

She overheard the conversation and determined that she would pay back that church. As a young adult, she saved enough money to pay the church everything the revival had cost them. The woman went on to be a missionary, an outstanding children's worker, and a member of the pastoral staff of a church. No one understood the value of reaching that one girl for Christ.

What is the worth of a soul? We say we believe it is worth more than the whole world, for Jesus said, "What is a man profited, if he shall gain the whole world, and lose his own soul?" (Matt. 16:26a KJV).

If one soul is worth so much, it would seem that every church, and every Christian, would be doing all within their power to reach every person possible for Jesus.

Do we really believe souls are so valuable, or do we just say we believe that?

LIFE RESPONSE:
Am I doing my part to win souls for Christ?

THROUGH THE BIBLE
Isaiah 65-66

COMMUNICATION OVERLOAD

We are an over-communicated society. The average American family sees more than 750,000 television pictures a day (TV is really a series of still pictures changing thirty times a second). Newspapers, books, magazines, radio, stereo or CD players, computers and telephones all pour information into our eyes and ears.

I now write all of my sermons on a personal computer, which has greatly facilitated my work. But occasionally, in my attempts to get my thoughts written down as quickly as possible, I inadvertently hit two or three function keys at the same time. When that happens, my screen goes blank and everything shuts down. The computer simply will not accept any more commands.

Everyone should be quick to listen . . .

James 1:19 (NIV)

Something like that may be happening in our over-communicated society. The circuits are overloaded and not every message is getting through. Studies on the human brain have established the existence of a phenomenon called "sensory overload." Beyond a certain point, the brain goes blank and refuses to function normally.

Is it possible we have become so over-communicated that we do not hear the voice of God speaking?

LIFE RESPONSE:
"Lord, help me to tune out the world's noise and really listen to You."

THROUGH THE BIBLE

James 1-5

Anybody Here Want To Live Forever?

A crusty old Marine sergeant, while attacking a beachhead during World War II, stood up and challenged his men, "Come on, men, do you want to live forever?"

Emboldened by his bravery, his men charged into the face of the enemy. Many of them died on that beach. But if they had taken just a moment to reflect on his question, they would have answered, "Yes, we do want to live forever. We want to know that when our threescore years and ten, more or less, of this life are over, we will go on living throughout eternity!"

> *God has given us eternal life, and this life is in his Son.*
>
> *1 John 5:11 (NIV)*

This longing to live forever seems to be a universal human trait. The idea of reincarnation was created to satisfy this yearning. Some people even experiment with deep-freezing human bodies, hoping someday to bring them back to life.

Many people who are suffering, however, would not want this life to last forever. With the idea of eternal life goes the qualification that it be a good life, a paradise — or at least better than the present one.

God created us with that longing for eternal life and He alone makes it possible. Those who believe in Him and put their lives under His control have the hope of eternal life in a better world. Is that your hope today?

LIFE RESPONSE:
I will hope above the horrors of this life.

THROUGH THE BIBLE
Jeremiah 1-3

AN ORDINARY HUMAN BEING

Muretus, a Christian scholar of the sixteenth century, became very ill while on a trip and was forced to seek the help of physicians. To the doctors — who did not know him — Muretus looked like a very ordinary citizen. They said, "Let's try an experiment on him, for he looks of no importance."

In the next room, Muretus overheard their discussion and called out to them, "Call not any man cheap for whom Christ died."

Unlike the previous creatures God had made, man was created in the image of the Creator. That image makes man special, set apart from the rest of creation.

The Apostle Paul spoke to this special nature of man. "'The first man, Adam, became a living being'; the last Adam became a life-giving spirit" (1 Cor. 15:45 NIV).

God had wonderful plans for His crowning creation, upon whom He bestowed glory and honor. Even though His highest plan was spoiled by sin, He arranged through His marvelous redemption to make human beings part of His family.

What an honor to be an "ordinary human being!"

> *Let us make man in our image, in our likeness . . .*
>
> Genesis 1:26 (NIV)

LIFE RESPONSE:

I will praise God that while I am made in His spiritual image, I am fully human as well.

THROUGH THE BIBLE

Jeremiah 4–5

THE ONE WHO NEVER CHANGES

I personally think that television has brought about as much change as any other single aspect of modern technology. First of all, it rearranged our homes. The television set is the center of attraction, with the chairs arranged for convenient viewing.

Television has also altered our family habits. Many families eat their meals in front of the TV. Conversation has become a lost art and reading is nearly a thing of the past. As for recreation, we have become a generation of spectators. We can even shop by television. Our morals have been tainted by the soap operas and films that picture every kind of perversion as the norm. Advocacy entertainment uses the sitcom format to constantly brainwash us with its humanistic philosophy.

I the Lord do not change.

Malachi 3:6 (NIV)

Even the way we worship has felt the impact of television and the new age. Before they go to church on Sunday, many people have already watched a Hollywood-style religious production, with choreographed choirs, professional musicians and a celebrity preacher.

We need a reminder that amidst all the changes in our society, Jesus never changes.

LIFE RESPONSE:
I will praise the Lord for His unchanging character.

THROUGH THE BIBLE

Jeremiah 6-8

COMMITMENT

Wanting to talk, a young college student once came to my office. He slouched down in a chair, and with tears in his eyes said, "Wow! My whole life is falling apart."

"What's wrong?" I asked.

He said, "I thought I knew what I wanted to do with my life and what I wanted to become. Now I'm not sure anymore, and everything is falling apart on me."

As long as he had a commitment, he was all right; but without it, he was in conflict and had no peace.

Jesus had such peace early in His life. As a boy of twelve, He was in the Temple discussing questions with the teachers of the law. When His mother and Joseph found Him and scolded Him for worrying them, He said, "Don't you know I must be about my Father's business?"

After He was involved in His ministry, He said, "I must work the works of Him that sent Me, while it is day" (John 9:4 KJV). And when His earthly life was ending, He could look up to the Heavenly Father and say, "It is finished" (19:30). He knew the calling of God for His life and He was committed to doing it.

I must be about My Father's business?

Luke 2:49 (NKJV)

The same is true for every human being. Commitment to God's business brings peace.

LIFE RESPONSE:

I will put my Father's business first.

LEARN TO TRUST

D r. E. Stanley Jones tells about a poor man who had an overnight guest. As he showed his visitor to the humble bedroom in the hayloft, the poor man said, "If there is anything else you want, let us know, and we'll show you how to get along without it."

Our children sometimes compared our living standard with that of businessmen and professional people in the churches we pastored. They would ask, "Are we poor?" We always answered, "No, we're not poor, we're rich! We have each other, love and God. What more would you want in life?"

During a dry spring in Indiana some years ago, I watched the farmers work their fields and plant their crops. But despite all the things they were able to do with equipment and hard work, they could not produce the rain. We are much more dependent on God and His provision than many will admit.

Your heavenly Father knows that you need all these things.

Matthew 6:32 (NKJV)

Yet, why be anxious about those things that your Heavenly Father knows you have need of?

Some railroad workers in England found a bird's nest under one of the rails. The little thrush sat peacefully on her eggs, undisturbed by the roar of the trains above her.

Like that thrush, the child of God has learned the simple reality of trust.

LIFE RESPONSE:
"Father, I bring my needs to you in childlike trust."

THROUGH THE BIBLE

Jeremiah 12-14

HE CAME
TO SAVE SINNERS

When the Methodist circuit-riding preachers traveled across America in pioneer days, they met with derision and opposition in many places. Sometimes, no one would rent them a building or hall in which to hold their meetings. Frequently the preachers would target their message and their prayers toward the worst and hardest sinner in town — the owner of the saloon or the leading gambler, the bootlegger or town drunkard. By winning the most notorious among them to their cause, these evangelists often saw revivals spread throughout the area until entire communities were converted. Today, there is a Methodist church on nearly every crossroads and in every town in America.

All the people saw this and began to mutter, 'He has gone to be the guest of a "sinner."'

Luke 19:7 (NIV)

When Jesus called Zacchaeus out of the sycamore tree, He was welcomed into the home of one of the richest and best-known men in Jericho. But Zacchaeus needed Christ. Willing to make restitution and to obey God, he became a sincere follower. The up-and-out need God as much as the down-and-out!

What sinners are you "targeting" for the Lord?

LIFE RESPONSE:

I will introduce the needy in spirit to the One who meets every need, the Lord Jesus Christ.

WHO IS YOUR BROTHER?

C harles Spurgeon once found a boy, ragged and hungry, on the streets. Taking him home with him, the pastor fed and clothed the boy. Then he knelt down and prayed for the lad. Throughout his prayer, he referred to the Almighty as "our Father."

When the prayer was ended the boy asked, "Did you say 'our Father?'"

"Yes, our Father, yours and mine."

Am I my brother's keeper?

Genesis 4:9 (NIV)

Who are my mother and my brothers?

Mark 3:33 (NIV)

"Does that mean we are brothers?" asked the boy.

"Well, yes, son, it does," the great pastor said. Then he gave the boy a note to take to a shoe shop for a pair of boots.

A few days later, the cobbler saw Spurgeon and asked him about the boy who had come in wanting a pair of boots.

"When I asked him, he said you were his brother," the cobbler said.

"Yes, he's yours too. And if you would like to share the cost of our brother's boots, that is fine with me!" said Spurgeon.

Who is your brother? Jesus considered His brother to be the very least among us (Matt. 25:40).

How are we treating our brothers? Jesus will ask us about that some day!

LIFE RESPONSE:

Am I treating others as members of the family?

THROUGH THE BIBLE

Jeremiah 18-21

OUR OWN DECISION

Whether or not we accept God's will for our lives is our own personal decision. Like Jesus, we want to have spiritual support from friends, but the decision is ours alone.

Parents sometimes are tempted to make decisions for their children. But the time comes when the children must take that responsibility for themselves.

One recent Christmas, my boys reminded me of something annoying I had done when they were young. Every year, one of their presents was a model car that had to be put together. They said, "Dad, you never let us build our own models. You always put them together for us."

I admit that I did. It wasn't that I wanted to spoil their fun, I just wanted them to do a good job. The problem was when it was finished, it was not their job, but mine.

We may try to do the job for our children, or for others, when they are putting together what they believe to be God's will for their lives. But each person must discover His will for themselves. The decision to undertake His will is theirs alone to make.

Not my will, but thine, be done.

Luke 22:42 (KJV)

Jesus, in His hour of loneliness, had to say, "Your will be done." Each person who decides to follow Jesus comes to that place of lonely decision.

LIFE RESPONSE:

I will make spiritual decisions, not based on someone else's standard, but on what I consider to be God's will for my life.

ALL STORMS ULTIMATELY PASS

I was sitting in an airplane in Louisville, Kentucky, waiting to return home. Since a storm was directly over the airport and planes were trying to land, we were not permitted to take off. It reminded me of another situation, when the pilot had told the passengers, "Don't worry. We will go eventually. All storms ultimately pass."

When the blizzard of 1978 hit Indiana, I was in Washington D.C., attending a convention. I waited four days in Washington, calling home, trying the airlines and the train station, all to no avail. No one was getting into Indiana.

> *Weeping may endure for a night, but joy cometh in the morning.*
>
> *Psalms 30:5 (KJV)*

When I finally got home, I saw the snow had drifted as high as the eaves of the house. A few months later, I walked along the front of my house and saw tulips blooming where the snow drift had been. The tulip bulbs had been there all along. The potential for their spring beauty was locked beneath the winter's blast, but the hope never died.

No matter how difficult the storm we are going through, we can anchor our souls in God and wait for Him to bring us out. People may fail us in our times of need, but God will never fail. We may be tempted to think He has, but He will not go back on His Word. All storms ultimately pass.

LIFE RESPONSE:

"Lord, I praise You for the fact that the storms in my life are not permanent."

THROUGH THE BIBLE

Jeremiah 24-26

THE HOLY SPIRIT AT WORK

While touring Israel, we rode in a bus from Jerusalem to Bethlehem. We passed through a checkpoint where soldiers stood with guns ready, stopping all traffic. I asked the guide why there was so much security. He whispered to me (so that the members of our group would not hear), that a bomb had exploded in Jerusalem early that morning. The soldiers were checking for terrorists trying to leave the city. He said, "We don't want to alarm anyone, so nothing is being said about it." It amazed me that a bomb could explode and no one know about it!

On a different day in Jerusalem, something could *not* be kept quiet. It began with the sound of a mighty rushing wind that sounded like a tornado. Then, flames of fire rested upon the heads of everyone present in a certain upper room. It was the day of Pentecost and the Holy Spirit was being poured out upon the infant church. Before long, as the King James Version puts it (Acts 2:6), it was "noised abroad," and people everywhere began to hear what was going on. That day, three thousand people were baptized into the church, the beginning of the ministry of the Holy Spirit in the hearts of the believers.

When the day of Pentecost came . . . All of them were filled with the Holy Spirit . . .

Acts 2:1, 4 (NIV)

Is He working in your church? If He is, you won't be able to hide it!

LIFE RESPONSE:
I will allow the Holy Spirit to work through me.

Get Off The Fence!

When the great chemist Faraday was a boy, he climbed a fence one day and put his hands and head through, just beneath the top rail. Then he began to speculate. "On which side of the fence am I? My hands and head are on one side, but my body and my heart are on the other." Just then someone came along and opened the gate, pinning him painfully between the gate and the post. He concluded it was better to be completely on one side or the other.

Jesus was saying that your hands and your head must be on the same side as your heart. You cannot love the world and serve God. Not only can we choose our master, we change masters as well.

No man can serve two masters . . .

Matthew 6:24 (KJV)

When I visited a former pastorate, I rejoiced to see a couple I had called on repeatedly. Held by chains of sin at that time, it seemed they would never come to Christ. Now they had been converted. They were new creatures in Christ Jesus.

Are you trying to sit on the fence? It is a miserable place to be. Get off on God's side of the fence and let Him bring a new way of living.

LIFE RESPONSE:

I will be on God's side with all of my heart, soul, mind and strength.

THROUGH THE BIBLE

Jeremiah 30-31

IS YOUR CHURCH LUKEWARM?

The pastor of a large, downtown church told me that many of his mainline denomination's churches in eastern cities have almost no members anymore. Through endowments, wills and bequests they have enough money to maintain the buildings, pay the pastor and meet the obligations of the church for many years to come. But the sanctuaries are nearly empty on Sunday morning. It would seem these rich churches need nothing — not even people.

But Jesus says such churches are, in reality, poor, blind and naked. He wishes they were either cold or hot, but because they are lukewarm, He finds them nauseating (Rev. 3:15-16).

The history of the Christian church is filled with men and women who were so hot in their zeal and faith, they were thought to be mad by their generation. Their dedication was beyond the understanding of those who loved the smugness and ease of an uncommitted life.

You say, I am rich . . . But you do not realize you are wretched, pitiful, poor . . .

Revelation 3:17 (NIV)

Christianity has become so respectable and so conventional that it is lukewarm and insipid. Wouldn't it be great if, once again, the world found the church dangerous enough to call us mad?

LIFE RESPONSE:

"Lord, help me to keep the spiritual fires burning in my own heart so that I may influence my church."

THROUGH THE BIBLE

Jeremiah 32-34

WHAT IS YOUR POTENTIAL?

While my brother was visiting a nursing home, one of the residents showed him her oil paintings. They were beautiful. "How long have you been an artist?" he asked.

"Just a little while," she answered. "I never painted a picture until I came here."

Actually, she had been an artist all her life — she just didn't know it because she had never tried.

Gideon asked, 'how can I save Israel? . . . I am the least in my family.'

Judges 6:15 (NIV)

Very few people really know their full potential. Gideon didn't know he was a leader who could command an army. Most of us settle for mediocrity, not attempting anything beyond our normal routine. When someone suggests we try to accomplish some project, we think we are incapable or unqualified.

Even when God taps us and asks us to use our resources and abilities, we shrink back like Gideon — afraid to trust God's judgment.

For many years I had wanted to paint. This desire became a longing and I finally decided to take lessons in oil painting. I'll never forget the thrill of completing my first painting.

Are you using your abilities or letting them lie dormant? The greatest failure is the person who never attempts anything.

LIFE RESPONSE:
I will use my interests and abilities for the glory of God.

THROUGH THE BIBLE
Jeremiah 35-37

AIM AT HEAVEN

In his book *Mere Christianity,* C. S. Lewis says, "If you read history, you will find that the Christians who did most for the present world were just those who thought most of the next . . . It is since Christians have largely ceased to think of the other world that they have become so ineffective in this. Aim at heaven, and you will get earth thrown in. Aim at earth, and you will get neither."

Are modern Christians thinking much about heaven? Have you wondered where heaven is? Although the Bible doesn't give us its location, heaven is a real place.

When I consider that in the vast night sky there are at least one thousand million galaxies, and that each galaxy is one hundred thousand light years or more in diameter, I can easily believe that somewhere in that vastness God can find a place for us.

Some have criticized preachers who talk about heaven, saying that there are very real problems to be dealt with right here on earth. That is true. But the people who have believed most firmly in heaven are the very ones who have done the most to improve things here on earth.

> *. . . there before me was a door standing open in heaven.*
>
> *Revelation 4:1 (NIV)*

LIFE RESPONSE:

Am I thinking more about opening doors on earth than the "open door" of Heaven.

LONELINESS CAN BE CURED

Ernest Hemingway said, "I live in a vacuum that is as lonely as a radio tube when the battery is dead and there is no current to plug into."

A leading psychologist says that there is an *epidemic* of loneliness today. Loneliness is more than merely being alone. Loneliness may be associated with suffering and with sorrow, as well as with solitude. Yet a person may experience all three and not be lonely.

A missionary whose husband was killed while piloting a plane in New Guinea wrote, "God's grace is sufficient for me. His loving arms are around me."

It is not good that man should be alone . . .

Genesis 2:18 (NKJV)

Loneliness is often caused by separation, not only a physical separation from loved ones, but a sense of emotional isolation, a lack of understanding by loved ones as well. What can cure such loneliness? It involves more than merely treating the symptoms. It is not found in increased activity or in such things as alcohol or drugs. If the underlying cause of loneliness is separation, then the solution must be reconciliation.

"God was in Christ, reconciling the world to himself" (2 Cor. 5:19 NKJV). Because of that reconciliation, the Apostle Paul could rejoice, even while experiencing the loneliness of a prison cell.

LIFE RESPONSE:
Have I done MY PART to be reconciled to someone separated from me.

THROUGH THE BIBLE
Jeremiah 42-45

CALLED ALONGSIDE TO HELP

A large freighter loaded with ore had made its way through Lake Erie into the Saint Clair River near Detroit. The captain somehow veered away from the deep channel and ran aground in shallow water. Tugboats were not able to move such a tremendous load. Then, another freighter was brought in alongside the stranded vessel, and cargo was transferred from it to the "helper." As the freighter alongside took on more and more of the weight, the stranded freighter began to rise and was soon back in the main channel again.

Jesus promised, "I will not leave you as orphans." He would send the Holy Spirit to us to be right alongside to help. Sometimes, life pushes us to the breaking point. No tugboat can move us out of our "slough of despond." But just as Help saved Christian from the bog in *Pilgrim's Progress*, so too Jesus reminds us that we're not stranded, not left alone.

I will not leave you as orphans; I will come to you.

John 14:18 (NIV)

If you will study Scripture, you will find that the Holy Spirit teaches, guides, comforts, helps and empowers. He also speaks to unsaved people and convicts them of their need of salvation. He comes to reveal Jesus Christ to every soul. He comes alongside to help.

LIFE RESPONSE:

I will praise the Lord for the help the Holy Spirit makes available to me.

THROUGH THE BIBLE

Jeremiah 46-48

How Much Is Enough?

This prosperous man, whom Jesus called a fool, was thinking only of himself. Money had snared his soul. All he wanted was more.

There is a legend of a miser who had a precious gold piece in a secret hiding place. Every day he took it out and held it in his hands. He did not invest it, spend it, or use it. His only delight was in possessing it.

Then one day someone discovered his hiding place and stole his gold piece. The miser was heartsick. A friend gave him a stone and said, "Here, use this in place of your gold."

The ground of a certain rich man yielded plentifully.

Luke 12:16 (NKJV)

The miser was furious. "But that is just a stone. What value is a stone compared with my precious gold?"

His friend said, "You can do with a stone all that you did with the gold."

Someone has suggested, "The use of money is all the advantage there is in having it." Some rare individuals believe that and practice it. One such man told a financial planner, "I have enough. I don't want to continue to amass more and more money. I want you to devise a plan whereby I can give away my entire income from this point on."

Ralph Waldo Emerson said, "Money often costs too much."

Don't let it steal your soul away!

LIFE RESPONSE:

I will keep possessions in their proper place . . . second to the things that really matter.

THE EVIDENCE IS THE FRUIT

A boy who had just committed his life to Christ asked his father, "How can I believe in the Holy Spirit when I have never seen Him?"

His father, an electrician, took his son to the power plant and showed him the great generators and thick power lines. "Son, this is where all the electricity comes from that produces heat for our house, cooks our food and brightens our house with light. You don't see any electricity here, do you?"

The boy said he didn't. "But you do believe in electricity, don't you?" the father continued.

The boy said yes. "Why?" his father asked.

"Because I can see the things it does in our house," was the boy's reply.

"You cannot see the Holy Spirit," explained the father, "but you can see what He does in your life and in mine."

The fruit of the Spirit is evidence of the indwelling of the Spirit. Love, joy, peace,

> *By their fruits ye shall know them.*
>
> *Matthew 7:20 (KJV)*

longsuffering, gentleness, goodness, faith, meekness and temperance are produced by the Holy Spirit (Gal. 5:22).

It is amazing that God chooses to dwell not in elaborate cathedrals but in the hearts of committed believers. We need to keep our commitment strong so the fruit can be produced in our lives day by day.

LIFE RESPONSE:

Am I teaching others about the Holy Spirit by the evidence of His presence in my life?

THROUGH THE BIBLE

Jeremiah 50

A SURE FOUNDATION

While visiting a town we had once lived in, I noticed a building lot that was empty except for the "For Sale" sign in the middle of it. That same empty lot had been for sale for a number of years. There was a good reason for that. Anyone knowing its history would certainly not want to build on it.

Underneath the lot is a substrata weakness of some kind. Years ago a man built a house there. He had been warned about the weakness and was told that the lot would not bear the weight of a house. But he insisted that he could build a foundation that would carry it. Ignoring the warnings, he built his house. And true to the gloomy predictions, it began to sink. Finally, it had to be torn down altogether, and the lot has stood vacant ever since.

For no one can lay any foundation other than the one already laid, which is Jesus Christ.

1 Corinthians 3:11 (NIV)

The church of the Lord Jesus Christ is not built on shaky ground. A sure foundation has been laid. The apostles and prophets contributed to it, but Jesus Christ is the bedrock — the foundation stone. It is upon basic, elementary and eternal truth that the church stands as it rises high and endures the beating winds of opposition.

To endure, a house, a church, or a life must be built on solid ground.

LIFE RESPONSE:
Am I building my life on the truths of Christ and His Word?

THROUGH THE BIBLE
Jeremiah 51-52

THE GIFT OR THE GIVER?

Overemphasis by some, or underemphasis by others, on the gifts of the Spirit has caused the gifts themselves to become controversial. That should not be. In fact, the work of the Holy Spirit ought to be the unifying power of the church. Perhaps some are so desirous of the spiritual gifts that they fail to recognize the Giver. After all, it is not His *gifts* that we need, but the presence of the *Giver*, the Holy Spirit.

When my children were small, I was sometimes gone for a week or ten days preaching in a revival. The first thing they asked when I got home was, "What did you bring me?" They weren't anxious to see me; they first wanted the gifts I had for them.

My wife, on the other hand, did not look or ask for gifts. She just wanted to see me.

Now I'm not faulting my children. They were only acting the way most little ones do. But perhaps that immaturity carries over into our spiritual lives. If we are concerned only with the gifts of the Spirit, we may be missing the most wonderful gift of all, the Spirit Himself! He is the Gift *and* the Giver. Thirst for Him . . . He will pour water on the one who is thirsty.

> *There are different kinds of gifts, but the same Spirit.*
>
> *1 Corinthians 12:4 (NIV)*

LIFE RESPONSE:

I will seek the Giver more than His gifts.

SHINE AS STARS

L ight shines best in the midst of darkness. Take a small candle into the glaring light of the noonday sun, and its humble glow is lost, its usefulness diminished. But take that same small candle into the darkness of an underground cavern, and it will gleam with remarkable power.

. . . sons of God . . . in the midst of a crooked and perverse nation, among whom ye shine as lights in the world; holding forth the word of life . . .

Philippians 2:15-16 (KJV)

A Christian may feel more comfortable in the security of the sanctuary, with other Christians around him. But his light is needed *outside* the sanctuary where the world is dark and full of sin.

Jesus said, "I am the light of the world" (John 8:12). He also said to His disciples, "You are the light of the world" (Matt. 5:14). Like the sun, Jesus is the primary source of light. Like the moon, Christians are a secondary source. Our light comes not from our own energy but from Jesus. The moon reflects the sun's light when it is in proper relationship to it. As Christians, we reflect the light of Jesus when we are in right relationship to Him.

LIFE RESPONSE:

I will check to see that my "light" is properly adjusted by a right relationship to Christ.

THROUGH THE BIBLE
Lamentations 3-5

IDLE WORDS

W hat are idle words? Does Jesus mean we are never to use humorous words? Are we never to answer anything but "Yes" and "No," as some interpret Matthew 5:39? I knew a man who took this scripture literally. While working with him one day, I quickly learned that conversation was possible only if I asked questions to which he could answer yes or no.

Jesus does not teach that all use of language is bad. The weight of our words is determined not by volume but by value.

As a young pastor, I felt inadequate when speaking to people during times of sorrow. One day, I was sitting with the family of a young man who had been killed in an automobile accident. I listened as people offered their condolences. One after another expressed love and sympathy with just a few words. Then a man came who talked from the time he entered the room until the time he left. Little of what he said was comforting, and much would have been better left unsaid.

Every idle word that men shall speak, they shall give account thereof in the day of judgment.

Matthew 12:36 (KJV)

Idle words are those that are without profit. But, "A good man out of the good treasure of his heart, bringeth forth good things" (Matt. 12:35 KJV).

LIFE RESPONSE:

"Lord, help me to give as much attention to *what* I say, as to *how* I say it and *when* I say it."

Prayer:
A Cry For Help

At the conclusion of a camp meeting service in which I had preached a message about prayer, a boy of about ten or twelve years of age came to me with a great message. Having heard someone else preach about prayer, he had retained much of the truth. He said, "There is a prayer that needs no introduction, contains no preamble and no conclusion. There is no problem with grammar, and it is contained in one word."

I asked, "What is that one word?"

He said, "Help!"

Men always ought to pray . . .
Luke 18:1 (NKJV)

And that is just as acceptable a prayer to God as an eloquent petition. Jesus teaches a lesson on prayer in the Sermon on the Mount (Matt. 6:5-13). He began by saying, "But when you pray . . . " He gave no certain hours or days. Prayer can occur any time, day or night, any day of the week. Prayers are important for us and we should have them regularly, but the time of day is immaterial.

The length is also unimportant. What *does* matter is the relationship to God of the one who prays — the faith exercised, the earnestness and sincerity with which the prayer is made.

Oh, what peace we often forfeit; oh, what needless pain we bear/ All because we do not carry everything to God in prayer.

LIFE RESPONSE:
Am I filling my *days* with *prayers*?

THROUGH THE BIBLE
1 Peter 3-5

HOW FORGIVEN ARE YOU?

As the new pastor of a church in Pennsylvania some years ago, I was asked to call on an elderly man who lived about two blocks from the church. When I introduced myself, he became so angry that — if he hadn't been over eighty years of age and rather infirm — I think he would have thrown me bodily out of his house.

Gently but persistently I questioned him about his strong reaction. In time, he told me of some injustice the church had committed against him and his family.

"When did this happen?" I asked.

To my surprise, it was something that had occurred nearly fifty years earlier. Through all those years, he had harbored ill will and anger, blocking the avenue of forgiveness from God. This man thought more about how he had been wronged than he did about his own sins.

Forgive us our debts, As we forgive our debtors.

Matthew 6:12 (KJV)

God's forgiveness is directly related to our forgiveness of others. Have you refused to forgive sins committed against you? Have you kept a record of these wrongs?

How forgiven are you?

LIFE RESPONSE:

"Lord, help me to forgive as much as I have been forgiven."

DON'T BE A HYPOCRITE!

We attended a high school play in which my son played a part. The young people were quite convincing in their portrayals of the characters in the play. In make-up and costumes, some of them appeared elderly, with gray hair. One carried a cane and walked with a limp.

Afterward, we saw these same young people — still in make-up and costumes — standing in the hall. How different, how unreal they looked! At close range, they neither looked like themselves nor like the characters they had portrayed.

> *When you give to the needy, do not announce it with trumpets, as the hypocrites do . . .*
>
> *Matthew 6:2 (NIV)*

Hypocrites are play actors, pretending to be something they are not. A close-up look reveals their pretenses. What a great disappointment it is to see what they really are!

Many people pretend to be good Christians. They may pray in public, give generously and seem sincere. They may even fool other church members for a while — maybe even the pastor. But no hypocrite ever fools God, for He looks at the heart.

There are two kinds of hypocrites: those who want to appear superspiritual before the church, and those who want to be known as religious in the world. They want the praise of men. Jesus says they have their reward.

LIFE RESPONSE:

I will seek the praise of Christ over the praises of the world.

THROUGH THE BIBLE

Ezekiel 5-9

WORK WITH MIGHT AND DELIGHT

There is a saying at our house that doesn't make much sense to others, but it helps us through some difficult tasks. It arose from an incident when our two oldest children, then in their early teens, were painting a fence. Having had enough of their complaining, my wife said, "If you dread it, you'll dread it. Let's just get the fence painted."

One of the children responded with some disgust, "Of course, Mom, if you dread it, you'll dread it." But at the same time, they began to laugh and finished the fence with delight. Now that saying is a rallying cry every time there is an unpleasant task to be done. It helps us get over our dread and enables us to work with delight.

Whatever your hand finds to do, do it with all your might . . .
Ecclesiastes 9:10 (NIV)

Working with might and delight is not the usual attitude. Many people seem to want to do as little as possible, take off as much time as they can, never volunteer for anything, and face each workday with dread.

One employer said that most men work about four hours out of eight. In other words, they're paid twice as much as they're worth.

Learning to work with might and delight will make your witness strong in the workplace.

LIFE RESPONSE:

I will "just get the fence painted" and not concentrate on the unpleasantness of the task.

THROUGH THE BIBLE
Ezekiel 10-13

OVERCOME EVIL WITH GOOD

My backyard garden has been a source of pleasure and pride over the years. After the hard work of weeding, I enjoy telling my wife, "I don't believe there is a single weed left in that garden. It is absolutely clean."

But I have discovered something. The best garden in the neighborhood is not necessarily the one with the fewest weeds, but the one that is the most fruitful — the one that produces the highest yield.

> *Do not be overcome by evil, but overcome evil with good.*
>
> Romans 12:21 (NIV)

Many people succeed in fighting temptation, resisting the devil and abstaining from certain sins. But what of the necessity of growing in grace and producing the fruit of the Spirit? Don't be overcome by evil but take the offensive. Take the initiative. Overcome evil with good.

One woman distributed booklets on prayer in each room of the local hotel. She wrote a personal message in the booklets and included her name and address. One day, a woman called her from another state. She told how, while passing through the city, she had checked into one of those hotel rooms with the intention of committing suicide. Instead she found the booklet, read it and turned her life over to Jesus.

Positive good can overcome evil!

LIFE RESPONSE:

Am I overcoming evil by bearing fruit?

THROUGH THE BIBLE

Ezekiel 14-16

ALMOST!

S everal years ago, three of my friends were killed when the small plane in which they were traveling crashed into a house and burned. Two of the men were pastors. They had attended a conference and were planning to be in their pulpits on Sunday morning.

In the darkness, the wing of the plane struck the top of a tree. If only they had left before dark. If only they had been a few feet higher. If only they had missed the house. Many of the tragedies of life are footnoted by laments of "if only" or "almost."

I'm convinced that many people who are lost, were almost saved. They were almost persuaded. They didn't miss entering the kingdom by much, but they missed it nonetheless.

Almost thou persuadest me to be a Christian.

Acts 26:28 (KJV)

"Almost" reflects missed opportunities, wasted time, procrastination and rationalization. There is no future in "almost." That is why the key word of the Bible is "now." Today is the day of salvation. A better time never comes. Excuses become habitual, life goes by, and people never take the crucial step.

Don't let ALMOST be the story of your life!

LIFE RESPONSE:

I am determined to do the things that *need* to be done *now*.

THROUGH THE BIBLE
Ezekiel 17-19

THIS WORLD NEEDS SALT

As Jesus spoke these words He was on a hill, perhaps overlooking the Sea of Galilee. It may be that as He spoke, local fishermen were bringing in the catch of the day. Unloading their boats, they prepared to transport the fish to Jerusalem or to other markets. In the mideastern heat, the fish would not stay fresh long. In fact, the strong stench of decaying fish would soon fill the air, except for one thing — salt!

As the fishermen loaded the fish they packed them in salt, knowing that the salt would prevent decay. Jesus may have pointed to the fishermen as He spoke the words, "You are the salt of the earth." You are the preserving influence, He was saying. Just as the salt keeps the fish from rotting, you are what keeps this world from putrefaction.

You are the salt of the earth.

Matthew 5:13 (NIV)

Ever since sin entered, the course of the world has spiraled downward. Left to run unhindered, sin would result in the total destruction of everything good. It is only by the influence of the Christians in this world that the decaying process is halted.

Jesus also warned, however, that salt can lose its saltiness. How tragic when the salt that is needed so desperately in this world loses its power to preserve.

LIFE RESPONSE:

I will seek to retain spiritual power in prayer and Bible study.

THROUGH THE BIBLE
Ezekiel 20-21

IMITATING JESUS

Wherever young people gather — in malls, on practice fields, at football games — you will probably notice some individuals whose hairstyles, clothing or mannerisms mimic popular athletes, television celebrities, or rock stars.

Someone has said, "We paste bits and pieces of others on ourselves." Imitation has been called the sincerest form of flattery. But we must be careful who we imitate. Christ is our Savior, and He is also our example. Obviously, we are very limited in our ability to imitate Christ. We cannot expect to be all that He was, or to demonstrate the perfection of His character. Nor are we to interpret this imitation as an attempt to be Christian. We are not Christians by imitation. We are Christians only by regeneration. We do not imitate Christ to become a Christian. We imitate Christ because we are Christians.

Be imitators of God . . .

Ephesians 5:1 (NIV)

Imitating Jesus means walking the pathways of selfless love, holiness, light and obedience. How carefully we should walk in His footsteps, knowing that we are His representatives, His ambassadors.

LIFE RESPONSE:

What I know about Jesus Christ, I will seek to duplicate in my words and actions.

FAILURE WITHOUT GOD

A noted spokesperson for the feminist movement said, "By the year 2000, we will, I hope, raise our children to believe in human potential, not God."

I want to tell her, and all those who think like her, that if we enter the third millennium believing in human potential instead of God, we are doomed to dismal failure. If men think they can navigate the new society of the third millennium with man at the helm, with human potential as our highest wisdom, and with God relegated to some dim and dusty place in the annals of history, they will awaken one day to the sad truth that without God, man can do nothing.

> *In him we live, and move, and have our being . . .*
>
> *Acts 17:28 (KJV)*

How can a society endure without the elementary guiding principles of God's Word? These truths have stood the test of time and have guided civilization through its development across the centuries. Nothing has been found to improve upon them. Governments that think they can shape a new society without these principles will collapse. They will learn too late that God knew what He was doing when He based the relationships of men to men upon the relationship of men to God.

What is true for governments is also true for individuals. No one can build a meaningful personal life without following God's blueprint.

LIFE RESPONSE:
"Lord, I praise You for the completeness I have found in You."

THROUGH THE BIBLE
Ezekiel 24-26

YOU CAST A SHADOW

I once rode on a plane with two young men who had never flown before. They were excited and nervous — straining to see all they could. The boy seated next to the window exclaimed, "Look! There is our shadow!" Gliding along the landscape beneath us was the shadow of the plane. The shadow was there all the time, but not always visible from the plane. When you are in a plane, you don't usually think about the shadow the plane casts on the ground.

You may not always be aware of your influence, but it is always there. Often, others are more conscious of it than you are. You can't help casting a shadow, and you cannot prevent your influence from falling upon others.

The godly influence of David Livingstone brought Henry Stanley to faith in God after he had lived

> *The things you have heard me say . . . entrust to reliable men who will also be qualified to teach others.*
>
> *2 Timothy 2:2 (NIV)*

with the missionary for some time. A Christian father was surprised when his grown children told him how they had "tuned him out" when he lectured them about honesty, truthfulness and other Christian principles. What really helped them learn those truths was seeing them demonstrated in their parents' lives day after day.

Let's make sure that the shadow of our influence is positive for good and for God.

LIFE RESPONSE:

Is my influence casting a positive "shadow?"

THROUGH THE BIBLE

Ezekiel 27-28

PROMISES, PROMISES

What promises have you made and kept? What promises have you *not* kept? Someone has said, "A promise is the one thing that, after giving it, you had better keep." Just as God's promise-keeping is a reflection of His character, so our faithfulness or failure to keep our word reflects our character as well.

I have a few suggestions and observations about making promises. First, make only those promises you have every intention of keeping. Second, it never pays to make promises to impress others. Third, don't make promises under pressure. That goes for vows made in storms, in foxholes, at deathbeds or sickbeds — these are apt to be forgotten when the trouble is past.

Whatever your lips utter you must be sure to do . . .

Deuteronomy 23:23 (NIV)

Promises made to God are serious business. People promise to tithe, to attend church faithfully, to make restitution, to quit bad habits, to do any number of things. But often years go by and the promises remain unfulfilled.

God may seem to be slow about keeping His promises. But He has not forgotten. His clock keeps perfect time. "God is not a man, that he should lie; neither the son of man, that he should repent: hath he said, and shall he not do it? or hath he spoken, and shall he not make it good?" (Num. 23:19 KJV).

LIFE RESPONSE:

Am I keeping my promises?

THROUGH THE BIBLE

Ezekiel 29-31

A Diligent Worker: A Good Witness

A man once asked me to pray for him because he had lost his job. Since he was a member of my church, I also attempted to intercede for him. Then I found out a few things that put the situation in a different light.

He often reported late to work. His excuse was that he needed to have family prayer in the morning.

He was often late with his deliveries. His excuse was that many times during the day he felt the need to pull over to the side of the road and read his Bible.

He interfered with other workers and their jobs. His defense was that he felt an obligation to witness to the men and try to lead them to Christ.

The soul of the diligent shall be made fat.
Proverbs 13:4 (KJV)

He would have been a far better witness for Christ if he had been a more diligent, honest, industrious worker — doing his Bible reading, praying and witnessing on his own time rather than on company time. After hearing all of the complaints against the man, I wondered why his employer hadn't fired him sooner.

Christianity at work demands integrity, faithfulness, punctuality and doing a good job.

LIFE RESPONSE:
"Lord, help me to be a witness for You in my diligent work habits."

THROUGH THE BIBLE
Ezekiel 32-33

AN ATTITUDE OF GRATITUDE

The first two funeral services I conducted as a pastor were those of an elderly couple. They were seventy-nine and eighty years of age. He was blind and she suffered from an incurable disease. During the year that I was their pastor, I spent more time with them in the hospital than anywhere else. I would take him to the hospital, lead him to her bedside and then leave him there while I went to make other calls. Often, when I was driving him home he would say, "Mama was in awful pain today. She doesn't say anything, but I could feel the tension in her hands."

Bless the Lord, O my soul, and forget not all his benefits.

Psalms 103:2 (KJV)

Many times I had heard that dear lady say, "Oh, I have so much to thank God for. When I look around this hospital ward and see the way these poor people are suffering, it just makes me grateful for all that God does for me." She was probably the most seriously ill person there, but she kept an attitude of gratitude by rejoicing over the benefits God had given her.

Thanksgiving does not come about by presidential decree or historical custom. Although it is good to be reminded of our need to give thanks, this cannot be limited to one day or one week. It should be our daily routine as we learn to develop our attitude of gratitude.

LIFE RESPONSE:
Am I thankful *in* all things, as well as *for* all things?

THROUGH THE BIBLE
Ezekiel 34-36

ARE YOU GOD?

O ne morning, a man received a phone call from a friend, asking him to take a mother and her four-year-old son to the hospital. That phone call changed the man's life.

He picked up the mother, who held the pale boy on her lap as they drove. The boy's big dark eyes stared wonderingly at the man. "Sir, are you God?"

The man was startled. "No, I'm not God. Why do you ask?"

The boy said, "My mother told me God would come and take me to a beautiful place. I wondered if you were God and if you're taking me there."

The man was deeply shaken. Four days later, God did come and take that boy to Himself. But the man could not get the boy and his question out of his mind. He began to think of other children who were sick and suffering. "I'm not God," he said, "but I can live for God and work for God." He gave himself to Christ and consecrated himself to work for children. God has used him to bless thousands of unfortunate little ones.

God lived in him and through him.

> *I have been crucified with Christ and I no longer live, but Christ lives in me.*
>
> Galatians 2:20 (NIV)

LIFE RESPONSE:

Is it evident to others that Christ is living in me?

WHAT'S THE DIFFERENCE?

Is becoming a Christian simply a matter of turning over a new leaf? Or is there really a difference in your life when you become a Christian?

A young and committed Communist was debating a young and enthusiastic Christian in Hyde Park, London. The Communist boasted of his ideology with its social concerns for the poor and downtrodden, and what he would accomplish through the redistribution of wealth. He pointed to a derelict lounging listlessly on a park bench nearby and said with pride, "Communism will put a new suit on that man."

The Christian responded, "That may be, but Christ will put a new man in the suit."

It isn't enough to improve the educational level, or the social standing, or even the financial position of an individual. There must be a basic change in his moral character. Jesus did not come to earth to live among men, to suffer and die, so that we could enjoy a higher standard of living. He came that we might rise to walk on a new plane of life altogether.

> *Just as Christ was raised from the dead . . . we too may live a new life.*
>
> Romans 6:4 (NIV)

LIFE RESPONSE:

I will seek to live a "resurrected life," not just a "reformed life."

COMETS OR CANDLES?

In the 1980s, many people put forth great effort to see Halley's Comet, which comes around an average of every 77 years. The phenomenon this most recent time around proved to be disappointing.

The same was true of Comet Kohoutek. Announced in 1973, it was billed as a spectacle of unprecedented splendor. The only thing spectacular about it, however, was the size of the disappointment it created.

A dark place needs a good, steady light. A glowing candle makes a dark room seem friendly and cozy. What good would a comet be for lighting a house, or even a city? A flash or streak of blinding light is soon gone, followed by darkness.

Some people shine like comets, others like candles. Some begin with an exciting commotion that promises greatness, but then dwindle into dying embers. Others burn with consistency and faithfulness, lighting the way through the darkness.

A crooked and perverse nation needs the witness of many steady lights. But those lights need to be dispersed into dark corners, not concentrated in one well-lighted location.

Is your candle lighting a dark corner?

> *. . . in the midst of a crooked and perverse nation, among whom ye shine as lights in the world.*
>
> *Philippians 2:15 (KJV)*

LIFE RESPONSE:

"Lord, help me to be a 'steady light' to some area of darkness."

THROUGH THE BIBLE

Ezekiel 43–45

BUILDING MONUMENTS

A farmer in Kansas, a self-made man, amassed a considerable fortune, but in the process made few friends. His wife's family treated him badly because they thought she had married beneath herself. When his wife died, he erected an elaborate statue in her memory. It portrayed his wife and him sitting on a love seat. Later, he had another statue made of himself kneeling at her grave. He commissioned still a third monument of his wife kneeling at his future grave.

By the time he was finished, he had spent a quarter of a million dollars on monuments. When someone from the town suggested that he help support a community project, the old miser frowned and shouted, "What's this town ever done for me?" When the man died, it is said that the only person at his funeral was the tombstone salesman! Today, those monuments are sinking slowly into the Kansas soil, sad reminders of a self-centered, unsympathetic life.

During his lifetime Absalom had taken a pillar and erected it in the King's Valley as a monument to himself . . .

2 Samuel 18:18 (NIV)

The best monuments we can erect are well-spent lives, memories of faith and love. Like Abel we, though dead, can speak (Heb. 11:4). Such monuments are built throughout a lifetime of service to others and devotion to God.

LIFE RESPONSE:

Am I spending more time building monuments than I am building relationships?

THROUGH THE BIBLE
Ezekiel 46-48

BEWARE!

During eighteen years as a pastor, I called on thousands of homes. One thing I learned right away was to read the signs posted on the doors of houses. One that never failed to gain my attention was "Beware of the dog." More than once I have walked away simply because of that sign. The reason goes back to my childhood.

As a boy of nine, trying to deliver the evening newspaper, I learned there are all kinds of dogs. There are loud, boisterous, barking dogs; snarling, growling, unfriendly dogs; bouncing, tail-wagging, hand-licking dogs; and sneaky, sulking, heel-nipping dogs. I learned to deal with almost all of them — except those for which people put out the sign "Beware!" I approached such houses with great caution, ready to run at any moment.

The Apostle Paul told the Philippians to "beware of dogs." He was warning them of evil-workers. He was saying, "There is danger here. Keep your eyes open, be alert and ready to take action." The word Paul used means to be aware of, to be on guard against, to see — not just with the physical eyes, but with the eyes of your understanding.

Beware of dogs . . .
Philippians 3:2 (KJV)

Too often, we become numb to the dangers around us. We live in a world which threatens the very existence of Christianity. A battle wages constantly for the hearts and minds of men. Are you alert and ready for action?

LIFE RESPONSE:

I will be mindful of the Holy Spirit's warnings about my associations.

NOTHING BUT THE TRUTH

C hildren often attempt to reinforce the truthfulness of their statements or convince their friends that they're telling the truth by saying, "Cross my heart, hope to die." I've heard men say, "Honest to God" or, "May God strike me dead if I'm lying."

Someone has said, "Perhaps the saddest commentary on our age is that the word honesty must be preceded by the adjective, 'old-fashioned.'"

> *Each of you must put off falsehood and speak truthfully to his neighbor . . .*
>
> Ephesians 4:25 (NIV)

David Livingstone asked an African chief for twenty-seven young men to accompany him more than a thousand miles through the jungle. He needed helpers, but the chief was reluctant to let them go. Livingstone promised to return with them. "My life will be as a pledge," he said.

It was not an easy trip. When they reached the coast, a British warship was there to take Livingstone back to England to be honored by Queen Victoria. But Livingstone refused to go. He was determined to keep his promise. After an absence of two and a half years, he brought the men back to their village. The Africans knew him as a man who kept his word.

Is that kind of honesty and trustworthiness part of your life?

LIFE RESPONSE:
Do my neighbors see honesty and trustworthiness in me?

PRACTICE WHAT YOU PREACH

Two bachelor brothers named Smythe lived together in London. Both of them were doctors — one was a doctor of medicine and the other a doctor of theology. They hired a housekeeper to look after their domestic needs.

One day, a visitor rang the doorbell. When the housekeeper answered, the visitor said, "I would like to see Doctor Smythe, please." After a moment of hesitation, the housekeeper said, "Which Doctor Smythe would you see, the one who preaches or the one who practices?"

Of course, there isn't any question that the one who preaches had also better be the one who practices. "Physician, heal thyself" is directed as much — or perhaps even more so — to the doctor of theology as to the doctor of medicine. It is possible for a doctor to heal someone else of the same disease that is killing him. But when a man preaches the gospel he had better be living according to the doctrine he preaches.

> *Whatever you have learned or received or heard from me, or seen in me — put it into practice.*
>
> *Philippians 4:9 (NIV)*

Much damage has been done to the kingdom of God by those who have not practiced what they preached. Paul, the apostle-preacher, practiced his messages in daily life until he could challenge his converts to live as he did! How does your life measure up to your beliefs?

LIFE RESPONSE:

I will make sure my "practice" matches, or exceeds, my "preaching."

THROUGH THE BIBLE

Daniel 3-4

IS IT "THEM" AND "US"?

Christians have the tendency to be exclusive, to consider as outsiders those who are not part of their group. I remember my first introduction to such a separatist attitude. As a new pastor in town, I was invited to attend a pastors' prayer fellowship. I met many of the town's pastors and shared in the prayer time with them.

When I went back to the next meeting, one of the pastors — whose church was near mine — was missing. I asked about him and was told, "He won't come because you are here."

. . . we tried to stop him, because he is not one of us.

Luke 9:49 (NIV)

Confused, I said, "I've never done anything to him that I know of. I just met him at the last meeting." A pastor explained that the absent preacher wouldn't fellowship with anyone who was not of his doctrinal persuasion. He would not join me in prayer because we held different views on some minute matters of doctrine. Ironically, his church was called The Church of the Open Door. But his door was open only to those who agreed with him!

Jesus told James and John not to forbid others to honor His name just because they were not of their group. Those who are not against us are for us, Jesus explained. How is your attitude toward those of other denominations?

LIFE RESPONSE:

I will not reject those whom Christ has accepted.

THROUGH THE BIBLE

Daniel 5-6

A Good Name

As a boy in upstate New York during World War II, I remember that many people were ashamed of their German heritage. Like them, I didn't want the other children at school to know that my maternal grandparents had come from Germany, or that I had an uncle named Adolph. Hitler had spoiled that name for me.

Certain names are remembered for the conduct or character of the people who bore them. Rockefeller or Vanderbilt may remind you of money. J. C. Penney might bring to mind success in business. Pullman means railroad and Carnegie means steel. Henry Ford will always be associated with cars and Bell with telephones. Edison means inventor, Capone means mobster and Roosevelt, politics. Disney says entertainment and Billy Graham, evangelism.

Do you know anyone named Judas? Even the dictionary defines a Judas as one who is a traitor.

A good name is to be chosen rather than great riches.

Proverbs 22:1 (NKJV)

What do people think when they hear your name? Your reputation, your character, your job, your home, your family may all come to mind. You are twice blessed if your friends — and God — agree that you have a "good name!"

LIFE RESPONSE:

"Lord, give me grace to life my live worthy of the name 'Christian.'"

YOU ARE THE LIGHT

A sick and weary African made his way to a mission hospital where he had been treated earlier. He remembered the kindness and compassion of the doctor who had cared for him. He said, "I want to see Jesus again." The doctor had so modeled the life of Christ that he was not seen — only Christ was seen in Him.

Under a picture of Peter Milne, which hangs in the church he founded on a small island in the New Hebrides, is the quote, "When he came there was no light, when he left there was no darkness."

Jesus said: 'I am the light of the world.'

John 9:5

You are the light of the world.

Matthew 5:14 (NIV)

That is the challenge of the light — to let Christ shine in us so that we reflect His glory to others.

Most of the world's people are groping around in darkness and despair, searching for a way out of the misery and heartache their sinful condition has brought upon them. They languish in the cold deadness of winter where the sun doesn't shine. But we can experience the light. We can walk in the light as He is in the light and have fellowship with Him, and the blood of Jesus Christ, God's Son, will cleanse us from all iniquity (1 John 1:7).

Whatever the darkness in our lives, Jesus can penetrate it, lighten it, displace it.

LIFE RESPONSE:

I will bring light to someone's darkness and despair today.

FIGHT THE ENEMY, NOT EACH OTHER!

Between battles in the Civil War, soldiers frequently sat around the campfires and discussed such subjects as religion and politics. One soldier said, "Sometimes the discussions would get very heated, even to the point of coming to blows. But then, off in the distance would be heard that unmistakable and unforgettable roll of unnatural thunder. We would recognize it immediately as the roar of distant cannon," the soldier recalled. "At once, everyone would be on his feet; handshakes and embraces, and words of apology would be exchanged all around. When we were idle, we might fuss and fight with each other, but now we faced a common enemy and in war, we were once again brothers."

We face a formidable foe. Arrayed against the church of Jesus Christ are all the powers of darkness. Joining them are those who have chosen to give themselves to the side of evil.

Is thine heart right, as my heart is with thy heart?

2 Kings 10:15 (KJV)

We who are on God's side must have unity. We must say to every Bible-believing Christian who shares our faith in the essentials, "Is your heart right, as my heart is with your heart?" And if he says, "It is," our response must be, "Give me your hand" (2 Kings 10:15).

LIFE RESPONSE:

"Lord, remind me that I am at war with the Enemy — not my brothers and sisters in the faith."

THROUGH THE BIBLE
Hosea 1-4

DOES IT REALLY HAPPEN?

While a pastor was speaking, a woman entered the church and walked down the aisle. As she approached the front, she called out in a loud voice, "Does it happen here? Does it really happen here?" She walked onto the platform and stood looking at the pastor, as she continued asking, "Does it happen here?"

"Does what happen here?" asked the pastor.

The blind receive sight, the lame walk, those who have leprosy are cured, the deaf hear, the dead are raised, and the good news is preached to the poor.

Matthew 11:5 (NIV)

"What it says on the sign."

The pastor suddenly remembered the motto printed on the church's sign out front. The sign said, "Miracles happen here." The church had adapted those words from Matthew, chapter eleven, verse five. The woman was in need, and in her desperation had turned to the church. She wanted to know if the church lived up to that claim.

We make some tremendous claims as Christians. The world has every right to know if we live up to those claims. It is our responsibility, and our privilege, to demonstrate to a watching world that our faith is genuine.

LIFE RESPONSE:
Is the "miracle" of salvation revealed to others by my Christ-like living?

THROUGH THE BIBLE
Hosea 5-9

LEADERS, LIVE THE LIFE!

A television talk show featured a marriage counselor. In the course of giving advice, the counselor referred to his former wife. The talk show host acted confused. "Wait a minute. What do you mean, your former wife?"

The marriage counselor said, "I mean just that. She is no longer my wife; we are divorced."

The host was shocked. "Divorced! But you're the expert. You're the marriage counselor giving advice to others."

"Yes," he responded. "I'm not ashamed of my divorce. Many marriage counselors are divorced."

A well-known entertainer, who professes faith in the Lord Jesus Christ, appeared on Christian television. She, along with others, was giving family counsel on a program dedicated to saving the family. Less than a month later, I read in the newspaper that this same person was marrying her third husband.

> *Since an overseer is entrusted with God's work, he must be blameless . . .*
>
> Titus 1:7 (NIV)

If I had money to invest, I don't believe I would turn it over to an investment counselor who had already declared bankruptcy! Neither would I listen to a marriage counselor whose own marriage had failed.

A Christian leader must live the life!

LIFE RESPONSE:

"Lord, help me to live my life above reproach."

THROUGH THE BIBLE

Hosea 10-14

LINE UP
FOR INSPECTION!

Whenever I read the words spoken by God to Abraham, "Walk before me and be blameless," the picture that comes to mind is that of a military parade. I envision a reviewing stand upon which stand the commander-in-chief, generals, and other top brass ready to observe the troops as they march by. Every soldier is carefully and meticulously dressed. Each column is perfectly straight, as with practiced precision the soldiers march in rhythmic step. The troops pass in review. On display, their preparations are being evaluated. The commander inspects them for precision, appearance and readiness.

I am God Almighty; walk before me and be blameless.

Genesis 17:1 (NIV)

The Apostle Paul urged the Ephesians to "walk worthy of the vocation wherewith ye are called" (Eph. 4:1 KJV). He meant they were to live a life worthy of the calling they had received as Christians.

Someday we will be called to the judgment seat of Christ, where we will have to "pass inspection." How can we be ready? By walking daily "in the light of the Lord" (Isa. 2:5). Because "if we walk in the light" we can count on "the blood of Jesus his Son" to cleanse us from all sin (1 John 1:7).

LIFE RESPONSE:

I pledge to live *here* so that I will not be ashamed to stand before Christ *there*.

THROUGH THE BIBLE
Joel 1–3

DON'T TALK TO THE DEVIL

I once heard someone pray in public and, as he was talking to the Lord, he suddenly switched and began talking to the devil. He told the devil what he could and could not do. He bound him. He rebuked him. His prayer jumped back and forth between the Lord and the devil, until I was not sure to whom he addressed some of his comments.

This disturbed me. Jude says that even Michael the archangel dared not bring a reviling accusation against the devil, but let the Lord rebuke him (Jude 9). We should not be talking to Satan, nor should we be listening to him. The Apostle Paul warned Timothy that some would depart from the faith and listen to deceiving spirits and doctrines of devils (1 Tim. 4:1).

Jesus rebuked the devil . . .

Matthew 17:18 (KJV)

In my opinion, many Christians — and some pastors and evangelists — are giving too much attention to the devil and not enough to the power of the cross of Jesus.

Satan must not be resisted in our own strength or wisdom, but through the power of the cross and the blood of Jesus. When you pray, concentrate on the Lord, not Satan. Jesus Christ has defeated him. Let your victory over the devil be in Christ.

Never forget, the outcome of this war is already settled!

LIFE RESPONSE:

Am I giving Christ and His Kingdom preeminence in my speech?

SOW YOUR SEED

A minister in colonial America felt led by the Holy Spirit to preach a sermon as he passed through a wilderness. He obeyed, though he felt foolish preaching to the trees.

Many years later, that minister was visiting in London when a man stopped him on the street. "Aren't you Rev. So-and-So, who used to live in America?" the stranger asked.

"Yes, I am he."

"Do you remember preaching a sermon out in the wilderness several years ago?"

Sow your seed . . . for you do not know which will succeed whether this or that.

Ecclesiastes 11:6 (NIV)

"I remember that day very well. But how did you know about that?" the preacher wondered.

"I was passing through the woods that day and heard a voice. I stopped to listen and it was you preaching. I never let you know I was there, but I heard your entire sermon. The Holy Spirit convicted me that day, and I knelt there in the forest and gave my heart and life to God."

Maybe you have felt that your witness, your ministry, or your service to God has been in vain. But we do not know where all the seed has fallen. Someday, we will learn that it falls in surprising places and produces a harvest.

LIFE RESPONSE:

I will sow the seeds of the gospel where I live, work, or play.

LIVE
THE LIGHT

When a small community contains both a Christian college and a seminary, it is only natural for many townspeople to be connected to the institutions — whether through jobs or related businesses and services. About one such town someone joked that "the nearest known sin is twenty miles away." I'm sure it's much closer than that! But Christians often feel comfortable in such cloistered settings, areas that are permeated with a Christian atmosphere.

Still, light shines best in the midst of darkness. You have heard the saying, "It's better to light a candle than to curse the darkness." While living surrounded by sin's darkness, we can shine with the light Jesus brought. We once were involved in the world's darkness, but Jesus has called us out of darkness to His light. Now He wants to use us to spread His light to others.

For you were once darkness, but now you are light in the Lord. Live as children of light.

Ephesians 5:8 (NIV)

A small light can drive out a great darkness, but it must maintain its distinction as light. When Christians become entangled in the sin and darkness of the world around them, their light soon goes out. When you become part of the darkness, you lose the power to shine. Light shines brightest by contrast, not by compromise.

LIFE RESPONSE:
"Lord, strengthen me so that I will not compromise."

❖

FIND GOD IN THE EVERYDAY ROUTINE

Where do you look for an omnipresent God? In the temple, the cathedral, the sanctuary? Yes, He can be found there. But you will also find Him in less splendid circumstances.

My first church was a small, wood-frame building that stood at the end of a dirt road in a patch of trees. It was not very impressive if you were to judge it by its architecture, but I saw many people find God there.

Some say God is found in a solemn worship service accompanied by fine organ music and choir — and I have found Him there. But I have heard an African congregation sing God's praise — without benefit of organ or piano — as they sat on backless benches in a little mountaintop building that did not even have glass in its windows. And I found He was there, too.

> *Jesus was recognized by them when he broke the bread.*
>
> Luke 24:35 (NIV)

He was revealed to the disciples at Emmaus in the breaking of bread. Some people may not find God because they don't look for Him in the ordinary, everyday routine. They expect to see Him in the spectacular, in the miraculous, in the unusual. But we probably will not see God there until we find Him in everyday life. He is walking the road with us, talking with us as a Friend, breaking bread.

LIFE RESPONSE:

Do I look for the Master in my daily, mundane routines . . . and fellowship with Him there?

THROUGH THE BIBLE

Obadiah & Jonah

A
CHEERFUL HEART

Some people seem to live in perpetual sunshine. On cloudy, dreary days the warmth of their spirit makes everyone feel better. The world brightens and burdens lighten because of their cheerful smiles.

Then there are those who bring a cloud of doom with them wherever they go. A certain cartoon character always has a storm cloud over his head. It constantly rains on him. People who live in the shadow of a cloud are a discouragement to others. Their crushed spirit "dries up *our* bones."

How can we be cheerful? We must understand that a cheerful heart does not depend on outward circumstances. In the midst of a storm Jesus said to His disciples, "Be of good cheer" (Matt. 14:27 KJV).

Cheerfulness does not come from artificial stimulation or through the gratification of the senses. It comes from recognizing the goodness of God and the greatness of His provision.

> *A cheerful heart is good medicine, but a crushed spirit dries up the bones.*
>
> Proverbs 17:22 (NIV)

It is not that we deny the realities of our situation, but that we come to know the One who is greater than our circumstances.

When trouble comes we are better prepared to meet it with a cheerful heart.

LIFE RESPONSE:

I am determined to bring "sunshine" rather than "clouds" to people around me.

PRAISE THE LORD!

I n the great Sunday school conventions that were held yearly at Cobo Hall in Detroit, Michigan, a banner was given to representatives of the fastest growing Sunday school in each state. At first, almost all the banners went to Baptist churches. After a few years, however, nearly all of the banners were going to Pentecostal or charismatic churches. Some of my denomination's pastors wondered about the success and growth of these churches.

I believe one reason for their growth is the spontaneity of their worship — the freedom of the Spirit — which draws people in. I recognize that there are cultural differences and varying tastes that affect our styles of worship. But when determining our attitude toward praise and worship, we must be guided by Scripture and not our own personal preferences. If culture and Scripture conflict, it is culture that needs to adjust.

In the midst of the church will I sing praise unto thee.

Hebrews 2:12 (KJV)

Hand-clapping and shouting are biblical expressions of worship, as are silence and prostration before God. Two things are certain. Praise is not an option; God expects it. And praise is not passive; all the words for praise in the Bible are action verbs. God never intended praise to be a spectator sport. No one can praise the Lord for someone else.

Obviously, God is not interested in empty emotionalism. But the person who truly loves God will find a way to praise Him.

LIFE RESPONSE:
I will not let someone else do my praising for me.

THROUGH THE BIBLE
Micah 1-4

PLAYING WITH DIAMONDS

A missionary who served in a diamond mining area, saw a group of boys playing marbles. As he got closer, he saw that they were playing marbles with diamonds!

When the wise men came to Jerusalem in search of the newborn King, King Herod asked the Jewish leaders where Christ was to be born. Aware of what the prophets had foretold, these Jewish leaders had the diamonds of the Old Testament writings. Yet they "played marbles" with these wonderful prophecies.

Did any of them go to Bethlehem to search for the King? The wise men had told them about the star. But even though they were only a few miles from Bethlehem, they didn't bother to try to find the Messiah.

How often are those who have the most truth, the most light, the least likely to follow it. At times, those who hear the Word frequently become insensitive to it.

> *[King Herod] asked them where the Christ was to be born. 'In Bethlehem in Judea,' they replied, 'for this is what the prophet has written.'*
>
> *Matthew 2:4-5 (NIV)*

We have the *diamonds* of the Word of God. Are we playing marbles with them? Or are we hiding His riches in our hearts and minds?

LIFE RESPONSE:

"Holy Spirit, guide me in the 'mining' of Your Word. Show me the 'diamonds of truth.'"

THROUGH THE BIBLE

Micah 5-7

YOU ARE
AN HEIR

I was talking with my dad one day, and he said, "I want to leave my children more than was left to me."

I said, "Dad, you shouldn't worry about leaving your children anything. You have already given us so much, we don't need anything more."

A godly heritage from our earthly parents is a wonderful inheritance. Yet the inheritance God, our Heavenly Father, has prepared for His children is imperishable, inexhaustible and incorruptible (1 Pet. 1:4).

Blessed are the meek: for they shall inherit the earth.

Matthew 5:5 (KJV)

How much of an inheritance would it take to provide an inexhaustible supply for you? Andrew Carnegie found it was hard work to distribute 300 million dollars. He gave an organ to a church. By the time he died, he was getting so many requests from churches for free organs that it kept two men busy, full time, answering the mail and making the decisions. He gave 7,689 organs to churches, at a cost of six million dollars. Earthly inheritances are worrisome.

The meek may suffer now, but when the will is read, it is the meek who will inherit the earth — a new heaven and a new earth!

LIFE RESPONSE:

How much time have I spent "reading the will" — searching the Bible for the promises of my inheritance?

THROUGH THE BIBLE
Nahum 1-3

THE RIGHT TIME

According to *The Guinness Book of World Records,* the most accurate and complicated timepiece in the world is the Olsen clock, located in the Copenhagen Town Hall, Denmark. The clock, which has more than 14,000 units, took ten years to make. The mechanism of the clock functions in 570,000 different ways. The celestial pole motion of the clock will take 25,753 years to complete a full circle, the slowest-moving designed mechanism in the world. The clock is accurate to a half a second in 300 years.

But even more marvelous than this feat of human ingenuity, are God's clock and calendar. The birth of Jesus Christ came with exact precision. There was a time ordained on God's prophetic calendar, and when that moment arrived, Christ was born.

When the fullness of the time was come, God sent forth His Son . . .

Galatians 4:4 (KJV)

God arranged for Christ to come when the Roman Empire had built a worldwide system of communication and travel. The world was uniquely prepared under this complex and efficient system to mark Christ's coming and disseminate the gospel.

God is in control of the times and seasons of our lives as well.

LIFE RESPONSE:

I will trust the Lord to order the "seasons" of my life.

WHO IS ON YOUR GIFT LIST?

The wise men's gift-giving is a pattern for our own. The first Christmas presents were given to Jesus; the wise men did not have a gift exchange among themselves. While there is nothing wrong with exchanging gifts with those we love, it would be a greater blessing if we concerned ourselves more with giving to the Lord than to each other.

The first and best gift, of course, was God's gift, His only Son, our Savior. And yet, Christmas may be the only birthday party at which the guest of honor is ignored, while the invited guests give presents to each other! When your Christmas bills come due, take a moment and add up the total cost. How much did you spend on presents, party items, special meals and all the rest? Compare that sum with what you gave to the Lord.

> *When they had opened their treasures, they presented unto him gifts; gold, and frankincense, and myrrh.*
>
> Matthew 2:11 (KJV)

How *do* we give to the Lord? Jesus tells us that by giving to the needy, the hungry, the thirsty, the prisoners and the strangers, we are giving to Him. What would happen if all Christians gave Christmas gifts only to those who could never repay them?

Remember, when the wise men gave, they worshiped!

LIFE RESPONSE:
"Heavenly Father, give me 'sense' in spending my Christmas 'dollars.'"

THROUGH THE BIBLE
Zephaniah 1-3

THE GRACE OF GIVING

I remember the Christmas our children discovered the blessing of giving. They had carefully selected gifts for their parents and wrapped the presents themselves. That Christmas morning, instead of running downstairs and tearing into their own gifts, they proudly handed us our gifts. Then, almost bursting with excitement, they insisted we open our gifts before they turned to their own. When it is motivated by love, what a blessing giving is.

But how do you give when you don't have money? You give what you have. Do you have time? Give some by helping others. Do you have a telephone? Use it to encourage and cheer someone. Do you have an ability, such as knitting or woodworking? Use that talent to make something for someone else.

See that you also excel in this grace of giving.

2 Corinthians 8:7b (NIV)

What skills do you have? Have you thought about giving those? Perhaps you are a mechanic who could fix someone's car or change the oil. Are you a teacher? Maybe you could tutor someone with a special need.

When you give what you have, there is no limit to what you can do. And that's what Christmas is all about, for God gave what He had. He demonstrated the grace of giving when He gave His only begotten Son.

LIFE RESPONSE:

I will seek to "excel in the grace of giving."

KNOWING ABOUT CHRISTMAS

Millions of people know about Christmas, but do they know what Christmas is about? Many children think Christmas is about presents, toys and treats, about decorating the tree and seeing Santa, making lists and hanging stockings. It's about getting everything you want, and then finding out what you want isn't all that satisfying.

Most parents think they know what Christmas is about. It's spending money you don't have, running all over town to find the most popular toy, worrying over what to get the "hard-to-buy-for" people, and dreading the bills that come later.

> *For unto you is born this day . . . a Saviour, which is Christ the Lord.*
>
> Luke 2:11 (KJV)

I noticed several display ads in a leading magazine: "What greater treasure of Christmas could you give than sheets and pillowcases?" said one. Another read, "Crowning gift of all, our lovebird scarf of Russian sable, just $9000." And this one, "Christmas everywhere! And in America it's — Cashmere."

Do we really know what Christmas is about, or do we just know about Christmas? When all the celebrating is over, one fact stands above it all — *unto you is born a Savior.* If you don't know Him, you do not know the real meaning of Christmas.

LIFE RESPONSE:
I will seek the *Christ* of Christmas above the *celebration* of Christmas.

THROUGH THE BIBLE

2 John, 3 John, Jude

Peace On Earth

After Germany surrendered during World War II, a girl who had been in Hitler's youth movement escaped imprisonment in her homeland. She walked across East Germany toward West Germany, only to find the border blocked by Russian patrols. She and another girl paid someone to take them across what was known as "no-man's-land" to West Germany. With their guide, they walked through the pre-dawn darkness to freedom. Suddenly, guns roared, people screamed, and then there was an eerie silence.

Out of the woods came the cry of a little child who had been separated from her mother. The two girls found the child and, as morning light broke, ran across an open meadow, holding the child by her hands. They expected Russian gunfire, but none came. Could it be that the sight of a little child — her blond hair blowing in the wind, the first streaks of dawn shining around her — kept the soldiers from firing?

Glory to God in the highest and on earth peace, good will toward men.

Luke 2:14 (KJV)

Across a "no-man's-land" of political strife and war a little child ran unmolested. For those few moments there was peace.

When God looked down on a hate-filled and strife-torn world, He sent a baby Boy in order to bring peace.

LIFE RESPONSE:

Am I seeking "peace on earth" by introducing the "Prince of Peace" to others?

THROUGH THE BIBLE

Zechariah 1-6

THE LITTLE TOWN OF BETHLEHEM

The Church of the Nativity in Bethlehem was built over the traditional site of Jesus' birthplace. When I visited the church some years ago, I sensed a sacredness, not because of the church standing there, or because of the ornately decorated grotto. It was because I realized the significance of what had taken place there.

Bethlehem is a place that underscores how God kept His promises regarding the Messiah. When God became flesh, everything He said He would do was realized. Here, at the place of His Incarnation, we became aware of how much God loved the world. Here, where Jesus took on the form of a servant, God's promise of salvation became visible.

> *Bethlehem . . . While they were there . . . she gave birth to her firstborn . . . and placed him in a manger.*
>
> Luke 2:4, 6-7 (NIV)

Bethlehem is the place where, as a helpless infant, Jesus became what I am. He understands our weakness because He was weak. Bethlehem is the place where God repaired the fellowship that was shattered in Eden. God sacrificed His Son to make it happen.

The Christmas story is the most incredible story ever told. At Bethlehem, God wrapped himself in human flesh, Mary wrapped her newborn in swaddling clothes, and Jesus wrapped himself in the stains of sin in order to reconcile us to God.

LIFE RESPONSE:
"Father, let me see clearly the beauty of the Bethlehem Gift."

THROUGH THE BIBLE
Zechariah 7-10

A NEWSWORTHY EVENT

If Peter Jennings or Tom Brokaw had been around in the year 1809, their nightly broadcasts would have included news about Austria. Most evenings, their top stories would have been about the Napoleonic wars. They would not have bothered to report the birth of babies that year.

Yet the year 1809 included the births of William Gladstone, Alfred Lord Tennyson, Oliver Wendell Holmes, Edgar Allen Poe, Charles Darwin and Abraham Lincoln! What a significant year! What news! But at the time — who cared?

Go back eighteen centuries before that. The world was watching Rome in all her splendor and might. Most people were thinking of Caesar Augustus, and increased taxation. What could be more newsworthy than decrees issued by the emperor of Rome?

The news written on the pages of eternal history, however, was that a woman from Nazareth gave birth to her firstborn son in Bethlehem, and laid him in a manger.

She gave birth to her firstborn, a son . . . and placed him in a manger . . .

Luke 2:7 (NIV)

Who noticed? A few shepherds. Yet that homeless child born in Bethlehem is still changing the course of history, as He has done from that day forward.

Has He made a difference in your life?

LIFE RESPONSE:
"Jesus, thank You for the wonderful sacrifice You made for me."

THROUGH THE BIBLE
Zechariah 11-14

A PERSONAL GIFT

One Christmas, my brother and I had to share our *main* gift. It was too expensive to be given to one child alone. Somehow, that present didn't seem quite the same as the others. It was mine and yet it wasn't mine!

I had the privilege of visiting Pacific Garden Mission in Chicago. I was amazed at the size and scope of their hundred-year-old ministry. I stood in one of the dormitories with its rows of cots. Hundreds of people sleep at the mission every night and between 800 and 1,000 meals are served every day. Many of those meals are eaten by forgotten men with no families, no homes, no one to care about them. But God cares. That is the reason the mission is there. The Word of God comes to each of them and says, "Unto you, this gift is given." The gift is personal and individual.

Thanks be unto God for his unspeakable gift.

2 Corinthians 9:15 (KJV)

Yes, God so loved the world. But He loves each person of the world, not just a "population" or a group of nations or tribes. The Bible teaches that each person is precious in God's sight. Not one is overlooked or forgotten. Each is known by name and each one is offered a gift of great worth. Salvation is God's free gift, offered without a price tag attached. Money cannot buy it. All you must do is to come to God on His terms.

Have you received His great gift?

LIFE RESPONSE:
"Father, reveal Your Gift to my heart in a fresh new way today."

AFTER CHRISTMAS, WHAT?

After the angels had gone . . . the shepherds returned. I imagine they never got over that experience. How many times do you suppose their children and grandchildren heard them tell and retell the story of that incredible night? I can imagine them as old men, with their grandchildren pleading at their feet, "Grandpa, tell us again about that night the angels sang."

But the shepherds could not stay in the light of that glory forever. What happened when the angels left and the shepherds returned?

Christmas comes and goes. The parties end. The lights and ornaments are packed away. What then?

It is time then to think of the prospects and the hope Christmas gives us. We have the prospect of a transformed life made possible by the coming of the Savior. We have the hope of a better country — that country, in fact, to which the angels returned.

> *When the angels had left them and gone into heaven . . . The shepherds returned . . .*
>
> *Luke 2:15, 20 (NIV)*

Christmas means hope for lost humanity and peace made possible by the coming of the Prince of Peace. The darkness of this present evil world is extinguished by the coming of the *Light of the world*.

Yes, the holiday may be over for another year, but the celebration must continue!

LIFE RESPONSE:

I will take Christmas with me into the new year.

THROUGH THE BIBLE

Revelation 1-3

BE STILL!

Most people today are surrounded by noise. They awaken to the sound of the radio in the morning and then turn the television on for company. When making a phone call, they are often put on hold and forced to listen to music.

Now more than ever God says to us, "Be still." Taking time to be quiet is crucial to our physical and spiritual well-being. In this quiet time, we can get to know God. But like Elijah, we must listen to the still, small voice.

A quiet time gives us an opportunity to not only get to know ourselves but to hear sounds that are normally drowned out by our activities. We need to listen to the beautiful sounds of God's creation — birds singing, the wind whistling, water lapping the river's bank. Families, too, need quiet times when they can listen to each other.

Be still, and know that I am God . . .
Psalms 46:10 (KJV)

It has been said that in times of quietness, our hearts should be like trees lifting their branches to the sky to draw down strength — strength which they will need to face the storms that will surely come. An inability to stay quiet is one of the conspicuous failings of mankind.

Put God first in your day with a time of quietness in His presence.

So I think I know the secret/Learned from many a troubled way/You must seek Him in the morning/If you want Him through the day!

LIFE RESPONSE:

I will open my heart to the presence of Christ at the start of every day.

THROUGH THE BIBLE
Revelation 4-7

WHY PRAY?

A woman came to my office one day with a frustrated look on her face and an anxious tone in her voice. "Pastor, when we pray, are we supposed to expect fairy-tale answers? Or should we go on as though it isn't going to make any difference?"

The atheist doesn't pray. He thinks there is no God to answer him. The fatalist doesn't pray. He thinks, "Whatever will be, will be." The ambitious man doesn't "waste time and energy" praying. He gets busy and does things himself. Even some Christians ask, "Why pray?"

Questions about the value of prayer arise from a misconception of God. Too many people think of Him as a spiritual "Houdini" who can open any door, or as a kind of "cosmic bellhop" who will answer their call every time they ring a bell.

The prayer of a righteous man is powerful and effective.

James 5:16b (NIV)

Jesus taught that we are praying to a Heavenly Father who offers the wonderful privilege of coming to Him at any time. Our Father knows just what we need.

But prayer is more than getting what we need. It is communication with One who loves us, and is based on a right relationship with Him. The prayer of a righteous person avails much, James says. Let's make sure we are keeping our part of the relationship!

LIFE RESPONSE:
I will keep my prayer life *alive* by giving it attention.

THE GREATEST CONTRAST

Life is full of contrasts: black and white, light and shadow, good and evil, joy and sorrow.

I have tried a little oil painting during the last few years. On more than one occasion I have mixed what I thought was a very good color on my palette. Once applied to the canvas, however, I have been very disappointed. This was because I had applied a light color against another light color or a dark color against another dark color. There must be a contrast to make the colors stand out.

For the wages of sin is death; but the gift of God is eternal life through Jesus Christ our Lord.

Romans 6:23 (KJV)

Of course the greatest contrast the world has ever known is the contrast between good and evil, the battle between Satan and God. Romans 6:23 sets forth this great contrast.

There is a contrast between rulers. Who, or what, is going to rule your life — sin or God?

There is the contrast of reward: *The wages of sin* or *the gift of God.* One is earned, the other is undeserved.

Then, there is the contrast of results: *death* or *eternal life.*

This great *contrast* becomes a great *choice* which each of us must make.

LIFE RESPONSE:

I have made my choice. Jesus is Lord of my life.

WANT TO KNOW THE FUTURE?

During the last half of December and the first part of January, the newspapers and magazines — especially those that specialize in the sensational — are flooded with the predictions of self-proclaimed psychics and so-called prophets of our day. Their prognostications for the new year are often front-page news.

From the attention they receive, one would almost believe there is some ` degree of accuracy in their predictions. One of the best known of such people in recent years, however, admits to being wrong at least thirty-five percent of the time. On the other hand, the standard for a prophet in the Old Testament was a 100 percent accuracy rate. If a prophet was ever wrong, he was not to be believed at all.

The reason such "predictors" are popular has nothing to do with the validity of their prophecies. The fascination comes from the nearly universal inner desire to know the future. It is obvious from Scripture that God does not want us to know much about the future, nor should we be unduly concerned about it. "Do not worry about tomorrow . . ." (Matt. 6:34).

> *It is not for you to know the times or dates the Father has set by his own authority.*
>
> *Acts 1:7 (NIV)*

LIFE RESPONSE:

I will trust my future to the One Who has already been there.

FOLLOWING JESUS

O n his daughter's college application, a father was asked to list her leadership characteristics. He wrote, "She has no leadership characteristics that I know of, but she is a first-rate follower." Upon reviewing her application, the president of the college called the father personally to accept his daughter as a student. He said, "Of the thousands of applicants we have received, and of the hundreds of students we have accepted, your daughter is the only one who was not 'a born leader.'"

And he said unto them, 'Follow me . . .'

Matthew 4:19 (KJV)

Perhaps most people would prefer to be leaders, but Jesus says to be a Christian, we must be followers. Following in the footsteps of Jesus is not a passive activity. If we are true followers of Jesus Christ, we will become strong, dynamic Christians who live for Him seven days a week.

A newspaper reporter took his car to several garages. He had deliberately pulled a spark plug wire loose and wanted to report on how different mechanics would diagnose and repair the problem. One after another pretended to fix some major problem. But at one garage, the mechanic reattached the wire and did not charge anything. He told the reporter he was a Christian. He was a follower of Jesus and that made the difference.

LIFE RESPONSE:
I will seek to be a "first-rate follower" of Jesus.

THROUGH THE BIBLE
Revelation 20-22

TOPICAL INDEX